RISK MANAGEMENT AND REGULATION IN BANKING

RISK MANAGEMENT AND REGULATION IN BANKING

PROCEEDINGS OF THE INTERNATIONAL CONFERENCE ON RISK MANAGEMENT AND REGULATION IN BANKING (1997)

Edited by
DAN GALAI
DAVID RUTHENBERG
MARSHALL SARNAT
BEN Z. SCHREIBER

SPRINGER-SCIENCE+BUSINESS MEDIA, LLC

Library of Congress Cataloging-in-Publication Data
International Conference on Risk Mangement and Regulation in Banking
(1997: Jerusalem)
Risk management and regulation in banking: proceedings of the
International Conference on Risk Mangement and Regulation in
Banking (1997) / edited by Dan Galai . . . [et al.].
p. cm.
Includes bibliographical references.
ISBN 978-1-4613-7292-9 ISBN 978-1-4615-5043-3 (eBook)
DOI 10.1007/978-1-4615-5043-3
1. Bank management—Congresses. 2. Risk management—Congresses.
3. Banking law—Congresses. I. Galai, Dan. II. Title.
HG1615.I78 1999
368. 1'068—dc21 99-13964
CIP

Originally published by Kluwer Academic Publishers in 1999
Softcover reprint of the hardcover 1st edition 1999

Printed on acid-free paper.

TABLE OF CONTENTS

CONTRIBUTORS TO THE CONFERENCE

Michel Crouhy is Vice President, Global Analytics, Market Risk Management Division, at Canadian Imperial Bank of Commerce (CIBC). Prior to his current position at CIBC, Michel Crouhy was a professor of finance at the HEC School of Management. He has been a visiting professor at the Wharton School and at UCLA. Dr. Crouhy holds a Ph.D from the Wharton School and is a graduate of Ecole Nationale des Ponts et Chaussees, France. He has published extensively in academic journals in the areas of banking, options, and financial markets, and he is editor of the collection *Banque & Bourse* at Presses Universities de France. He has also served as a consultant to major financial institutions in Europe and in the United States in the areas of quantitative portfolio management, risk management, valuation and hedging of derivative products, forecasting volatility term structure, and correlations.

Dan Galai is the Abe Gray professor of finance and business administration at the Hebrew University, School of Business Administration in Jerusalem. He was a visiting professor of finance at INSEAD and has also taught at the University of California, Los Angeles, and the University of Chicago. Dr. Galai holds a Ph.D. from the University of Chicago and undergraduate and graduate degrees from the Hebrew University. He has served as a consultant for the Chicago Board of Options E-xchange and the American Stock Exchange, as well as for major banks. He has published numerous articles in leading business and finance journals on options, financial assets, and corporate finance, and was a winner of the First Annual

Pomeranze Prize for excellence in options research presented by the CBOE. Dr. Galai is a Principal in SIMGA P.C.M., which is engaged in portfolio management and corporate finance.

John G. Heimann is chairman of Global Financial Institutions and a member of the Executive Management Committee of Merrill Lynch & Co., where he is responsible for the senior relationship management for financial institutions worldwide. During his career, he has served in a number of governmental posts including U.S. Comptroller of the Currency, Superintendent and Community Development, and member of the Board of the Federal Deposit Insurance Corporation (FDIC) and Federal National Mortgage Association (FNMA). Presently, he is chairman of the Financial Services Council, a member of the Group to Thirty, a member of the Board and Executive Committee of the Institute of International Finance, a member of the New York Federal Reserve Banks International Capital Markets Advisory Committee, and a member of the Council on Foreign Relations.

Mark Britten-Jones is an assistant professor of finance and accounting at the London Business School. He received his Ph.D. in finance from the University of California, Los Angeles. His research fields include derivatives, fixed income securities, and risk aversion.

Yoram Landskroner is an associate professor of finance, School of Business administration at the Hebrew University of Jerusalem. He holds a Ph.D. from the University of Pennsylvania Wharton School, and undergraduate and graduate degrees from the Hebrew University. He was a visiting professor of finance at New York University, University of California, Berkeley and UCLA. Professor Landskroner's research interests include banking risks and capital standards, demand for money, and foreign exchange options. He has published numerous articles in leading business and finance journals on these topics. He serves as a consultant to the Supervisor of Banks at the Bank of Israel, Banking Supervision Department, and he was a member of the Board of Directors of the Tel Aviv Stock Exchange.

Robert M. Mark is Executive Vice President at the Canadian Imperial Bank of Commerce (CIBC). Lately he received the 1998 Financial Risk Manager of the Year award by Global Association of Risk Professionals (GARP) for his noteworthy contributions to the financial risk management profession. Prof. Mark has created a leading worldwide risk management practice at CIBC by implementing innovative procedures and integrating key functions throughout the organization. Furthermore, his numerous publications have created a body of work that has become valuable educational reference material.

Arie L. Melnik is a professor of finance and economics at the University of Haifa. He received his Ph.D. from Cornell University and taught at Michigan State University, Northwestern University, University of Texas, University of Toronto,

University of California, Berkeley, and N.Y.U. Prof. Melnik's major areas of interest are financial economics, banking, and corporate finance: in particular, the European loan market, segmentation in the credit market, packages of financial services, lending syndicates, and the structure of financial contracts. Professor Melnik served in a number of professional and public service posts. At the University of Haifa he was chairman of the Department of Economics and chairman of the Department of Business Administration. He also served as chairman of the University Computer Committee and the Executive Committee of the Board of Governors.

Yair E. Orgler assumed the position of chairman of the Tel Aviv Stock Exchange (TASE) Board of Directors in June 1996. He also retained his position of professor of finance at the Leon Recanati Graduate School of Business Administration, Tel-Aviv University. Prof. Orgler has a M.Sc in Industrial Engineering from the University of Southem California and a Ph.D. in Industrial Administration from Carnegie-Mellon University in Pittsburgh. In his previous positions, he served as the first chairman of Maalot, the Israel Securities Rating Company, which he founded in 1991, chairman of the Wage Committee of the Association of University Heads in Israel, vice-rector of Tel-Aviv University, and dean of the Leon Recanati Graduate School of Business Administration. In addition, Prof. Orgler has been, since 1982, the incumbent of the Goldreich Chair in International Banking at Tel-Aviv University.

David H. Pyle is Booth Professor of Banking & Finance (emeritus) at the Haas School of Business, University of California, Berkeley. During 1994–96, he was a visiting professor of finance at the London Business School. He has served as senior economic advisor to the U.S. Comptroller of the Currency and as a visiting scholar at the Federal Reserve Bank of San Francisco and the Banca d'Italia. Professor Pyle's more recent research and publications have focused on issues in bank regulation.

Jacob Paroush is a professor of economics at Bar-Ilan University and president-elect of the Israeli Economics Association. His research interests includes collective decision making, banking risks, and other topics in microeconomic theory. He has published a book and numerous articles in leading economic, business, finance, and banking journals on these topics.

David Ruthenberg is an assistant supervisor of banks and the head of research at the Banking Supervision Department Bank of Israel. He is also an associate professor at the School of Business Administration, the Hebrew University of Jerusalem. He was a visiting associate professor at New York University and at the University of California at Berkeley. Dr. Ruthenberg holds a Ph.D. (1976) from Wayne State University, Detroit, Michigan. He has published numerous articles in the field of banking in leading finance and economic journals. He serves on the editorial board of "Banking Review" and the "Banking Quarterly" (Israel).

Anthony M. Santomero is Richard K. Mellon Professor of Finance and Director, Wharton Financial Institutions Center at the Wharton School, University of Pennsylvania. He is a leading authority on financial institution risk management and financial structure and a recognized consultant to major financial institutions and regulatory agencies throughout North America, Europe, and the Far East. He has written more than 90 articles and monographs on financial sector regulation and economic performance. Dr. Santomero received his B.A. in economics from Fordham University, his Ph.D. in economics from Brown University, and has recently received an honorary doctorate from the Stockholm School of Economics.

Marshall Sarnat is Dean of the Faculty of Business Administration at the Israeli Center for Academic Studies, and Alberston and Waltuch Professor of Finance emeritus at the Hebrew University of Jeruslem. He is president of the Financial Institute of Israel, editor of the Bank of Israel's *Banking Review*, co-editor of the *Journal of Banking and Finance*, and consultant to several corporations and government agencies. Professor Sarnat is a member of the executive committee and past president of the European Finance Association. He was a member of the advisory committee of the Bank of Israel and of the National Judicial Commission on the manipulation of trading in bank shares. He has also served as visiting professor at New York University, UCLA, the University of California at Berkeley, New University of Lisbon, and the University of Toronto. Professor Samat is the author of numerous articles and books on financial economics, investments and capital markets.

Stephen M. Schaefer is Esmee Fairbairn Professor of Finance at the London Business School. Formerly on the faculty of the Graduate School of Business at Stanford University, he has also been a visiting professor at the Universities of British Columbia, California (Berkeley), Chicago, Venice, and Cape Town. Between 1991 and 1997 Prof. Schaefer was an independent member of the board of the Securities and Futures Authority.

Ben Z. Schreiber is an economist at the bank of Israel and teaches at Bar-Ilan University. He holds a Ph.D. from the Hebrew University of Jerusalem. Dr. Schreiber's research interests include deposit insurance, risk management in financial institutions, and top management compensation.

Arie L. Shapiro is a managing director of Marine Lendlease Limited, a privately held investment banking firm providing financial services to the shipping and offshore oil industries. Mr. Shapiro held executive positions and directorships with subsidiaries of GATX Corporation and served as president and chief executive officer of GATX Ship Leasing and Mortgage Corporation. He is a director of several shipping companies and a member of the Baltic Exchange. Until its merger with Diamond Offshore Drilling in 1996, Mr. Shapiro was a director of Arethusa (Off-Shore) Limited, previously Zapata Off-Shore Company. Mr. Shapiro has a B.A.

degree in economics from Hebrew University, Jerusalem, and was a member of the founding committee of its School of Business. He has an M.B.A. degree from the University of Michigan.

Brian Smouha is a senior partner in the UK firm of Deloitte & Touche, part of the international firm Deloitte Touch Tohmatsu International. He has recently relocated from London to Washington, D.C., as lead audit partner on the external audit of the World Bank. In 1983, Mr. Smouha was appointed lead liquidator for the collapsed Banco Ambrosiano at the request of 109 creditor banks. He was later appointed by the Bank of England inspector to report on the defense against the attempted takeover of Standard Chartered Bank by Lloyds Bank (1987). In 1991, Mr. Smouha was appointed by the courts on the recommendation of the Bank of England and the Luxembourg Monetary Institute to lead the closure and liquidation of the Bank of Credit and Commerce International. BCCI was operating in 70 countries, had a group balance sheet of over $20 billion, and 14,000 employees. It is reputed to be the world's largest and most complex bank liquidation in history.

Clifford Smout is a graduate student in economics from Clare College, Cambridge. He joined the Bank of England in 1978, and at present is Head, Regulatory and Supervisory Policy Division. He has served as private secretary to the Deputy Governor, Sir George Blunden, as a reserve manager in the Foreign Exchange Division, and as Deputy Head of Banking Supervision. Mr. Smout has been a member of Basle Committee since 1993, and currently chairs its interest rate risk subgroup. He also serves on the SFA Capital Committee.

Giorgio Szego is a professor of mathematical finance at the University of Rome. He received his Ph.D. in mathematics from the University of Pavia, Italy. Dr. Szego is a member of the Board of the Bank of Naples and an editor of the *Journal of Banking and Finance*. His main research interest is economics of financial regulation. His book, *The Financial System: Economics and Regulation* won the 1996 Award for Economic Literature.

Zvi Wiener is a member of the faculty at the Hebrew University of Jerusalem. He received his Ph.D. in mathematics from the Weizmann Institute of Science, Rehovot, Israel. He has served as a Rothschild postdoctoral fellow at the Wharton School, as Alon fellow at the Hebrew University, and as a visiting fellow at Wolfram Research, Inc. His research interests include risk management, pricing and hedging of derivative financial instruments, and interest rate models.

David Zaken is an assistant to the Supervisor of Banks at the Bank of Israel and teaches at the Hebrew University of Jerusalem. His research interests include risk management in financial institutions, in particular market risks and VaR models.

Ben-Zion Zilberfarb is the Director General of the Ministry of Finance and a professor of economics at Bar-Ilan University. He received his Ph.D. degree from University of Pennsylvania under the supervision of Prof. Lawrence Klein (Nobel Laureate). Prof. Zilberfarb has written more than 50 articles and two books dealing mainly with the Israeli economy in the following areas: inflation, privatization, indexation, demand for money, and international trade. He was a member of many public committees, such as the Economic Planning Authority, the Steering Committee for Research in the Social Sciences, and an advisor to many governmental bodies.

I. INTRODUCTION

The birth of finance as a modern academic discipline can be dated from the publication, in 1952, of Harry Markowitz's pathbreaking article on the risk return tradeoff and portfolio selection. Subsequently, the Nobel Memorial Prize in Economics was awarded to six scholars—Franco Modigliani, Harry Markowitz, Merton Miller, William Sharpe, Robert Merton, and Myron Scholes—all of whom have provided seminal insights into risk analysis and contributed to the development and recognition of finance as an academic discipline capable of fruitful application in practice. (We sadly note, as did the 1997 Nobel Committee, that Fischer Black did not live to share the honor.)

The period following the publication of the Markowitz article has been characterized by far-reaching innovations that have reshaped our understanding of financial theory and its application to the real world. Few professions have experienced greater change in so short a period of time as has risk management, which originally dealt with the implementation of corporate safety procedures, the avoidance of litigation, and the purchase of insurance. Although the hedging of risk has been around for a long time, a veritable arsenal of new and often sophisticated tools and techniques for risk management has been forged, in no small measure due to the work of the above-mentioned scholars and their disciples. And while numerous cases of the successful mitigation of risks can be cited, the public is all too aware of the widely publicized instances in which both banks and corporations sustained very large losses due to poor risk management.

Similarly, the vigorous regulation of banking and financial institutions has been with us for a considerable time, at least since the Great Depression of the 1930s. However, here too we have witnessed in recent years, far-reaching changes in regulatory climate and practices across the globe. The EEC edicts on the harmonization of financial markets and the Basle Accord on the capital requirements of banks are two cases in point.

In view of these fundamental changes and their world-wide impact on banking and financial intermediaries, Israel's Banking Supervision Department and the Hebrew University's School of Business decided to invite an outstanding group of academics and practitioners to an international conference on risk management and regulation in banking. The conference, which was jointly sponsored by five of Israel's leading banks (Hapoalim, Leumi, Discount, Mizrachi, and First International), was convened in Jerusalem on May 18, 1997. This volume of selected conference papers is a result of that conference.

The first two articles, by David Pyle and Anthony Santomero, respectively, provide a broad overview of risk management in banking. In his paper, Pyle addresses the question of why bank risk management is needed and then goes on to examine the theoretical bases for bank risk management. He emphasizes that meeting regulatory requirements does not appear to be the most important reason for establishing a sound risk management framework. In today's world, reliable measures of market risk, credit risk, operational risk, and performance risk, as well as the ability to monitor positions and create incentives for prudent risk-taking, are a *sine qua non* for efficient management.

Santomero presents a summary of major findings from the comprehensive study of risk management in the financial sector carried out by the Wharton Financial Institutions Center with support from the Sloan Foundation. He reports on the state of risk management techniques employed by a sample of relatively sophisticated banks in the United States. Santomero outlines and evaluates the standard practice and then offers a critique of current risk management policies by pointing out shortcomings in the methodology used to analyze risk and the elements that are missing in risk management and control.

The next three papers examine and evaluate alternative techniques for the management of market risk. In his paper, "Introduction to VaR," Zvi Wiener describes the concept of Value-at-Risk and shows how it can be used for supervision and internal control. Several alternative methods for the measurement of Value-at-Risk are discussed. The nonparametric approach is represented by historical simulations and Monte-Carlo techniques. Variance-covariance and some analytical models are used to demonstrate the parametric approach. The paper concludes with a brief comment on the backtesting required by the Basle regulations.

The primary purpose of the 1988 Basle Accord and its 1996 amendment was to set minimum international capital guidelines that link banks' capital requirement to both market risk and credit risk. In the first of their two papers, Michel Crouhy, Dan Galai, and Robert Mark compare the two alternatives to assess market risk as proposed by BIS. The first uses the standardized approach, which sets factors as determined by BIS for various financial instruments. The alternative internal model approach is based on the proprietary models of individual banks to value securities and the probability distributions for changes in the value of claims. The two methods, and the BIS rules and guidelines for approving internal models, are critically examined and evaluated. The authors conclude their paper with a numerical example illustrating the potential savings in capital requirement due to the use of internal models rather than the standardized approach.

In their second paper, Crouhy, Galai, and Mark employ the option-pricing approach, pioneered by the two 1997 Nobel laureates and Fischer Black, to the problem of credit risk. The authors present a model in which the credit spread on a corporate bond is the product of the probability of default. They present this as a put option, and a numerical example is used to illustrate the application of option pricing theory to the assessment of credit risk.

Stephen Schaefer introduces an approximation method to estimate the market risk of nonlinear financial instruments. The increasing use of derivatives by financial institutions emphasizes the need to recognize their special features and their influence on the risk exposure of the bank. Schaefer suggests a computationally convenient method to combine derivatives in the VaR estimation.

The next two articles deal directly with the implementation of the 1996 Basle Accord on market risk. In a thought-provoking paper, Giorgio Szego offers an outspoken critique of the Basle capital regulations. Citing recent troubles and crises that have plagued the world's banking system, Szego casts some doubts on the meaningfulness of prudential regulation, the effectiveness of supervision, the underlying rationale of solvency ratios, and the very survival of traditional banks as financial intermediaries.

Clifford Smout, Head of the Foreign Exchange Division at the Bank of England, discusses problems relating to the implementation of the Basle Accord on Market Risk in the UK. He suggests that smaller banks in the UK are likely to use the standardized approach but expects larger firms with diversified portfolios to opt for the Value-at-Risk approach. After an examination of the numerous problems confronting the implementation of an internal VaR model, he urges that we not lose sight of the very real advantages of the VaR approach: reduction of compliance costs, greater flexibility and ease of adjustment, greater accuracy in dealing with hedged and partially hedged positions, and an even-handed treatment (at least in theory) of different types of risk.

The next two papers deal with financial regulation in general, an area in which traditional approaches and practices have been significantly affected by financial theory. John Heimann, Chairman of Global Financial Institutions at Merrill Lynch and former U.S. Comptroller of the Currency, draws upon his experience, both as regulator and as practitioner, to examine the role of risk management in today's volatile world. He notes that due to the globalization of finance, risk and therefore risk management have become world-wide phenomena. Confronted by the complexities of some of the newer financial techniques and models, Heimann offers top management a simple rule of thumb, "if you don't understand it, don't do it." He stresses the need to organize for risk management, starting at the top with the board of directors and the need to ensure that compensation does not become a one-way street in which traders are rewarded for successful risk taking but are not penalized for loss.

From a somewhat different viewpoint, Brian Smouha, Senior Partner at Deloitte & Touche, takes a long look at bank fraud, in general, and at Banco Ambrosiano and the Bank of Credit and Commerce International (BCCI) crises, in particular. Using insights gained when he served as lead liquidator for the collapsed Banco Ambrosiano and for BCCI, which had the world's largest and most complex bank liquidation in history, Smouha presents a cogent discussion and analysis of the biggest and most frightening of all risks: fraud.

The final section of the book contains two papers dealing with risk management in Israel. Yoram Landskroner, David Ruthenberg, and David Zaken set out the approach to risk management that has evolved at the Bank Supervision Department at the Bank of Israel. They present an internal model based on a portfolio approach, which takes the covariances of the different risks into account. The estimation of overall market risk considers a bank's total balance sheet (including off-balance sheet items), not only its trading portfolio. Their proposed risk-adjusted capital requirement standard is comprised of an objective factor derived empirically from money and capital market data, and a subjective factor that reflects the degree of risk tolerance of the Bank Supervisor (or of a bank's management, if the model is used for internal risk control).

The book concludes with a paper by Yair Orgler, Chairman of the Tel Aviv Stock Exchange, on risk management with derivatives traded at the TASE. The objective of the paper is to describe the financial derivatives available at the TASE and those planned for introduction in the near future. Orgler discusses the main features of all these derivatives and provides data on those presently traded. In addition, he provides insights on the perplexing question of why certain contracts did not take off.

Finally, it is a pleasant duty to thank Prof. Arie Melnik; Prof. Jacob Paroush; Mr. Arie Shapiro; Prof. Itzhak Swary; Prof. Ben-Zion Zilberfarb, who chaired the various conference sessions; the former supervisor of Israel's banks, Mr. Zeev Abeles; and the senior executives of four leading banks of Israel: Mr. Gidon Lahav, Mrs. Galia Maor, Mr. Amiram Sivan, and Mr. Shlomo Peutrokovsky, who served as participants in the panel discussion that concluded the conference; as well as the other members of the organizing committee: Prof. Dan Galai, Prof. David Ruthenberg, and Dr. Ben Schreiber.

Marshall Sarnat

II. RISK MANAGEMENT IN BANKING: AN OVERVIEW

1. BANK RISK MANAGEMENT: THEORY

DAVID H. PYLE

INTRODUCTION[1]

Not too many years ago, the then Chairman of the U.S. House Banking Committee told me it was out of the question to require banks and savings and loans to mark their assets to market. Would anyone responsible for financial regulatory oversight have the temerity to be similarly dismissive today? I suspect the answer is yes. However, the increased attention that formal, scientific appraisal of bank risk has received since then is gratifying to most financial economists. The fact that contemporary bank-risk management employs many of the important theoretical and methodological advances in our field is a source of collective pride. My role on this program is to outline some of the theoretical underpinnings of contemporary bank-risk management. I shall begin with a discussion of why bank-risk management is needed. Then I shall provide some of the theoretical bases for bank-risk management with an emphasis on market and credit risks.

WHY IS RISK MANAGEMENT NEEDED?

Recent financial disasters in financial and nonfinancial firms and in governmental agencies point to the need for various forms of risk management. Financial misadventures are hardly a new phenomenon, but the rapidity with which economic entities can get into trouble is. The savings and loan (S&L) crisis in the United States took two decades, plus serious regulatory ineptness and legislative cupidity, to develop into the debacle it became. The manager of the Orange County

Investment Pool (OCIP) took less than three years to increase that quasibank's potential one-month loss from a significant but perhaps manageable 1.8% to a disastrous 5% of its investors' deposit-like claims.[2] Anyone who is aware of the leverage inherent in various interest-rate derivatives knows he could have done this faster and even more ruinously had he set his mind to it. To their credit, most regulatory authorities appear to recognize that the core of the problem is not derivatives per se but inadequate risk management.

Banks and similar financial institutions need to meet forthcoming regulatory requirements for risk measurement and capital.[3] However, it is a serious error to think that meeting regulatory requirements is the sole or even the most important reason for establishing a sound, scientific risk management system. Managers need reliable risk measures to direct capital to activities with the best risk/reward ratios. They need estimates of the size of potential losses to stay within limits imposed by readily available liquidity, by creditors, customers, and regulators. They need mechanisms to monitor positions and create incentives for prudent risk-taking by divisions and individuals.

Risk management is the process by which managers satisfy these needs by identifying key risks, obtaining consistent, understandable, operational risk measures, choosing which risks to reduce and which to increase and by what means, and establishing procedures to monitor the resulting risk position.

WHAT ARE THE KEY RISKS?

Risk, in this context, may be defined as "reductions in firm value due to changes in the business environment." Typically, the major sources of value loss are identified as

Market risk is the change in net asset value due to changes in underlying economic factors, such as interest rates, exchange rates, and equity and commodity prices.

Credit risk is the change in net asset value due to changes in the perceived or actual ability of counter-parties to meet their contractual obligations.

Operational risk results from costs incurred through mistakes made in carrying out transactions such as settlement failures, failures to meet regulatory requirements, and untimely collections.

Performance risk encompasses losses resulting from the failure to properly monitor employees or to use appropriate methods (including model risk).

With the exception of model risk, financial theory does not have a lot to say about the latter two types of risk, although as the managers of various firms have discovered to their regret, they can be highly important.[4] Consequently, in what follows, I focus on the theoretical underpinnings of market risk management with a few comments on credit risk.

MEASURING MARKET RISK

Significant differences exist in the internal and external views of what is a satisfactory market risk measure. Internally, bank managers need a measure that allows active, efficient management of the bank's risk position. Bank regulators want to be sure a bank's potential for catastrophic net worth loss is accurately measured and that the bank's capital is sufficient to survive such a loss. Consider the differences in desired risk measure characteristics that these two views engender.

Timeliness and scope

Both managers and regulators want up-to-date measures of risk. For banks active in trading, this may mean selective intraday risk measurement as well as a daily measurement of the total risk of the bank. Note, however, that the intraday measures that are relevant for asset allocation and hedging decisions are measures of the marginal effect of a trade on total bank risk and not the stand-alone riskiness of the trade. Regulators, on the other hand, are concerned with the overall riskiness of a bank and have less concern with the risk of individual portfolio components. Nonetheless, given the ability of a sophisticated manager to window dress a bank's position on short notice, regulators might also like to monitor the intraday total risk. As a practical matter, they probably must be satisfied with a daily measure of total bank risk.

The need for a total risk measure implies that risk measurement cannot be decentralized. For parametric measures of risk, such as standard deviation, this follows from the theory of portfolio selection (Markowitz, 1952) and the well-known fact that the risk of a portfolio is not, in general, the sum of the component risks. More generally, imperfect correlation among portfolio components implies that simulations of portfolio risk must be driven by the portfolio return distribution, which will not be invariant to changes in portfolio composition. Finally, given costly regulatory capital requirements, choices among alternative assets require managers to consider risk/return or risk/cost tradeoffs, where risk is measured as the change in portfolio risk resulting from a given change in portfolio composition. The appropriate risk scaling measure depends on the type of change being made. For example, the pertinent choice criterion for pure hedging transactions might be to maximize the marginal risk reduction to transaction cost ratio over the available instruments while the choice among proprietary transactions would involve minimizing marginal risk per unit of excess return.

Efficiency

Risk measurement is costly and time consuming. Consequently, bank managers compromise between measurement precision on the one hand and the cost and timeliness of reporting on the other.[5] This tradeoff will have a profound effect on the risk measurement method a bank will adopt. Bank regulators have their own problem with the cost of accurate risk measurement, which is probably one reason they have chosen to monitor and stress test bank risk measurement systems rather than undertaking their own risk measurements.

Information content

Bank regulators have a singular risk measurement goal. They want to know, to a high degree of precision, the maximum loss a bank is likely to experience over a given horizon. They then can set the bank's required capital (i.e., its economic net worth) to be greater than the estimated maximum loss and be almost sure that the bank will not fail over that horizon. In other words, regulators should focus on the extreme tail of the bank's return distribution and on the size of that tail in adverse circumstances. Bank managers have a more complex set of risk information needs. In addition to shared concerns over sustainable losses, they must consider risk/return tradeoffs. That calls for a different risk measure than the tail statistic, a different horizon, and a focus on more usual market conditions. Furthermore, even when concerned with the level of sustainable losses, the bank manager may want to monitor on the basis of a probability of loss that can be observed with some frequency (e.g., over a month rather than over a year). This allows managers to use the risk measurement model to answer questions such as

Is the model currently valid? For example, if the loss probability is set at 5%, do we observe a violation once every 20 days on average?

Are traders correctly motivated to manage and not just avoid risk? How often does Trader I's position violate his risk limit relative to the likelihood of that event?

Market risk measurement alternatives

There are two principle approaches to risk measurement, scenario analysis and value-at-risk analysis.

Scenario analysis: In scenario analysis, the analyst postulates changes in the underlying determinants of portfolio value (e.g., interest rates, exchange rates, equity prices, and commodity prices) and revalues the portfolio given those changes. The resulting change in value is the loss estimate. A typical procedure, often called stress testing, is to use a scenario based on an historically adverse market move. This approach has the advantage of not requiring a distributional assumption for the risk calculation. On the other hand, it is subjective and incorporates a strong assumption that future financial upsets will strongly resemble those of the past. Given the earlier discussion, it should be clear that stress testing can provide regulators with the desired lower tail estimates but is of limited utility in day-to-day risk management.[6] It should also be clear that meaningful scenario analysis is dependent on having valuation models that are accurate over a wide range of input parameters, a characteristic that is shared to a considerable extent by value-at-risk models. Pioneering research on capital asset pricing (Sharpe, 1964), option pricing (Black and Scholes, 1973; Merton, 1973), and term structure modeling (Vasicek, 1977) has provided the basis for reliable valuation models, models that have become increasingly accurate and applicable with subsequent modification and extension by other researchers.

Value-at-Risk (VaR) analyses use asset return distributions and predicted return parameters to estimate potential portfolio losses. The specific measure used is the loss in value over X days that will not be exceeded more than Y% of the time. The Basle Committee on Banking Supervision's rule sets Y equal to 1 percent, and X equal to 10 days. In contrast, the standard in RiskMetrics™ (the J.P. Morgan/Reuters VaR method) is 5 percent over a horizon sufficiently long for the position to be unwound which, in many cases, is one day. The difference in probability levels reflects the differences in informational objectives discussed above. The differences in horizon might appear to reflect differences in the uses to which the risk measure is put, in particular the desire of regulators to set capital rules that provide protection from failure over a longer period. This conclusion may be correct, but it is somewhat contradicted by the arbitrary multiplication of the resulting VaR figure by three to get regulatory required capital. The Basle Committee could have gotten about the same result using a one-day horizon and multiplying by 9.5. Perhaps order of magnitude arbitrariness is less palatable than single digit arbitrariness.

There are two principle methods for estimating VaR: the analytical method and Monte Carlo simulation, each with advantages and disadvantages.[7] There are implementation problems common to both methods, namely choosing appropriate return distributions for the instruments in the portfolio and obtaining good forecasts of their parameters. The literature on volatility estimation is large and seemingly subject to unending growth, especially in acronyms (Arch, Grach, Egarch, et al.). Since I am not an expert on forecasting, it will be safest and perhaps sufficient to make two comments on forecasting for VaR analysis. Firstly, the risk manager with a large book to manage needs daily and, in some cases, intraday forecasts of the relevant parameters. This puts a premium on using a forecasting method that can be quickly and economically updated. Secondly, forecasting models that incorporate sound economic theory, including market microstructure factors, are likely to outperform purely mechanical models.[8]

Modeling portfolio returns as a multivariate normal distribution has many advantages in terms of computational efficiency and tractability. Unfortunately, there is evidence going back to Mandelbrot (1963) and beyond that some asset returns display nonnormal characteristic. The fact that they display fat tails, more extreme values than would be predicted for a normal variable, is particularly disturbing when one is trying to estimate potential value loss. To some degree, these fat tails in unconditional return distributions reflect the inconstancy of return volatility and the problem can be mitigated by modeling individual returns as a function of volatility as in the RiskMetrics™ model:

$$r_{i,t} = \sigma_{i,t}\varepsilon_{i,t}$$

where $\varepsilon_{i,t}$ *is* $N(0,1)$.

Another alternative is to assume that returns follow a nonnormal distribution with fat tails (e.g., the Student's t distribution), but only if one is prepared to accept the concomitant portfolio return computation problems. Danielson and de Vries (1997) have proposed a method for explicit modeling of the tails of financial returns. Since VaR analysis is intended to describe the behavior of portfolio returns in the lower tail, this is obviously an intriguing approach. Furthermore, the authors show that the tail behavior of data from almost any distribution follows a single limit law, which adds to the attractiveness of the method. However, estimating tail densities is not a trivial matter so, while promising, there are computational issues to be resolved if this is to become a mainstream VaR method.

Analytical VaR: The analytical method for VaR uses standard portfolio theory. The portfolio in question is described in terms of a position vector containing cash flow present values representing all components of the portfolio. The return distribution is described in terms of a matrix of variance and covariance forecasts (covariance matrix) representing the risk attributes of the portfolio over the chosen horizon. The standard deviation of portfolio value (v) is obtained by pre- and post-multiplying the covariance matrix (Q) by the position vector (p) and taking the square root of the resulting scalar:[9]

$$v = \sqrt{p'Qp}.$$

This standard deviation is then scaled to find the desired centile of portfolio value that is the predicted maximum loss for the portfolio or VaR:

$$VaR = vf(Y)$$

where, f(Y) is the scale factor for pecentile Y.

For example, for a multivariate normal return distribution, $f(Y) = 1.65$ for $Y = 5\%$, or 2.33 for $Y = 1\%$. Analytical VaR is attractive in that it is fast and not terribly demanding of computational resources. As the following algebra demonstrates, analytical VaR also lends itself readily to the calculation of the marginal risk of candidate trades:[10]

$$\Delta v_i = \frac{p'Q}{v} a_i$$

where a_i is a given candidate trade an Δv_i is its marginal risk.

Given trade cash flow descriptions, the information needed to calculate the marginal risk of any candidate trade can be accumulated during a single calculation of portfolio standard deviation (v).

Analytical VaR has a number of weaknesses. In its simplest form, options and other nonlinear instruments are delta-approximated, which is to say the representative cash flow vector is a linear approximation of position that is inherently nonlinear. In some cases, this approximation can be improved by including a second-order term in the cash flow representation.[11] However, this does not always improve the risk estimate and can only be done with the sacrifice of some of the computational efficiency that recommends analytical VaR to bank managers.

Monte Carlo Simulation: Monte Carlo simulation of VaR begins with a random draw on all the distributions describing price and rate movements taking into account the correlations among these variates. Mark-to-model and maturation values for all portfolio components at the VaR horizon are determined based on that price/rate path. This process is repeated enough times to achieve significance in the resulting end-of-horizon portfolio values. Then the differences between the initial portfolio value and these end-of-horizon values are ranked and the loss level at the Yth centile is reported as the VaR of the portfolio.

To avoid bias in this calculation, the analyst must use risk-neutral equivalent distributions and, if the horizon is sufficiently long, be concerned with bias introduced by the return on capital. If model error is not significant, the use of Monte Carlo simulation solves the problem of nonlinearity though there are some technical difficulties such as how to deal with time-varying parameters and how to generate maturation values for instruments that mature before the VaR horizon. From the risk manager's viewpoint, the main problem is the cost of this method and the time it takes to get reliable estimates.

MEASURING CREDIT RISK

To be consistent with market-risk measurement, credit risks are defined as changes in portfolio value due to the failure of counter-parties to meet their obligations or due to changes in the market's perception of their ability to continue to do so. Ideally, a bank-risk management system would integrate this source of risk with the market risks discussed above to produce an overall measure of the bank's loss potential. Traditionally, banks have used a number of methods—credit scoring, ratings, credit committees—to assess the creditworthiness of counter-parties. At first glance, these approaches do not appear to be compatible with the market risk methods. However, some banks are aware of the need for parallel treatment of all measurable risks and are doing something about it.[12] Unfortunately, current bank regulations treat these two sources of risk quite differently subjecting credit risk to arbitrary capital requirements that have no scientific validity. There is danger in this since it can lead to capital misallocation and imprudent risk-taking.

If banks can score loans, they can determine how loan values change as scores change. If codified, these changes would produce over time a probability distribution of value changes due to credit risk. With such a distribution, the time series of credit risk changes could be related to the market risk and we would be able to integrating market risk and credit risk into a single estimate of value change over a given horizon.

This is not a pipe dream. Considerable research on the credit risk of derivatives, including a paper at this conference, is available. Obviously, banks themselves are in the best position to produce the data series necessary for broader application of this approach. If it is reasonable to require banks to produce and justify market risk measurement systems, why can't they be required to do the same for credit risk and to integrate the two? The House Banking Committee chairman I mentioned at the start of this talk probably would have rejected this idea out of hand. I hope today's regulatory authorities won't.

NOTES

1. In writing this paper, I have benefited from a set of notes on risk management by Hayne Leland.
2. Potential one-month losses estimated at a 5% probability of occurrence. See Jorion (1995) for a thorough and entertaining discussion of the Orange County fiasco.
3. Regulatory capital requirements result from the need to control the moral hazard inherent in the bank/depositor relationship when there are governmental deposit guarantees (explicit or implicit). Merton (1977) provided the classic theoretical demonstration of this moral hazard and its determinants.
4. Perhaps, conventional wisdom is more relevant than theory for many of these risks. For example, Barings might have benefited from an intelligent application of the adage "Don't put the fox in charge of the hen house."
5. See Pritsker (1996).
6. Even for the regulators, reliance on a given scenario carries the risk of establishing a Maginot line defense against catastrophe.
7. It is also possible to use the Cox-Ross-Rubinstein (1979) tree-based methods to generate a VaR estimate, but the use of this method is limited to a small number of risk sources and thus it is an unlikely candidate for use in bank-risk management.
8. See Figleski (1997) for evidence on the relative accuracy of various volatility forecasting methods.
9. To keep this method manageable in terms of parameter estimation and speed of calculation, the size of the covariance matrix can be constrained and the portfolio position vector described in terms of a subset of the actual risks being faced. For example, in the RiskMetrics data base, equity risk appears as the variances and covariances of 32 equity indices and a given equity position is made to correspond to this description by scaling its present values by the equity's beta.
10. Incremental VaR, as defined here, is a first-order approximation of the change in risk due to a candidate trade and is applicable when the cash flows for such trades are small relative to the aggregate cash flow of the existing portfolio. See Garman (1996).
11. See Fallon (1996) and JP Morgan (1996).
12. See. J.P. Morgan (1997).

REFERENCES

Black, F., and M. Scholes (1973). "The Pricing of Options and Corporate Liabilities," *J. Political Economy* 81, 637–59.

Cox, J.C., S.A. Ross, and M. Rubinstein (1979). "Option Pricing: A Simplified Approach," *J. Financial Economics* 7, 229–63.

Danielson, J., and C.G. de Vries (1997). "Extreme Returns, Tail Estimation, and Value-at-risk," Working Paper, University of Iceland (http://www.hag.hi.is/~jond/research).

Fallon, W. (1996). "Calculating Value-at-risk." Working Paper, Columbia University (bfallon@groucho.gsb.columbia.edu).

Figlewski, S. (1997). "Forecasting Volatility," *Financial Markets, Institutions, & Instruments* 6, No. 1.

Garman, M.B. (1996). "Improving on VaR," *Risk* 9, No. 5.

Jorion, P. (1995). *Big Bets Gone Bad*. Academic Press, San Diego, CA.

JP Morgan (1996). *RiskMetrics™—technical document*. 4th ed.

JP Morgan (1997). *CreditMetrics™—technical document*.

Mandelbrot, B. (1963). "The Variation of Certain Speculative Prices," *J. Business* 36, 394–419.

Markowitz, H. (1952). "Portfolio Selection." *J. Finance* 7, 77–91.

Merton, R.C. (1973). "Theory of Rational Option Pricing," *Bell Journal of Economics and Management Science* 4, 141–83.

Merton, R.C. (1997). "An Analytical Derivation of the Cost of Deposit Insurance and Loan Guarantees: An Application of Modern Option Pricing Theory," *J. of Banking & Finance* 1, 3–11.

Pritsker, M. (1996). "Evaluating Value-at-Risk Methodologies: Accuracy Versus Computational Time," unpublished Working Paper, Board of Governors of the Federal Reserve System (mpritsker@frb.gov).

Sharpe, W. (1964). "Capital Asset Prices: A Theory of Market Equilibrium under Conditions of Risk." *J. Finance* 19, 425–42.

Vasicek, O.A. (1977). "An Equilibrium Characterization of the Term Structure." *J. Financial Economics* 5, 177–88.

2. RISK MANAGEMENT IN BANKING: PRACTICE REVIEWED AND QUESTIONED

ANTHONY M. SANTOMERO

1. INTRODUCTION

Risk management has become a hot topic in the financial sector. Almost without exception, institutions have rushed headlong into major efforts to upgrade their risk management systems, and focus management attention on appropriate process for due consideration of the tradeoff between risk and return. For a long while, these systems were a patchwork of firm specific solutions to risk measurement and management, but recently this has all changed. The industry, worldwide, has begun to settle on standard approaches to risk management, as well as a consistent view of what is and is not possible in this domain. This is not to say the industry is completely happy with the results achieved thus far. Rather, it is to suggest that standards, or something like best practices, in this area are emerging.

We would like to think that Wharton was part of this process of convergence. At the very least, our work in this area has brought information to the attention of decision makers in the industry. As many of you may know, the Wharton Financial Institutions Center, with the support of the Sloan Foundation, has been actively involved in an analysis of financial risk management processes in the financial sector. Over the past two years, onsite visits were conducted to review and evaluate the risk management systems and the process of risk evaluation that are in place. In the banking sector, system evaluation was conducted, covering many of the major financial institutions, including universal banks, U.S.-style commercial banks, and a number of major investment banking firms.

These results were then presented to a much wider array of banking firms for reaction and verification. The resultant study, Santomero (1997), has been widely distributed and its results discussed in both academic and industry circles.[1] Presentations of our results have occurred at industry meetings as varied as the U.S. Bankers Roundtable and the International Bankers Summer School. They have also contributed to firm specific discussions of internal risk systems at some of the world's major financial institutions. Finally, they have been given to various regulatory agencies throughout the world in their quest for adequate understanding of internal risk management programs in light of their recently expanded responsibility to perform risk system examinations.

The purpose of the present paper is twofold. First, it will quickly outline the findings of our investigation. It will report on the state of risk management techniques in the industry, outlining the standard practice as well as evaluating how and why it is conducted in the particular way chosen. Second, it will offer a critique of the process, including a series of questions that are currently unanswered, or answered imprecisely in the current practice employed by this group of relatively sophisticated banks. Here, we discuss the problems which the industry finds most difficult to address, shortcomings of the current methodology used to analyze risk and the elements that are missing in the current procedures of risk management and risk control. To academics, this list can be seen as a broad research agenda, areas where work is clearly needed. To practitioners, it is a wake-up call. Problems remain in risk management systems, in spite of the money already spent.

2. REVIEWING THE INDUSTRY'S PERSPECTIVE ON FINANCIAL RISK

It has become trite to begin as analysis of risk management with the mantra "banking is a risky business," but it is true. Bankers worldwide have come to realize that the deregulation of local markets, the internationalization of financial market competition, and the underlying instability of the world economy have resulted in an environment in which operating a financial institution is substantially more risky than it had been in the past. This has led institutions to question many of their assumptions about what risks are appropriately taken and how they should view their role in the financial sector. Elsewhere[2] we have argued that this has led to two different responses by member institutions in the financial sector. First, they have moved to agency and off-balance sheet activity to a greater extent than before, and second, they have employed a number of standard techniques to reduce risk exposure for transactions that do involve the bank as principal.

The first of these points is uncontestable. Worldwide, the banking industry is generating more of its revenue from fee income than ever before. This has been fueled by financial innovations on both sides of the balance sheet. As financial markets become more competitive, larger corporate clients have moved to direct financing. This has caused their key financial institutions to increase their emphasis on placement, and decrease the importance of bank loans. Whether it is private placement, syndications, or direct underwriting, major financial institutions have clearly shifted their focus from loan generation to the facilitation of funding needs of their large corporate clients. On the consumer level, securitization has brought about a similar trend, albeit mostly in Anglo-Saxon countries. However, as this trend spreads, here too, the bank's direct exposure to consumer credit risk is substantially reduced. On the liability side, a similar move off balance sheet is occurring. The deregulation of deposit rates and the increasing sophistication of retail customers has led to increased emphasis on asset management and away from deposit gathering. Interest rate spread is giving way to fee income, and balance sheet activity is being sacrificed in favor of less risk, and a stable income stream from agency services.

Beyond all this, however, there is a second important trend. Even for those risks contained in the bank's principal activities, i.e., those involving their own balance sheets and the basic businesses of lending and borrowing, not all risks of these contracts are borne by the bank itself. In many instances the financial risk associated with a transaction are being mitigated or completely eliminated by risk reducing business practices; in others, the risk is being shifted to other parties through a combination of pricing and product design.

Banking institutions recognize that an institution should not engage in business in a manner that unnecessarily imposes risk upon them; nor should they absorb risks that can be efficiently transferred to other participants. Rather, the bank should manage only those risks at the firm level that are more efficiently managed there, rather than by the market itself or by owners in their own portfolios. In short, a financial institution should accept only those risks that are uniquely a part of the bank's array of unique value-added services.

Elsewhere, Oldfield and Santomero (1997), it has been argued that risks facing all financial institutions can be segmented into three separable types, from a management perspective. These are:

1. risks that can be eliminated or avoided by simple business practices,
2. risks that can be transferred to other participants, and,
3. risks that must be actively managed at the firm level.

In the first of these cases, the practice of risk avoidance involves actions to reduce the chances of idiosyncratic losses from standard banking activity by eliminating risks that are superfluous to the institution's business purpose. Common risk avoidance practices here include at least three types of actions. The standardization of process, contracts and procedures to prevent inefficient or incorrect financial decisions is the first of these. The construction of portfolios that benefit from diversification across borrowers and that reduce the effects of any one loss experience is another. Finally, the implementation of contracts with management that require employees to be held accountable. In each case, the goal is to rid the firm of risks that are not essential to the financial service provided, or to absorb only an optimal quantity of a particular kind of risk.

Banks are also using the technique of risk transfer to eliminate or substantially reduce the risks inherent in their positions. Markets exist for many of the risks borne by the banking firm. Interest rate risk can be transferred by rate sensitive products such as swaps or other derivatives. Borrowing terms can be altered to effect a change in asset duration. Finally, the bank can buy or sell financial claims to diversify or concentrate the risks that result from servicing its client base. To the extent that the financial risks of the assets created by the firm are understood by the market, these assets can be sold at their fair value. Unless the institution has a comparative advantage in managing the attendant risk or a desire for the embedded risk they contain, there is no reason for the bank to absorb such risks, rather than transfer them.

However, there are two classes of assets or activities where the risk inherent in the activity must and should be absorbed at the bank level. In these cases, good reasons exist for using firm resources to manage bank-level risk. The first of these includes financial assets or activities where the nature of the embedded risk may be complex and difficult to communicate to third parties. This is the case when the bank holds complex and proprietary assets that have thin, if not nonexistent, secondary markets. Communication in such cases may be difficult or too expensive to hedge the underlying risk.[3] The second case includes proprietary positions that are accepted because of their risks and expected return. Here, risk positions that are central to the bank's business purpose are absorbed because they are the raison d'être of the firm. Credit risk inherent in some lending activity is a clear case in point, as is market risk for the trading desk of banks active in certain markets. In all such circumstances, risk is absorbed and needs to be monitored and managed efficiently by the institution. Only then will the firm systematically achieve its financial performance goal.

In such cases, necessary procedures must be in place to carry out adequate monitoring and management of the accepted risky position. In essence, techniques must be employed to both limit and manage the different types of risk, and must be implemented in each area of accepted risk. The procedures employed by leading firms to manage the accepted risks rely on a sequence of steps to implement a risk management system. These can be seen as containing the following four parts:

1. standards and reports,
2. position limits or rules,
3. investment guidelines or strategies,
4. incentive contracts and compensation.

In general, these tools are established to measure exposure, define procedures to manage these exposures, limit individual positions to acceptable levels, and encourage decision makers to manage risk in a manner that is consistent with the firm's goals and objectives. To see how each of these four parts of basic risk management techniques achieves these ends, we refer the interested reader to Oldfield and Santomero (1997). In Section 3 we illustrate how these techniques are applied to manage the specific risks facing the banking community.

3. MANAGING RISKS IN PROVIDING BANKING SERVICES

How are the techniques of risk management employed by the commercial banking sector? To explain this, one must begin by enumerating the risks which the banking industry has chosen to manage and illustrate how risk management systems are applied in each area. Naturally, the risks associated with the provision of banking services differ by the type of service rendered. For the sector as a whole, however, our research has found that the industry has broken these risks into six generic types: *market risk, credit risk, counter-party risk, liquidity risk, operational risk,* and *legal risks.* The first of these is often divided between *trading risk* and *balance sheet rate risk.*

Yet even here, the industry does not have risk management systems in place for all of these concerns. Rather, they have limited their risk management systems implementation to the need to control four of the above risks which make up most, if not all, of their financial risk exposure, viz., credit, trading, balance sheet, and liquidity risk. While they recognize the other risks enumerated above, they view them as less central to their concerns.[4] Where counterparty risk is seen as significant, it is evaluated using standard credit risk procedures, and often within the credit department itself. Likewise, most bankers would view legal risks as arising from their credit decisions or, more likely, proper process not employed in financial contracting.

Accordingly, risk management systems are essentially aimed at managing these four risks. In each case, a procedure is established to standardize, measure, constrain and manage each of these risks. To illustrate how this is achieved, this review of firm-level risk management begins with a discussion of risk management systems in each area. The more difficult issues of implementation and omitted risks will be left to later sections.

3.A. Credit risk management procedures

In presenting the approach employed to manage credit risk, the key issue to recognize is the need to apply a consistent evaluation and rating scheme to all investment opportunities. This is essential in order for credit decisions to be made in the same manner across the firm and for the resultant aggregate reporting of credit risk exposure to be meaningful. To facilitate this, a substantial degree of standardization of process and documentation has developed. This has lead to standardized ratings across borrowers so that an aggregate portfolio report presents meaningful information on the overall quality of the credit portfolio. In Appendix 1 a credit-rating procedure is presented that is typical of those employed within the commercial banking industry.

The form reported here is a single rating system where a single value is given to each loan, which relates to the borrower's underlying credit quality. At some institutions, a dual system is in place where both the borrower and the credit facility are rated. In the latter, attention centers on collateral and covenants, while in the former, the general credit worthiness of the borrower is measured. In any case, the reader will note that in the reported system all loans are rated using a single numerical scale ranging between 1 and 10.[5] For each numerical category, a qualitative definition of the borrower and the loan's quality is offered and an analytic representation of the underlying financials of the borrower is presented. Such an approach, whether it is a single or a dual rating system, allows the credit committee some comfort in its knowledge of loan asset quality at any moment of time. It requires only that new loan officers be introduced to the system of loan ratings, through training and apprenticeship to achieve a standardization of ratings throughout the bank.

Given these standards, the bank can report the quality of its loan portfolio at any time, along the lines of the report presented in Table 1. Notice that total receivables, including loans, leases and commitments, and derivatives, are reported in a single format. Assuming adherence to standards, the entirety of the firm's credit quality is reported to senior management monthly via this reporting mechanism. Changes in this report from one period to another occur for two reasons, viz., loans have entered or exited the system, or the rating of individual loans has changed over the intervening time interval. The first reason is associated with standard loan turnover. Loans are repaid and new loans are made. The second cause for a change in the credit quality report is more substantive. Variations over time indicate changes in loan quality and expected loan losses from the credit portfolio. In fact, credit quality reports should signal changes in expected loan losses, if the rating system is meaningful.

For this type of credit quality report to be meaningful, all credits must be monitored, and reviewed periodically. It is, in fact, standard for all credits above some dollar volume to be reviewed on a quarterly or annual basis to ensure the accuracy of the rating associated with the lending facility. In addition, a material change in the conditions associated either with the borrower or the facility itself, such as a change in the value of collateral, will trigger a re-evaluation. This process, therefore, results in a periodic but timely report card on the quality of the credit portfolio and its change from month to month.

Absent from the discussion thus far is any analysis of systematic risk contained in the portfolio. Recently, many banks have begun to develop concentration reports, indicating industry composition of the loan portfolio. This process was initially hampered by the lack of a simple industry index. Broad industry classifications were employed at some institutions, but most found them unsatisfactory. Recently, however, Moody's has developed a system of 34 industry groups that may be used to report concentrations. Table 2 reports such an industry grouping to illustrate the kind of concentration reports that are emerging as standard in the banking industry. Notice that the report indicates the portfolio percentages by sector, as well as commitments to various industries. For the real estate portfolio, geography is also reported, as Table 3 suggests. While this may be insufficient to capture total geographic concentration, it is a beginning.

Table 1. Bank level loan credit quality report.

Type	Rating reservables	0	1	2	3	4	5	6	7	8	9	10	Total	
		Risk rating												
LOANS AND LEASES	1a. COMMERCIAL LOANS AND LEASES	2	4	201	252	511	2,000	3,374	937	1,856	231	48	9,426	1a
	1b. CONSUMER LOANS	0	5,139	0	0	1,629	521	65	15	45	0	0	7,414	1b
	1c. OTHER LOANS AND LEASES							481					481	1c
	TOTAL LOANS AND LEASES	2	5,143	201	252	2,140	2,521	3,920	952	1,901	231	48	17,311	
	1d. LESS: GROSS COMMERCIAL LOAN C/O ESTIMATE									0	−17	−47	−64	1d
	1e. LESS: GROSS COMMERCIAL LOAN C/O ESTIMATE									−24	0	0	−24	1e
	TOTAL LOAN AND LEASE CHARGE-OFFS	0	0	0	0	0	0	0	0	−24	−17	−47	−89	
	LOANS AND LEASE RESERVABLES	2	5,143	201	252	2,140	2,521	3,920	952	1,877	214	0	17,222	
OREO	2a. OREO									184	12	6	202	2a
	2b. LESS: OREO CHARGE-OFF ESTIMATE									0	0	−6	−6	2b
	OREO RESERVABLES	0	0	0	0	0	0	0	0	184	11	1	196	
CONTINGENT EXPOSURE	3a. UNUSED COMMITMENTS				1,959	1,959	980	980					5,878	3a
	@ 50%	0	0	0	980	980	490	490	0	0	0	0	2,939	
	3b. COMMERCIAL LETTERS OF CREDIT	0	1	1	3	19	51	83	5	2	0	0	165	3b
	@ 20%	0	0	0	1	4	10	17	1	1	0	0	33	
	3c. STAND-BY LETTERS OF CREDIT	18	1	27	44	76	141	183	78	50	15	0	632	3c
	@ 100%	18	1	27	44	76	141	183	78	50	15	0	632	
	3d. SWAPS	0		0	0	0	0	0	0	0	0	0	1	3d
	@ 100% OF CREDIT EQUIVALENT EXPOSURE	0		0	0	0	0	0	0	0	0	0	1	
	3e. BANKER'S ACCEPTANCES	0	0	0	13	1	47	80	6	0	0	0	146	3e
	@ 100%	0	0	0	13	1	47	80	6	0	0	0	146	
	CONTINGENT EXPOSURE RESERVABLES	18	1	27	1,037	1,060	688	770	85	51	15	0	3,751	
RESERVABLES	**TOTAL RESERVABLES**	20	5,144	288	1,288	3,200	3,209	4,690	1,037	2,111	240	1	21,169	

All items in millions of dollars.

Table 2. Credit Exposure by 34 Minor Industry Sectors.

	Outstandings			Unfunded Commitments			Commitments			
Moody's group	% of Total	Term to Mat.	Risk Rating	% of Total	Term to Mat.	Risk Rating	% of Total	Term to Mat.	Risk Rating	Utilization Rate
Aerospace and Defense	0.5	2.8	4.8	0.9	2.7	3.6	0.7	2.7	4.1	42
Automobile	2.8	2.9	4.5	2.6	1.8	3.6	2.7	2.4	4.1	60
Banking	3.1	1.3	3.6	14	1.3	2.6	7.7	1.3	2.8	23
Beverage, Food and Tobacco	4.3	2.9	4.7	4.7	2	3.3	4.5	2.5	4.1	55
Buildings and Real Estate	24.2	3	5	10.6	1.7	4.2	18.5	2.7	4.8	76
Cargo Transport	2.5	5.8	4.7	1.9	1.8	3.1	2.2	4.4	4.1	64
Chemicals, Plastics, and Rubber	2.3	2	4.4	2.7	1.8	3.6	2.5	1.9	4	53
Containers, Packaging, and Glass	0.7	2.4	5	0.6	2.2	4	0.7	2.3	4.6	61
Diversified Natural Resources, Precious Metals, and Minerals	0.7	1.6	5.1	0.6	1	4.8	0.7	1.4	5	59
Diversified/Conglomerate Manufacturing	0.6	2.7	4.7	0.6	2.5	4.3	0.6	2.6	4.5	59
Diversified/Conglomerate Sevice	5.1	2.2	4.3	2.9	0.9	3.6	4.1	1.8	4.1	71
Ecological	0.6	2.6	4.3	0.6	2.3	4	0.6	2.5	4.2	55
Electronics	2.5	2	4.4	5	1.7	3.9	3.6	1.8	4.1	41
Farming and Agriculture	2.8	2.4	4.7	1.6	1.1	3.5	2.3	2	4.4	71
Finance	3.4	3.3	3.5	3.6	1.3	2.5	3.5	2.4	3.1	56
Government	1.4	3.3	4.2	0.8	2	2.9	1.1	2.9	3.8	69
Grocery	0.9	3.2	5	1	2.4	3.8	0.9	2.8	4.4	53
Healthcare, Education, and Childcare	5.1	3.3	4.6	5.2	1.9	3.6	5.2	2.7	4.2	57
Home/Office Furnishings, Housewares, Durable Consum. Prods.	2.2	2.1	4.6	2	1.4	3.7	2.1	1.8	4.3	60
Hotels, Motels, Inns, and Gaming	1.3	3.4	5.3	0.4	4.2	4.3	1	3.6	5.1	82
Insurance	1.6	2.5	3.4	4	1.2	2	2.6	1.7	2.5	36
Leisure, Amusement, Motion Pictures, Entertainment	2.7	3.1	4.6	2.3	2.3	3.6	2.6	2.8	4.2	62
Machinery (Nonagri., Nonconstr., Nonelec.)	2.7	2.3	4.7	2.4	1.6	3.8	2.6	2	4.4	60
Mining, Steel, Iron, Nonprecious Metals	2.9	1.9	4.8	2.8	1.7	4	2.9	1.8	4.4	59
Oil and Gas	2.6	4.1	4.1	3.4	2.6	3.6	3	3.3	3.9	52
Other	2.2	3.3	4.7	1	2.5	3.2	1.6	3.1	4.3	76
Personal/Nondurable Consumer Prods.	1.6	1.9	4.7	1.7	2.1	3.6	1.6	1.9	4.2	56
Personal, Food, and Miscellaneous Servs.	1.2	2.7	4.7	0.7	1.3	3.7	1	2.3	4.5	71
Printing, Publishing, and Broadcasting	6.4	2.7	4.8	5.1	2.9	3.5	5.9	2.8	4.3	63
Retail Stores	2.3	2.1	4.3	3.7	1.8	3.5	2.9	2	3.8	46
Telecommunications	1	2.9	4.2	2	1.9	2.6	1.4	2.3	3.2	40
Textiles and Leather	2.5	1.6	4.6	2	1.6	4.1	2.3	1.6	4.4	63
Transportation	1.8	3.1	4.3	1.6	2.3	3.4	1.7	2.8	4	60
Utilities	1.6	2.9	3.5	4.7	1.9	2.7	2.9	2.2	2.9	32

"% of total" is the percentage concentration in loan portfolio at the end of the reporting period.
"Term to mat" is the term to maturity in years, as a weighted average of industry group.
"Risk Rating" is based upon a ten point scale.

Table 3. Composition of loan portfolio by geographic area distribution of domestic commercial real estate loans by region.

	Geographic Region						
Project Type	Central Atlantic	Southeast	Midwest	West	Southwest	Northeast	Total
Office complexes	$196	$46	$46	$36	$12	$6	$342
Retail	155	70	45	22	11	—	303
Hotels	72	49	10	6	12	—	149
Industrial	50	2	2	5	3	—	62
Apartments	31	—	17	—	3	—	51
Undeveloped land	6	18	10	9	—	—	43
Health care	11	9	—	4	4	—	28
Residential	17	—	—	3	4	—	24
Other project types	56	—	—	—	—	—	56
Total	$594	$194	$130	$85	$49	$6	$1,058

All items in millions of dollars.

3.B. Interest rate management procedures

The area of interest rate risk is the second area of major concern and ongoing risk monitoring and management. Here, the tradition has been for the banking industry to diverge somewhat from other parts of the financial sector in their treatment of interest rate risk. Most commercial banks make a clear distinction between their trading activity and their balance sheet interest rate exposure. For each type of exposure, a different approach to measurement and management is employed.

For their trading positions, banks generally have viewed interest rate risk as a classic part of market risk, and have developed elaborate trading risk management systems to measure and monitor exposure. For large commercial banks and European-style universal banks that have an active trading business, such systems have become a required part of the infrastructure. But, in fact, these trading risk management systems vary substantially from bank to bank and generally are less real than imagined. In many firms, standard value-at-risk models, now known by the acronym *VaR*, are up and running. But, in many more cases, they are still in the implementation phase. In the interim, simple and hoc limits and close monitoring substitute for elaborate real-time systems. This may be completely satisfactory for institutions that have little trading activity and work primarily on behalf of clients, but the absence of adequate trading systems elsewhere in the industry is worth noting.

For institutions that do have active trading businesses, value-at-risk has become the standard approach. This procedure has recently been publicly displayed with the release of *Riskmetrics*™ by J.P. Morgan, but similar systems are in place at other firms. In that much exists in the public record about these systems[6], there is little value to reviewing this technique here. Suffice it to say that the daily volatility of the market value of tradeable assets is incorporated into a measure of total portfolio

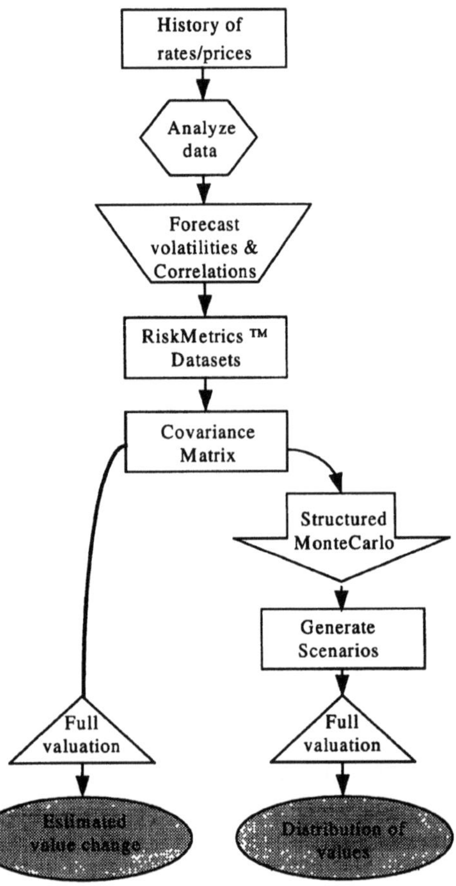

Figure 1. Introduction to RiskMetrics™. Procedure Use of the RiskMetrics™ datasets for VaR estimation. Source: Introduction to RiskMetrics™—Technical Document, JP Morgan, Fourth, Edition.

risk. Such systems generally include all fixed income instruments, equity positions and foreign-denominated assets. See Figure 1 for a quick review and example.

For balance sheet exposure to interest rate risk, commercial banking firms follow a different approach. Given the generally accepted accounting procedures (GAAP) established for bank assets, as well as the close correspondence of asset and liability structures, commercial banks tend not to use market value reports, guidelines or limits. Rather, their approach relies on cash flows and book values, at the expense of market values. Asset cash flows are reported in various repricing schedules along the line of Table 4. This system has been labeled traditionally a "gap reporting system," as the asymmetry of the repricing of assets and liabilities results in a gap.

This has classically been measured in ratio or percentage mismatch terms over a standardized interval such as a 30-day or one-year period.

This is sometimes supplemented with a duration analysis of the portfolio, as seen in Table 5. However, many assumptions are necessary to move from cash flows to duration. Asset categories that do not have fixed maturities, such as prime rate loans, must be assigned a duration measure based upon actual repricing flexibility. A similar problem exists for core liabilities, such as retail demand and savings balances. Nonetheless, the industry attempts to measure these estimates accurately, and include both on- and off-balance sheet exposures in this type of reporting procedure. The result of this exercise is a rather crude approximation of the duration gap.[7]

Currently, many banks are using balance sheet simulation models in addition to investigate the effect of interest rate variation on reported earnings over one-, three- and five-year horizons. These simulations require relatively informed repricing schedules, as well as estimates of prepayments and cash flows. In terms of the first issue, such an analysis requires an assumed response function to rate movement on the part of the bank, in which bank pricing decisions in both their local and national franchises are simulated for each rate environment. In terms of the second area, the simulations require precise prepayment models for proprietary products, such as middle market loans, as well as standard products such as residential mortgages or traditional consumer debt. In addition, these simulations require yield curve simulation over a presumed relevant range of rate movements and yield curve shifts.

Once completed, the simulation reports the resultant deviations in earnings associated with the rate scenarios considered. Whether or not this is acceptable depends upon the limits imposed by management, which are usually couched in terms of deviations of earnings from the expected or most likely outcome. This notion of Earnings At Risk, EaR, is a common benchmark for interest rate risk. The results are viewed as indicative of the effect of underlying interest rate mismatch contained in the balance sheet. Reports of these simulations, such as contained in Table 6, are now commonplace in the industry.

Bacause of concerns over the potential earnings outcomes of the simulations, treasury officials often make use of the cash, futures, and swap markets to reduce the implied earnings risk contained in the bank's embedded rate exposure. However, all institutions restrict the activity of the treasury to some extent by defining the set of activities it can employ to change the bank's interest rate position in both the cash and forward markets. Most will engage in some derivative activity, but all restrict their positions in swap, caps and floor markets to some degree.

3.C. Foreign exchange risk management procedures

In this area there is considerable difference in current practice. This can be explained by the different franchises that coexist in the banking industry. Most banking institutions view activity in the foreign exchange market to be beyond their franchise, while others are active participants. The former will take virtually no principal risk,

Table 4. Interest rate sensitivity typical gap report.

Assets	Prime loans and funding source	0–3 months	>3–6 months	>6–12 months	>1–5 years	>5 years	Nonmarket	Total
Investment securities	$ —	$533	$711	$3,085	$7,354	$1,315	$40	$13,058
Federal funds sold and securities purchased under resale agreements	—	1,668	—	—	—	—	—	1,668
Loans:								
Commercial	4,015	1,747	316	125	222	66	412	6,912
Real estate 1–4 family first mortgages	115	1,565	1,223	913	2,519	1,024	99	7,458
Other real estate mortgages	2,572	2,171	591	537	1,478	359	578	8,286
Real estate construction	732	112	1	12	18	—	235	1,110
Consumer	729	4,071	226	303	628	93	2,053	8,103
Lease financing	—	85	94	175	850	8	—	1,212
Foreign:	—	18	—	—	—	—	—	18
Total Loans (2)	8,163	9,769	3,162	2,065	5,715	1,550	3,386	33,099
Other earning assets:	—	—	—	—	—	—	52	52
Total earning assets	8,163	11,990	3,162	5,150	13,069	2,865	3,478	47,877
Noninterest-earning assets:	—	—	—	—	—	—	4,636	4,636
Total assets	8,163	11,990	3,162	5,150	13,069	2,865	8,114	52,513

All units in millions of U.S. dollars.

Table 4. (continued)

Liabilities and stockholder's equity	Prime loans and funding source	0–3 months	>3–6 months	>6–12 months	>1–5 years	>5 years	Non-market	Total
Deposits:								
Interest-bearing checks	$ —	$ —	$ —	$ —	$ —	$ —	$4,789	$4,789
Savings deposits	—	—	—	—	—	—	$2,544	$2,544
Market rate savings	8,163	5,905	1,005	2,011	—	—	—	17,084
Saving certificates	—	2,128	1,357	1,069	2,437	150	14	7,155
Other time deposits	—	65	13	31	191	13	2	315
Deposits in foreign offices:	—	38	—	—	—	—	—	38
Total interest bearing deposits	8,163	8,163	2,375	3,111	2,628	163	7,349	31,925
Federal funds purchased and securities sold under repurchase agreements	—	1,079	—	—	—	—	—	1,079
Commercial paper and other short-term borrowings	—	188	—	—	—	—	—	188
Senior debt	—	1,527	26	318	343	42	—	2,256
Subordinated debt	—	1,895	—	—	—	—	70	1,965
Total liabilities	8,163	12,825	2,401	3,429	2,971	205	7,419	37,413
Noninterest-bearing liabilities	—	—	—	—	—	—	10,785	10,785
Stockholders' equity	—	—	—	—	—	—	4,315	4,315
Total liability and stockholders' equity	8,163	12,825	2,401	3,429	2,971	205	22,519	52,513
Gap before interest rate financial contracts	—	−835.00	761	1,721	10,098	2,660	−14,405	—
Interest-bearing interest rate swaps	—	−652.00	193	214	245	—	—	—
Gap adjusted for interest rate financial contracts	$ —	($1,487)	$954	$1,935	$10,343	$2,660	$14,405	$ —
Cumulative gap	$ —	($1,487)	$533	$1,402	$11,745	$14,405	$ —	
Adjustments:								
Exclude noninterest-earning assets, noninterest-bearing liabilities and stockholders' equity	—	—	—	—	—	—	$10,464	
Move interest-bearing checking and savings deposits from nonmarket to shortest maturity	—	−7,333	—	—	—	—	$7,333	
Adjusted cumulative gap	$ —	($8,820)	($7,866)	($5,931)	$4,412	$7,072	$10,464	

1. The nonmarket column consists of marketable equities securities.
2. The nonmarket column consists of nonaccrual loans of $1,494 million, fixed-rate credit card loans of $2,062 million (including $39 million commercial credit card loans) and overdrafts of $130 million.

Table 5. A duration analysis of interest rate risk exposure.

As of December 31, 1995 $ (millions)	On Balance Sheet			Off Balance Sheet		Combined On & Off	
	Balance	Rate	Effective Duration Years	Notional Amount (1)	Net Spread	Adjusted Rate	Adjusted Effective Duration
Assets:							
Variable rate prime loans	$16,179.00	6.75(%)	0.29	$15,133.00	2.07(%)	8.73(%)	1.74
Other variable loans/investments	14,963.00	7.00	0.19	0.00		7.01	0.19
Total variable rate assets	31,342.00	6.90	0.24	15,133.00	2.07	7.91	1.00
Fixed rate loans	27,889.00	9.64	2.19	58.00	−5.15	9.63	2.19
Other fixed investements	12,259.00	6.82	2.95	1,205.00	−1.49	6.67	2.82
Total fixed rate assets	40,148.00	8.78	2.42	1,263.00	−1.66	8.73	2.38
Other assets	8,629.00		1.34	0.00			1.34
Total assets	$79,919.00	7.10	1.45	$16,396.00	1.78	7.47	1.73
Liabilities:							
Contractually repriceable	$27,479.00	2.41	2.08	$5,638.00	1.98	2.00	1.73
Variable borrowings	10,250.00	2.76	0.05	198.00	−8.90	2.93	0.08
Total variable liabilities	37,729.00	2.51	1.53	5,836.00	1.61	2.26	1.28
Total fixed liabilities	20,003.00	4.61	1.49	8,624.00	2.33	3.61	0.75
Non-interest bearing DDA	13,677.00		3.42		0.00		3.42
Total deposits/borrowings	71,409.00	2.62	1.88	14,460.00	2.04	2.21	1.54
Other liabilities	1,476.00		0.06	0.00			0.06
Total liabilities	$72,885.00	2.57	1.84	$14,460.00	2.04	2.17	1.51

1. $5.6 billion of basis swaps are excluded from variable rate prime notional amounts, but included in effective duration calculations.

Table 6. Net interest margin simulation.

	Rate Scenario					
	Unchanged	+100 bps	+200 bps	Limit	−200 bps	Limit
12 Months Net Interest Income:						
(a) W/Deposit rates unchanged from 9/94	$1,577.00	$1,560.50	$1,540.80		$1,545.40	
Total earning assets	32,892	32,912	34,420		32,346	
Net rate	4.79(%)	4.74(%)	4.75(%)		4.78(%)	
Change in net interest income		−16.50	−36.20	+/−78.90	−31.60	+/−78.9
% Net interest income		−1.0(%)	−2.3(%)	+/−5.0(%)	−2.0(%)	+/−5.0(%)
(b) W/Deposit rates reflecting 50 basis point tightening in unchanged	$1,551.00	$1,560.50	$1,540.80		$1,545.40	
Total earning assets	32,892	32,912	32,420		32,346	
Net rate	4.72(%)	4.74(%)	4.75(%)		4.78(%)	
Change in net interest income		9.50	−10.20	+/−78.90	−5.60	+/−78.9
% Net interest income		0.6(%)	−0.6(%)	+/−5.0(%)	−0.4(%)	+/−5.0(%)
Portfolio Equity:						
Market value	$5,727.00		$5,241.00		$6,109.00	
Change in market value			−486	+/−857	382	+/−857
% Shareholder's equity			11.1(%)	+/−20.0(%)	8.7(%)	+/−20.0(%)
Duration (years)	4.20		4.30		2.90	

no forward open positions, and have no expectations of trading volume. Within the latter group, there is a clear distinction between those that restrict themselves to acting as agents for corporate and/or retail clients and those that have active trading positions.

The most active banks in this area have large trading accounts and multiple trading locations. And, for these, reporting is rather straightforward. Currencies are kept in real time, with spot and forward positions marked-to-market. As is well known, however, reporting positions is easier than measuring and limiting risk. Here, limits are generally set by desk and by individual trader, with monitoring occurring in real time by some banks, and daily closing at other institutions. As a general characterization, those banks with more active trading positions tend to have invested in the real-time VaR systems discussed above, but there are exceptions.

Limits are key elements of risk management in foreign exchange trading, as they are for all trading businesses. As Table 7 illustrates by example, it is fairly standard for limits to be set by currency for both the spot and forward positions in the set of trading currencies. Institutions set limits currency-by-currency according to their subjective variance tolerance. At some institutions, attempts are made to derive the limits using the trading systems estimates of currency volatility, but this approach requires the bank to have a fully functioning trading system in place.

Table 7. Global foreign exchange trading limits.

Currency type	Currency short name	Net position		Net overall currency position		Daylight currency position	FX forward risk points (US$ Equivalent) CAP = 85,000				Sensivity to a 25 B.P. change in interest rates
							Overall 0–10 Yrs.		Med-long term 2–10 Yrs.		
		Limit	INCR./ (DECR.)	Limit	INCR./ (DECR.)	(2 × Net)	Limit	Increase	Limit	Decrease	
MAJOR CURRENCIES				540.00	−60.00						
U.S. DOLLAR	USD	275.00				150.00	55,000.00	23,000	3,000	−4,000	5,729,167
CANADIAN DOLLAR	CAD	220.00				840.00	25,000	2,720	2,000	−3,000	2,604,167
POUND STERLING	GBP	210.00				420.00	14,500	7,220	500	−1,500	1,510,417
SWISS FRANC	CHF	185.00				370.00	6,000	900	500	−1,000	625,000
GERMAN MARK	DEM	280.00	15.00			560.00	16,000	3,800	500	−1,500	1,666,667
DUTCH GUILDER	NLG	60.00				120.00	3,000	2,040			312,500
JAPANESE YEN	JPY	210.00				420.00	14,600	6,000	500	−1,500	1,520,833
ITALIAN LIRE	ITL	70.00	5.00			140.00	2,200	1,240			229,167
FRENCH FRANC	FRF	90.00	10.00			180.00	8,300	5,500	500	−500	864,583
BELGIAN FRANC	BEF	65.00	10.00			130.00	3,000	2,160			312,500
AUSTRALIAN DOLLAR	AUD	60.00				120.00	2,600	1,040			270,833
EUROPEAN CURRENCY UNIT (ECU)	XEU	65.00				130.00	7,150	6,670			744,792
MINOR CURRENCIES				160.00	60.00						
ARGENTINIAN AUSTRAL	ARP	5.00				10.00					
AUSTRIAN SCHILLING	ATS	30.00	10.00			60.00	750	510			78,125
BAHAMIAN DOLLAR	BSD	2.00				4.00					
BAHRAIN DINAR	BHD	2.00				4.00					
BARBADOS DOLLAR	BBD	2.00				4.00					
BERMUDA DOLLAR	BMD	2.00				4.00					
BRAZIL CRUZADO	BRC	5.00				10.00					
CAYMAN DOLLAR	KYD	2.00				4.00					
CHINESE RENMINBI	CNY	9.00				18.00	120				12,500
DANISH KRONE	DKK	45.00	5.00			90.00	1,000	640			104,167
E. CARIBBEAN DOLLAR	XCD	2.00				4.00					
FIJI DOLLAR	FJD	8.00				16.00	72				7,500
FINNISH MARKKA	FIM	30.00	14.00			60.00	250	130			26,042
GREEK DRACHMA	GRD	10.00	8.00			20.00					

For banks without a VaR system, some stress testing is conducted to evaluate the potential loss associated with changes in the exchange rate. This is done for small deviations in exchange rates as shown in Table 7, but it also may be investigated for historical maximum movements. The latter is investigated in two ways. Either historical events are captured, and worse-case scenario simulated, or the historical events are used to estimate a distribution from which the disturbances are drawn. In the latter case, a one or two standard deviation change in the exchange rate is considered. While some use these methods to estimate volatility, until recently most did not use co-variability in setting individual currency limits, or in aggregating exposure across multiple correlated currencies.

Incentive systems for foreign exchange traders are another area of significant differences between the average commercial bank and its investment banking counterpart. While, in the investment banking community trader performance is directly linked to compensation, this is less true in the banking industry. While some admit to significant correlation between trader income and trading profits, many argue that there is absolutely none.

3.D. Liquidity risk management procedures

Two different notions of liquidity risk have evolved in the banking sector. Each has some validity. The first, and the easiest in most regards, is a notion of liquidity risk as a need for continued funding. The counterpart of standard cash management, this liquidity need is predictable and easily analyzed. The type of liquidity risk that does present a real challenge is the need for funding when and if a sudden crisis arises. In this case, the issues are very different.

Standard reports on liquid assets and open lines of credit, which are germane to the first type of liquidity need, are substantially less relevant to the second. Rather, what is required is an analysis of funding demands under a series of worst-case scenarios. These include the liquidity needs associated with a bank-specific shock, such as a severe loss, and a crisis that is systemwide. In each case, the bank examines the extent to which it can be self-supporting in the event of a crisis, and tries to estimate the speed with which the shock will result in a funding crisis. Reports center on both features of the crisis with Table 8 illustrating one bank's attempt to estimate the immediate funding shortfall associated with a downgrade. Other institutions attempt to measure the speed with which assets can be liquidated to respond to the situation, using a report that indicates the speed with which the bank can acquire needed liquidity in a crisis. Response strategies considered include the extent to which the bank can accomplish substantial balance sheet shrinkage and estimates are made of the sources of funds that will remain available to the institution in a time of crisis. Results of such simulated crises are usually expressed in days of exposure or days to funding crisis.

3.E. Other risks considered but not modeled

Beyond the basic four financial risks, viz., credit, interest rate, foreign exchange, and liquidity risk, banks have a host of other concerns as was indicated above. Some of

Table 8. One-day Fallout Funding Scenario.

Category: overnight funds available			
Rating Movement Downward to:	**Total**	**Change**	**Pct. Change**
Thomson Bankwatch B	$16,229		
Thomson Bankwatch B/C	$13,365	($2,864)	(17.65%)
Thomson Bankwatch C	$6,291	($9,938)	(61.24%)
Category: term funds available			
Rating Movement Downward	**Total**	**Change**	**Pct. Change**
Thomson Bankwatch B	$19,299		
Thomson Bankwatch B/C	$17,020	($2,209)	(11.49%)
Thomson Bankwatch C	$12,458	($6,771)	(35.21%)

these, like operating risk, or system failure, are a natural outgrowth of their business, and banks employ standard risk avoidance techniques to mitigate them. Standard business judgment is used in this area to measure the costs and benefits of both risk reduction expenditures and system design, as well as operational redundancy. While generally referred to as risk management, this activity is substantially different from the management of financial risk addressed here.

Yet, there are still other risks, somewhat more amorphous but no less important. In this latter category are legal, regulatory, suitability, reputational, and environmental risk. In each of these risk areas, substantial time and resources are devoted to protecting the firm's franchise value from erosion. As these risks are less financially measurable, they are generally not addressed in any formal, structured way. Yet, they are not ignored at the senior management level of the bank.

4. RISK AGGREGATION AND THE KNOWLEDGE OF TOTAL EXPOSURE

Thus far, the techniques used to measure, report, limit, and manage the risks of various types have been presented. In each of these cases, a process has been developed or at least has evolved to measure the risk considered, and techniques have been deployed to control each of them. The analytical approaches that are subsumed in each of these analyses are complex, difficult and not easily communicated to nonspecialists in the risk considered. The bank, however, must select appropriate levels for each risk and by extension the level of total risk for the organization as a whole.

The question of how to specify and manage the firm's aggregate risk exposure is receiving increased scrutiny lately with two approaches receiving the most attention. The first of these, pioneered by Bankers Trust, is the RAROC system of risk analysis.[8] In this approach, risk is measured in terms of variability of outcome. Where possible, a frequency distribution of returns is estimated, from historical data, and the standard deviation of this distribution is estimated. Capital is allocated to activities as a function of this risk or volatility measure. Then, the risky position is required to carry an expected rate of return on allocated capital which compensates the firm for the associated incremental risk. By dimensioning all risk in terms of loss distributions, and allocating capital by the volatility of the proposed activity, risk is aggregated and priced in one and the same exercise.

A second approach is similar to RAROC, but depends less on a capital allocation scheme and more on cash flow or earnings effects of the implied risky position. This was referred to as the Earnings-At-Risk methodology above, when employed to analyze interest rate risk. When market values are used, the approach becomes identical to the VaR methodology employed for trading exposure. This method can be used to analyze total firm-level risk in a similar manner to the RAROC system. Again, a frequency distribution of returns for any one type of risk can be estimated from historical data. Extreme outcomes can then be estimated from the tail of the distribution. Either a worst-case historical example is used for this purpose, or a one- or two-standard deviation outcome is considered. Given the downside outcome associated with any risk position, the firm restricts its exposure so that, in the worst-case scenario, the bank does not lose more than a certain percentage of equity capital, current income, or market value. Therefore, rather than moving from volatility of value through capital, this approach goes directly to the current earnings implications from a risky position. The approach, however, has a very obvious shortcoming. If EaR is used, it is cash flow based, rather than market value driven.

Both measures, however, attempt to treat the issue of trade-offs among risks, using a common methodology to transform the specific risks to firm-level exposure. In addition, both can examine the correlation of different risks and the extent to which they can, or should be viewed as, offsetting. As a practical matter, however, most, if not all, of these models do not view this array of risks as a standard portfolio problem. Rather, they separately evaluate each risk and aggregate total exposure by simple addition. As a result, much is lost in the aggregation. Perhaps over time this issue will be addressed.

5. A CRITICAL REVIEW OF THE STATE OF RISK MANAGEMENT

The banking industry is clearly evolving to a higher level of risk management techniques and approaches than had been in place in the past. Yet, there is significant room for improvement. Before the areas of potential value added are enumerated, however, it is worthwhile to reiterate an earlier point. The risk management techniques reviewed here are not the average, but the techniques used by firms at the higher end of the market. The risk management approaches at smaller institutions, as well as larger but relatively less sophisticated ones, are less precise and significantly less analytic. In some cases they would need substantial upgrading to reach the level of those reported here. Accordingly, our review should be viewed as a glimpse at best practice, not average practices.

Nonetheless, the techniques employed by those that define the industry standard could use some improvement. In this section, the shortcomings of the currently implemented systems will be discussed at some length, perhaps this will lay the groundwork for further advances.

5.A. The credit risk area

The evaluation of credit rating continues to be an imprecise process. Over time, this approach needs to be standardized across institutions and across borrowers to a greater extent than it currently is. In fact, the current general consensus is that ratings are not comparable across financial institutions, and there is considerable debate as to the consistency of procedural implementation even within a single large institution. Over time, one should expect that the banking industry's rating procedures should be compatible with rating systems elsewhere in the capital market and have the same degree of objectivity. Without such consistency, the banking industry will continually be gamed by large borrowers who will turn to bank borrowing only when grading differences permit them a lower cost alternative.

Some would argue that this is not necessarily a problem. If banks have better information or a comparative advantage in analyzing a funding opportunity, then they ought to have differential ratings. In short, this gives them a comparative advantage in the lending market and represents their franchise value. While there is some truth to this, this view should not be pushed too far. For the overwhelming majority of loans, the lender offers little unique analysis capability. As a practical matter, therefore, the divergence of ratings and ratings methodologies rarely offers the bank a comparative advantage.

A second area where improvement seems warranted is the analysis of ex post outcomes from lending to both corporate and consumer borrowers. Credit losses, are currently only vaguely related to credit rating. They need to be more closely tracked by the industry than they currently are and incorporated into required bundle rates. In short, as in the bond market, credit pricing, credit rating and expected loss ought to be demonstrably linked. Studies by Moody's on their rating system have illustrated the relationship between credit rating and ex post default rates for open market credits.[9] A similar result should be expected from internal bank-rating schemes of this type as well. However, the lack of available industry data to do an appropriate aggregate migration study does not permit the industry the same degree of confidence in their expected loss calculations. Clearly this is an area where industry efforts are warranted. Only if accurate loss histories are created can you expect accurate and fair credit risk pricing. At the moment, the industry is working at a relative handicap in this area.

Generally accepted accounting principles require these data. The credit portfolio is subject to fair value accounting standards, which have recently been tightened by The Financial Accounting Standards Board (FASB) in the United States. Commercial banks are required to have a loan loss reserve account (a contra-asset), which accurately represents the diminution in market value for known or estimated credit losses. As an industry, banks have generally sought estimates of expected loss using a two-step process, including default probability, and an estimate of loss given default. This approach parallels the work of Moody's referred to above.[10] At least quarterly, the level of the reserve account must be re-assessed, in light of the current evidence of expected loss, which should be driven directly from credit quality reports, and internal studies of loan migration through various quality ratings.[11] To do this accurately, the industry needs better ex post loan data, and a sufficiently long history of both losses given default and migration from one quality rating to another.

The issue of optimal credit portfolio structure is the third area that warrants further study. In short, analysis is needed to evaluate the diversification gains associated with careful portfolio design. At this time, banks appear to be too concentrated in idiosyncratic areas, and not sufficiently managing their credit concentrations by either industrial or geographic areas. However, there are currently few tools available to address this problem.

For the investment management community, concentrations are generally benchmarked against some market indexes, and mutual funds will generally report not only the absolute percentage of their industry concentration, but also their positions relative to the broad market indexes. Unfortunately, there is no comparable benchmark for the loan portfolio. Accordingly, firms weigh the pros and cons of specialization and concentration by industry group and establish limits on their overall exposure in a purely subjective way. This is not the result of any analytical exercise to evaluate the potential downside loss, but rather, an hoc evaluation of management's tolerance, based upon rather imprecise recollections of previous downturns. Clearly this approach needs greater rigor.

5.B. The interest rate risk area

As noted above, interest rate risk approaches include both the trading risk systems and balance sheet rate risk analysis. Here we consider each in turn. On trading systems, there has been considerable improvement. The VaR methodology has converted a rather subjective hands-on process of risk control to a more quantitative approach.

However, several important issues remain. The first of these is that the whole approach of VaR is dependent upon estimated distributions of returns. These are the key inputs to the risk measure, but the true ex ante distribution is unknown. Estimates are obtained from either historical data or Monte Carlo simulation, but in either case, the estimated distribution is not unique. In addition, the well known existence of fat tails is particularly troublesome given that the risk measure obtained using VaR is dependent upon such tail estimates.

The second issue that arises in trading systems is the periodicity of the data. For trading risk systems, daily data are generally used to estimate the distribution, and the values are scaled by the square root of time for extended periods, e.g., weeks or months. However, the result is known to be an unreliable estimate of the variance over these periods. The implication of this problem is that resultant VaR measures may not be good measures of worst case loss estimates.

Finally, Heath,[12] among others, has argued quite convincingly that the use of VaR itself is not a very useful summary statistic of the underlying risk position. Collapsing all that is known about an estimated distribution into a single measure of the cumulative probability distribution may be neat, but it is hardly sufficiently informative. The industry must look beyond this single index number to gain more insight into the underlying estimated distribution.

Turning to balance sheet risk measurements, while simulation studies have substantially improved upon gap management, the use of both book value accounting measures and cash flow losses continues to be problematic. Movements to improve this methodology will require increased emphasis on market-based accounting. However, it must be remembered that the implementation of market value accounting must treat both sides of the balance sheet, not just the asset portfolio.

In addition, the simulations reported to management need to be improved. Here, bank balance sheet analyses must incorporate the advances in dynamic hedging that are used in complex fixed income pricing models.[13] As they stand, these simulations tend to be rather simplistic, and scenario testing rather limited.

5.C. The foreign exchange risk area

The VaR approach to market risk is a superior tool, even with all its shortcomings. Yet, much of the banking industry continues to use rather ad hoc approaches in setting foreign exchange and other trading limits. The value at risk methodology can and should be used to a greater degree than it is currently to set these limits. Such a movement would improve the management of foreign exchange risk in two important ways. First, open currency positions could be measured against one another using the appropriate metric of relative volatility, rather than dollar values. In addition, correlations across currencies could be taken into account in the basic variance-covariance structure that is a central part of the VaR technique.

Both these improvements are already in place in some of the banks we visited, but not many. In fact, while VaR approaches were talked about, we frequently found fewer institutions actually managed their trading desks, desk limits, and cross-currency holding using these risk management systems than one might have expected.

5.D. The liquidity risk area

Crisis models need to be better linked to operational details. In addition, the usefulness of such exercises is limited by the realism of the environment considered. If liquidity risk is to be managed, the price of illiquidity must be defined and built into illiquid positions. While this logic has been adopted by some institutions, this pricing of liquidity is not commonplace. All too frequently, liquidity risk scenarios are seen as a regulatory report, rather than part of strategic planning. By construction, therefore, they have been given little attention by senior officers and are likely to be of limited use in the time of crisis. This is not true everywhere we visited. Some very sophisticated players built equally rigorous analyses of a liquidity crisis, but they were the exception, not the rule.

5.E. Other risks need greater attention

As banks move more off balance sheet, the implied risk of agency activities must be better integrated into overall risk management and strategic decision making. Currently, they are ignored when bank risk management is considered. Risks embedded in operations, whether associated with agency transactions or balance sheet businesses, have remained in the operations area in most organizations.

Recently, however, several organizations have attempted to address these issues as part of firm level risk management, under the title of operating risk. Here, the whole panoply of other risks associated with running a financial service firm is examined with an eye toward estimated loss probabilities and the costs associated with such an operating failure. However, these efforts are at a fairly primitive stage at this point. Much more needs to be done if reasonable exposure estimates are to be obtained, and the true cost of risk absorption is to be embedded in many of the operating businesses.

5.F. The aggregation of risks

There has been much discussion of the RAROC and VaR methodologies as an approach to capture total risk management. Yet, frequently, the decisions to accept risk, along with the pricing of a risky position, is separated from firm level risk analysis. This appears to be the result of senior management not being completely comfortable with either methodology. If aggregate risk is to be controlled, it must be integrated better into the banking firm's strategic planning process.

Why then has the industry resisted using such global risk measures? For one thing, both aggregate risk methodologies presume that the time dimensions of all risks can be viewed as equivalent. A trading risk is similar to a credit risk, for example. This appears problematic when market prices are not readily available for some assets and the time dimensions of different risks are dissimilar. Yet, thus far no one has addressed this issue adequately. In addition, each approach to firm level risk control has unique shortcomings.

RAROC allocates capital to lines of business or transactions, but there is no clear way to assure aggregate consistency. If capital is allocated on a deal by deal basis, total available capital may exceed allocated capital. This leaves management with insufficient returns to compensate shareholders and no clear linkage to deploy excess capital within the firm. If capital is allocated proportionately, firms with excess capital will seek excessive margins and forego business that can add value to the organization's bottom line. In short, RAROC has a summation problem.

VaR, on the other hand, requires a reasonably stable estimate of the underlying distribution of firm level performance. Obtaining such a distribution is even more difficult than obtaining estimates for individual assets or lines of business. In fact, if one could credibly obtain reasonable estimates of the distribution associated with firm level performance, the problem of risk management for the firm as a whole would be substantially reduced. One can obtain such estimates for traded firms from stock market prices, but no one has even suggested that these estimates of firm level volatility could be decomposed or used credibly by management. In short, we are a long way from truly understanding firm level risk sufficiently to obtain even a primitive tool of management.

6. SUMMARY REMARKS

As noted at the outset, risk management systems have attracted considerable attention in the financial sector. Over the past decade, substantial progress has been made, and one can see a clear convergence of techniques used and systems employed. However, considerably more work needs to be done. The current state of risk management is merely a beginning, contrary to the views of many in senior management, and, most notably, those who have convinced firms to invest large amounts of money into risk management systems.

This money has not been lost, and in fact, it has been spent in many productive ways. Yet, there are many more questions still to be answered, many more questions that have been answered only superficially, and some questions for which we have no useful answers. While this may keep many banking executives up at night, it is in fact a fair representation of where we currently are.

ACKNOWLEDGMENT

This paper was prepared for the joint Bank of Israel, Hebrew University Conference on Risk Management and Regulation in Banking, May 17–19, 1997.

NOTES

1. A companion paper reports on risk management practices for insurance firms. See Babbel and Santomero (1997).
2. See Oldfield and Santomero (1997).
3. This point has been made in a different context by both Santomero and Trester (1997) and Berger and Udell (1993).
4. Some banking firms would also list regulatory and reputational risk in their set of concerns. Nonetheless, all would recognize the first four as key, and all would devote most of their risk management resources to constraining these key areas of exposure.
5. There is nothing unique about ten grades. Some have eight, others have twelve. The most important thing here is that there are sufficient gradations to permit accurate characterization of the underlying risk profile of a loan or a portfolio of loans.
6. See, for example, the work of Jorion (1997), Marshall and Siegel (1996), Fallon (1996), and Phelan (1997).
7. See Saunders (1996) or Hempel, Simonson, and Coleman (1994) for a discussion of duration gap, its construction and its usefulness.
8. See Salomon Brothers (1993) and Wee and Lee (1995) for the most complete public information on Bankers Trust RAROC systems.
9. See Moody's (1996) and Santomero and Babbel (1997) for evidence of the relationship between credit rating and default rates.
10. See Altman (1993) for a discussion of both the FASB standards and the methods employed to evaluate the level of the reserve account.
11. Accurately estimating loan losses from a loan quality report is, in fact, quite difficult because of the limited information available to the bank on future loan losses and the change in loan quality over time.

To see how the statistical properties of the time series of loan ratings can be used to obtain loan loss estimates, see Kim and Santomero (1993).

12. See Heath (1997).

13. See Garbade (1996) for an example.

REFERENCES

Allen, F., and Santomero, A. (1997). "The Theory of Financial Intermediation," *Journal of Banking and Finance*, December.

Altman, E. (1993). "Valuation, Loss Reserves and the Pricing of Corporate Bank Loans," *Journal of Commercial Bank Lending*, August, 8–25.

Babbel, D., and Santomero, A. (1997). "Financial Risk Management by Insurers: An Analysis of the Process," *Journal of Risk and Insurance*, June.

Berger, A., and Udell, G. (1995). "Relationship Lending and Lines of Credit in Small Firm Finance," *Journal of Business*, July.

Berger, A., and Udell, G. (1993). "Securitization, Risk, and the Liquidity Problem in Banking," *Structural Change in Banking*, M. Klausner and L. White, (eds), Illinois: Irwin Publisher.

Fallon, W. (1996). "Calculating Value-at-Risk," Working Paper 96–49, Wharton Financial Institutions Center, The Wharton School, University of Pennsylvania.

Froot, K., D. Scharfstein, and J. Stein (1993). "Risk Management: Coordinating Investment and Financing Policies," *Journal of Finance*, December.

Furash, E. (1994). "Organizing the Risk Management Process In Large Banks," Risk Management Planning Seminar, Federal Financial Institutions Examination Council, Washington, D.C., September 29.

Garbade, Kenneth D. (1996). *Fixed Income Analytics*, MIT Press.

Heath, David C. (1997). "A Characterization of the Measures of Risk," Presented at the Federal Reserve Bank of Atlanta Financial Markets Conference, February.

Hempel, G.H., D.G. Simonson, and A.B. Coleman (1994). *Bank Management*. New York: John Wiley and Sons, Inc.

Jorion, P. (1993). *Value at Risk: The New Benchmark for Control Market Risk*. Illinois: Irwin Professional Publications.

Kim, D., and A. Santomero (1993). "Forecasting Required Loan Loss Reserves," *Journal of Economics and Business*, August.

Marshall, C., and M. Siegel (1996). "Value at Risk: Implementing a Risk Measurement Standard," Working Paper 96–47, Wharton Financial Institutions Center, The Wharton School, University of Pennsylvania.

Moody's Investor Service (1996). *Corporate Bond Defaults and Default Rates 1970–1995*, Moody's Special Report.

Morsman, E. (1993). *Commercial Loan Portfolio Management*. Philadelphia: Robert Morris Associate.

Oldfield, G., and A. Santomero (1997). "The Place of Risk Management in Financial Institutions," *Sloan Management Review*, Summer.

Phelan, M. (1997). "Probability and Statistics Applied to the Practice of Financial Risk Management: The Case of JP Morgan's RiskMetrics™," *Journal of Financial Services Research*, June.

Salomon Brothers (1993). "Bankers Trust New York Corporation—Risk Management," United States Equity Research, February.

Santomero, A. (1997). "Commercial Bank Risk Management: An Analysis of the Process," *Journal of Financial Services Research*, June.

Santomero, A. (1995). "Financial Risk Management: The Whys and Hows," *Financial Markets, Institutions and Investments*, 4.

Santomero, A., and D. Babbel (1996). *Financial Markets, Instruments, and Institutions*. Illinois: Irwin Publishers.

Santomero, A., and J. Trester (1997). "Financial Innovation and Bank Risk Taking," *Journal of Economic Behavior and Organizations*, October.

Saunders, A. (1996). *Financial Institutions Management: A Modern Perspective*. Illinois: Irwin Publishers.

Smith, C., C. Smithson, and D. Wilford (1990). *Strategic Risk Management* (Institutional Investor Series in Finance). New York: Harper and Row.

Stultz, R. (1984). "Optimal Hedging Policies," *Journal of Financial and Quantitative Analysis*, 19.

Wee, L., and Lee, J. (1995). *RAROC and Risk Management—Quantifying the Risks of Business*. Bankers Trust New York Corporation.

APPENDIX 1

A typical credit rating system

The following are definitions of the risk levels of Borrowing Facility.

1. **Substantially Risk Free**
   Borrowers of unquestioned credit standing at the pinnacle of credit quality. Basically, governments of major industrialized countries, a few major world class banks and a few multinational corporations.
2. **Minimal Risk**
   Borrowers of the highest quality. Almost no risk in lending to this class. Cash flows over at least 5 years demonstrate exceptionally large or stable margins of protection and balance sheets are very conservative, strong and liquid. Projected cash flows (including anticipated credit extensions) will continue a strong trend, and provide continued wide margins of protection, liquidity and debt service coverage. Excellent asset quality and management. Typically large national corporations.
3. **Modest Risk**
   Borrowers in the lower end of the high quality range. Very good asset quality and liquidity; strong debt capacity and coverage; very good management. The credit extension is considered definitely sound; however, elements may be present which suggest the borrower may not be free from temporary impairments sometime in the future. Typically larger regional or national corporations.
4. **Below Average Risk**
   The high end of the medium range between the definitely sound and those situations where risk characteristics begin to appear. The margins of protection are satisfactory, but susceptible to more rapid deterioration than class 3 names. Some elements of reduced strength are present in such areas as liquidity, stability of margins and cash flows, concentration of assets, dependence upon one type of business, cyclical trends, etc., which may adversely affect the borrower. Typically good regional or excellent local companies.
5. **Average Risk**
   Borrowers with smaller margins of debt service coverage and where definite elements of reduced strength exist. Satisfactory asset quality and liquidity; good debt capacity and coverage; and good management in all critical positions. These names have sufficient margins of protection and will qualify as acceptable borrowers; however, historic earnings and/or cash flow patterns may be sometimes unstable. A loss year or a declining earnings trend may not be uncommon. Typically solid local companies. May or may not require collateral in the course of normal credit extensions.
6. **Management Attention Risk**
   Borrowers who are beginning to demonstrate above average risk through declining earnings trends, strained cash flow, increasing leverage, and/or weakening market fundamentals. Also, borrowers which are currently performing as agreed but could be adversely impacted by developing factors such as, but not limited to: Deteriorating industry conditions, operating problems,

pending litigation of a significant nature, or declining collateral quality/adequacy. Such borrowers or weaker typically require collateral in normal credit extensions.

Borrowers generally have somewhat strained liquidity; limited debt capacity and coverage; and some management weakness. Such borrowers may be highly leveraged companies which lack required margins or less leveraged companies with an erratic earnings records. Significant declines in earnings, frequent requests for waivers of covenants and extensions, increased reliance on bank debt, and slowing trade payments are some events which may occasion this categorization.

7. **Potential Weakness**
   Borrower exhibits potential credit weakness or a downward trend which, if not checked or corrected, will weaken the asset or inadequately protect the bank's position. While potentially weak, the borrower is currently marginally acceptable; no loss of principal or interest is envisioned. Included could be turnaround situations, as well as those previously rated 6 or 5, names that have shown deterioration, for whatever reason, indicating a downgrading from the better categories. These are names that have been or would normally be criticized "Special Mention" by regulatory authorities.
8. **Definite Weakness; No Loss**
   A borrower with well defined weakness(es) that jeopardize the orderly liquidation of the debt. Borrowers that have been or would normally be classified "Substandard" by regulatory authorities. A substandard loan is inadequately protected by the current sound worth and paying capacity of the obligor. Normal repayment from this borrower is in jeopardy, although no loss of principal is envisioned. There is a distinct possibility that a partial loss of interest and/or principal will occur if the deficiencies are not corrected.
9. **Potential Loss**
   A borrower classified here has all weaknesses inherent in the one classified above with the added provision that the weaknesses make collection of debt in full, on the basis of currently existing facts, conditions, and values, highly questionable and improbable. Serious problems exist to the point where a partial loss of principal is likely. The possibility of loss is extremely high, but because of certain important, reasonably specific pending factors, which may work to the advantage and strengthening of the assets, its classification as an estimated loss is deferred until its more exact status may be determined. Pending factors include proposed merger, acquisition, or liquidation, capital injection, perfecting liens on additional collateral, and refinancing plans.
10. **Loss**
    Borrowers deemed incapable of repayment of unsecured debt. Loans to such borrowers are considered uncollectible and of such little value that their continuance as active assets of the bank is not warranted. This classification does not mean that the loan has absolutely no recovery or salvage value, but rather it is not practical or desirable to defer writing off this basically worthless asset even though partial recovery may be effected in the future.

APPENDIX 2

An introduction to Value-at-Risk and RiskMetrics

Value-at-Risk is a measure of the maximum potential change in value of a portfolio of financial instruments with a given probability over a pre-set horizon. VaR answers the question: how much can I lose with *x*% probability over a given time horizon. For example, if you think that there is a 95% chance that the DEM/USD exchange rate will not fall by more than 1% of its current value over the next day, you can calculate the maximum potential loss on, say, a USD 100 million DEM/USD position by using the methodology and data provided by RiskMetrics. The following examples describe how to compute VaR using standard deviations and correlations of financial returns (provided by RiskMetrics) under the assumption that these returns are normally distributed. (RiskMetrics provides alternative methodological choices to address the inaccuracies resulting from this simplifying assumption).

Example 1. You are a USD-based corporation and hold a DEM 140 million FX position. What is your VaR over a 1-day horizon given that there is a 5% chance that the realized loss will be greater than what VaR projected? The choice of the 5% probability is discretionary and differs across institutions using the VaR framework.

What is your exposure? The first step in the calculation is to compute your exposure to market risk (i.e., mark-to-market your position). As a USD-based investor, your exposure is equal to the market value of the position in your base currency. If the foreign exchange rate is 1.40 DEM/USD, the market value of the position is USD100 million.

What is your risk? Moving from exposure to risk requires an estimate of how much the exchange rate can potentially move. The standard deviation of the return of the DEM/USD exchange rate, measured historically can provide an indication of the size of rate movements. In this example, we calculated the DEM/USD daily standard deviation to be 0.565%. Now, under the standard RiskMetrics assumption that standardized returns $((r_t/_t)$ on DEM/USD are normally distributed given the value of this standard deviation (that is, 1.65) or 0.932%, (see Figure A1.) 95% of the time. RiskMetrics provides users with the VaR statistics 1.65.

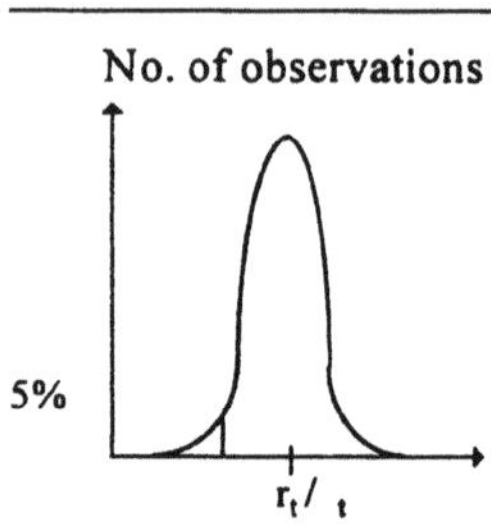

Figure A1. VaR statistics.

In USD, the VaR of the position[1] is equal to the market value of the position times the estimated volatility or:

FX Risk: \$100 million × 0.932% = \$932,000

What this number means is that 95% of the time, you will not lose more than \$932,000 over the next 24 hours.

Example 2. Let's complicate matters somewhat. You are a USD-based corporation and hold a DEM 140 million position in the 10-year German government bond. What is your VaR over a 1-day horizon period, again, given that there is a 5% chance of understanding the realized loss?

What is your exposure? The only difference versus the prvious example is that you now have both interest rate risk on the bond and FX risk resulting from the DEM exposure. The exposure is still USD 100 million but it is now at risk to two market risk factors.

What is your risk? If you use an estimate of 10-year German bond standard deviation of 0.605%, you can calculate:

Interest rate risk: \$100 million × 1.65 × 0.605% = \$999,000
FX Risk: \$100 million × 1.65 × 0.56% = \$932,000

Now, the total risk of the bond is not simply the sum of the interest rate and FX risk because the correlation between the return on the DEM/USD exchange rate the return on the 10-year German bond is relevant. In this case, we estimated the correlation between the returns on the DEM/USD exchange rate and the 10-year German government bond to be –0.27. Using a formula common in standard portfolio theory, the total risk of the position is given by:

$$VaR = [\sigma^2_{InterestRate} + \sigma^2_{FX} + (2 \times \rho_{InterestRateFx} \times \sigma_{InterestRate} \times \sigma_{FX})]^{1/2}$$

$$VaR = \left[(0.999)^2 + (0.932)^2 + (2 \times -0.27 \times 0.999 \times 0.932)\right]^{1/2}$$
$$= \$1.168\, million$$

To compute VaR in this example, RiskMetrics provides users with the VaR of the interest rate component (i.e., 1.65 × 0.605), the VaR of the foreign exchange position (i.e., 1.65 × 0.565) and the correlation between the two return series, –0.27.

NOTE

1. This is a simple approximation.

III. MANAGING MARKET AND CREDIT RISKS

3. INTRODUCTION TO VAR (VALUE-AT-RISK)

ZVI WIENER

1. AN OVERVIEW OF RISK MEASUREMENT TECHNIQUES

Modern financial theory is based on several important principles, two of which are no-arbitrage and risk aversion. The single major source of profit is risk. The expected return depends heavily on the level of risk of an investment. Although the idea of risk seems to be intuitively clear, it is difficult to formalize it. Several attempts to do so have been undertaken with various degree of success. There is an efficient way to quantify risk in almost every single market. However, each method is deeply associated with its specific market and can not be applied directly to other markets. Value-at-Risk (VaR) is an integrated way to deal with different markets and different risks and to combine all of the factors into a single number, which is a good indicator of the overall risk level.

For example, the major risk associated with a government bond is the interest rate risk. A simple way to measure it is by duration. More subtle dependence on the term structure can be estimated by convexity or by sensitivity to a nonparallel shift. The more detailed analysis of the term structure of interest rates usually involves a parametric term structure model. Within the framework of this model the corresponding risk factors can be quantified (at least numerically if not analytically).

However, as soon as corporate bonds are included in a portfolio there is a need to deal with default (credit) risk. This is a completely different type of uncertainty, which is correlated with all of the major indices of the economy. Therefore, to measure the risk we would need to analyze the counterparty. The simplest way to deal with this type of risk is by using credit rating systems (provided in many cases by credit agencies).

For more complicated financial instruments, like interest rates and currency swaps, there is a need to develop a model of default and recovery (see for example, Duffie and Pan, 1997). This type of model is necessary for measuring the risk of credit derivatives, an instrument that has become very popular recently.

For an equity portfolio the most useful way to measure risk is by volatility of returns. This parameter, together with the expected level of returns and correlations between different assets, leads to standard investment models like CAPM and APT. These models use diversification as the major tool to improve the risk-return ratio and some type of correlation (like beta) as a risk measuring tool. However, it is clear that the equity market is strongly correlated with other types of risks (like political events and litigation risk). Therefore, it is not sufficient to deal with stock markets in isolation.

Derivative instruments became one of the major sources of hedging strategies, as well as speculations. The risk associated with each single option, or a portfolio of options, can be measured by the whole set of the Greeks: delta, gamma, theta, etc. Each of them represents the rate of the change in price when only one of the parameters changes (like the underlying asset, volatility, time to maturity, etc.). Again, these indices are well suited to watch the very specific types of risk related to derivative instruments, but can not be applied directly to other instruments.

Foreign exchange is another area with its own risk indices. They typically include spreads and exchange rate volatilities. However, lately some other characteristics have been added, such as target zones and the term structure models of several related currencies.

We can summarize the major risk measurement tools in the Table 1.

The variety of different methods still does not give a simple answer to the most basic question, What is the current risk? which every financial institution should ask itself. There are several reasons this question cannot be answered in a simple way. First of all, there is no simple answer. Risk is something infinitely dimensional; it depends on all of the possible events in the world, and it is impossible to represent it precisely with a single number or any set of scenarios. For example, the only genuine answer to the question What is the maximal loss we can suffer over some time horizon? is unfortunately, We can lose everything! However, the probability of this event is very small. *Very small* must be quantified in some way. Whenever the

Table 1. ••.

Asset	Risk Measure
Bonds	duration, convexity, term-structure models
Credit	rating, default models
Stocks	volatility, correlations, beta
Derivatives	delta, gamma, vega
Forex	target zones, spreads

total risk is low this probability is quite small, however it is higher when we have a higher total risk.

Imagine a CFO of a company trying to explain the level of risk by giving the whole distribution of profits and losses under all possible scenarios. This can easily include many different parameters with complicated correlation between them. Even if he had such a graph, it would be extremely difficult to use it to compare even two different portfolios. This information must be reduced to a single number. VaR (Value-at-Risk) was introduced precisely with the purpose of providing a one dimensional approximation of the infinitely dimensional risk. Because of the simplifying nature of this index one should always take into account its limitations. However, it can be very useful for risk supervision, reporting, division of resources, and overall risk management. Some interesting applications can be found in Marshall and Siegel (1997).

2. THE CONCEPT OF VAR

This concept came from the industry and is relatively simple. In using VaR, one must take into account that as there is no precise answer, it will be only a rough approximation with limited usage. Imagine that we are interested in a simple risk measurement of a portfolio consisting of many different types of securities, Assume first that we can price the portfolio if we knew all major market characteristics. For example take a situation in which there are only two major factors—the stock market index and the interest rate. We can plot the value of the portfolio as a function of these parameters as for example shown in Figure 1.

However, this figure does not tell us what the probabilities of getting different values of the basic parameters are. Moreover it does not take into account correlations between different parameters. One needs to add a joint distribution of the two basic parameters and to consider the distribution together with the graph above. The picture has already become too complicated, even with only two basic factors.

Another way to represent the risky nature of the investment is to plot a graph, which gives the probabilities of changes in the market value of the whole portfolio. This can be done either as a density function as in Figure 2 or as a cumulative probability as in Figure 3.

This graph deals directly with the variable we are interested in—the probability of heavy losses. Since we are interested in the most unfavorable outcomes, we would like to measure the level of losses which will not be exceeded with some fixed probability. The critical level typically used for this fixed probability is either 5 percent or 1 percent. This quantile is the corresponding Value-at-Risk as shown in Figures 2 and 3. Thus the idea behind VaR is to measure the heaviest losses which will not occur by the end of the basic time interval with some fixed probability.

To draw such a graph of probabilities, the following steps should be taken:

1. Data must be gathered regarding the current position.
2. The basic time period must be set.

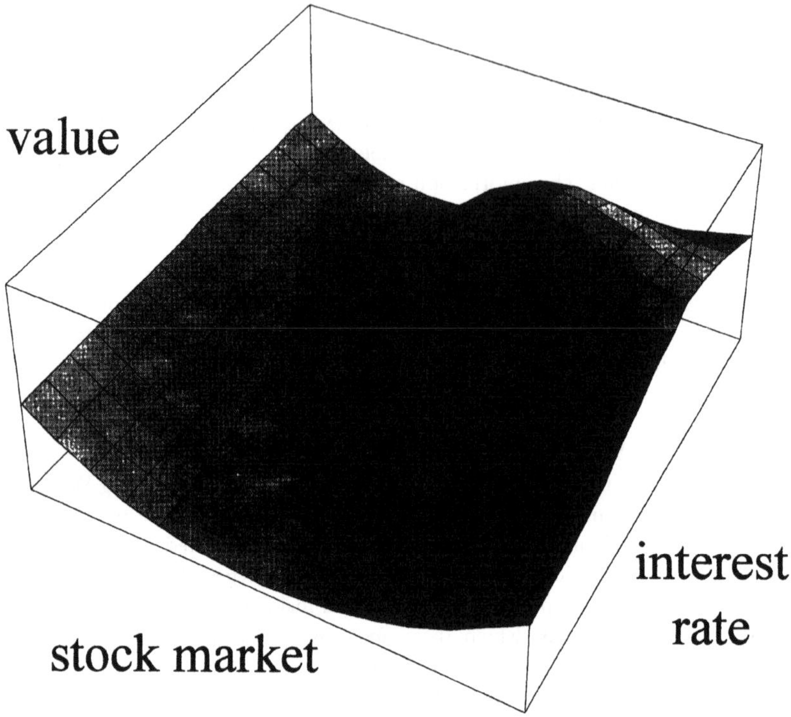

Figure 1. Value of the portfolio as a function of market parameters (which can be correlated).

3. A model must be built, predicting the distribution of the prices of the securities in the portfolio as a function of basic market parameters.

After these three steps are completed, one can draw the value-probability graph, at least in theory, since in practice this might require too much time and other resources.

Historically, VaR was introduced by financial companies in the late 80's. Since then this approach has become popular among practitioners, the academic community and—most significantly—among central banks. A more detailed description of the historical development of VaR can be found in Duffie and Pan (1997), Linsmeier and Pearson (1996), and http://www.gloriamundi.org. The RiskMetrics™ initiative of J.P.Morgan played a very positive role and made VaR a widely used risk management tool.

We want to emphasize that VaR itself is not the true way to measure risk in the absolute sense. There are many other risk measurements. The major advantage of VaR is that it has become a widely accepted standard! Once the industry and

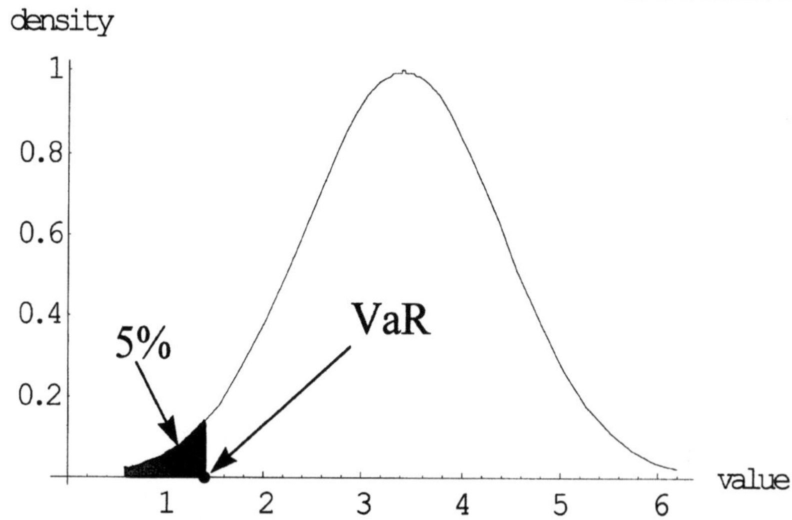

Figure 2. 5% VaR is defined on the probability density function.

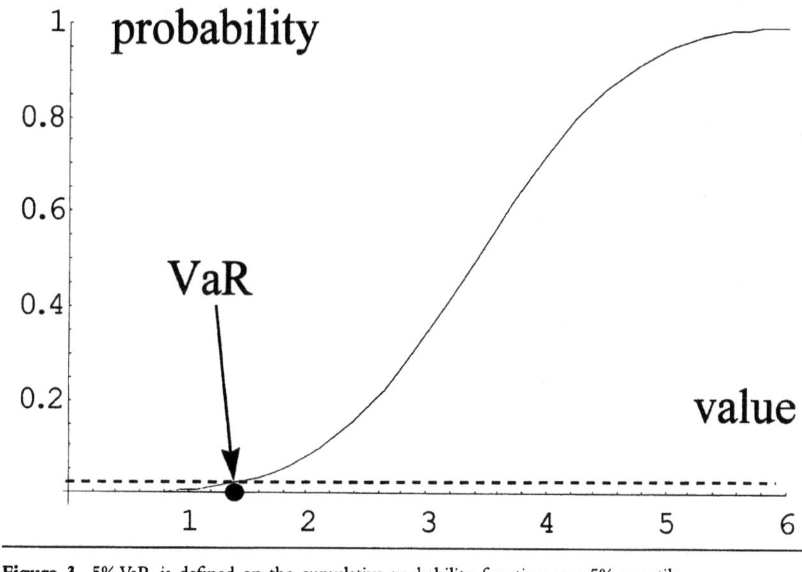

Figure 3. 5% VaR is defined on the cumulative probability function as a 5% quantile.

the regulators agreed to use it as the primary risk-management tool, it plays an important unifying role, and enables a good basis for comparison of risk between portfolios, institutions, and financial intermediaries. Two necessary conditions for the success of VaR are relative simplicity of implementation and stability of results. In what follows we will discuss some major methods of implementation of VaR.

3. CHOICE OF PARAMETERS AND CURRENT POSITION

Any risk management project should begin with meticulous collection of data. One can not expect a model to produce reasonable results when it has very inaccurate data. The data collection consists of three major steps.

First, we must know our current portfolio. Even this simple question is not as innocent as it seems. In the modern global financial system, trading is ongoing throughout the entire day. This raises the question: When do we collect data? The most popular method is to collect the data at the end of the working day on the major market (the market with major risk exposures for the financial institution). However, this approach cannot be used by intraday speculators or market makers who typically have large positions throughout the day but close or hedge most of them by the end of the day.

The second type of data one needs to collect is the current market data. Just to demonstrate that this is not a simple task, let us recall that equity prices are disclosed almost continuously, interest rates may have significant jumps around certain dates (for example, decisions of central banks), inflation rates are published with a delay of several weeks, and credit ratings of companies and countries are also typically published with a significant delay. This raises the question of data timing. The solution to this question mainly depends on the type of porfolio and the major goal of VaR measurement, which we will discuss later.

The third type of data is historical observations. The amount of historical information is huge. Moreover the historical information is needed to estimate the major market characteristics for the next basic period. In effect, we are basing our predictions on a very problematic assumption: that the future behavior of the markets can be predicted by its past behavior. Although this approach is problematic, there is no other way to study the market. Although there is no need to assume stationarity of markets, the models we discuss are typically based on historical estimates.

There is an alternative way to measure basic market characteristics without relying solely on historical data. In financial markets which are well developed, one can use the implied parameters (like implied volatilities, see Jackwerth and Rubinstein, 1997). However, this approach is problematic to the extent that by measuring VaR we are typically interested in estimating the maximal realistic losses. By using the implied parameters we rely heavily on market expectations and can suffer from underestimation of fat tails by the whole market.

The next question we have to deal with is: What level of confidence and basic time period do we use? The answer depends primarily on the final goal. When the primarily goal is to satisfy imposed restrictions, such as central bank requirements, there is not much choice. Most central banks have adopted the Basle requirements, which allow to chose between the standardized approach and an internal model (also called the alternative approach). The standardized approach is simple for implementation, but it does not account for correlations between different markets. In most situations it leads to a significant overestimation of risk. The alternative approach allows the use of correlations between markets. This method is more time consuming but much more flexible and typically leads to more realistic risk estimates. The alternative approach for banks requires a 99 percent confidence level (1 percent of worst outcomes) and a 10-day time horizon. A simple calculation shows that this leads to a very conservative estimate. An exception (a loss exceeding the predicted level) can be expected only once in every $100 \cdot 10$ days, i.e., very rarely (once every few years). However, when the primarily goal is to build an efficient internal risk management model, it is strongly recommended to use parameters that lead to an observable and verifiable result. Typically firms use a 95 percent confidence level (5 percent of worst outcomes) and a short time horizon, such as one day. In this case, losses greater than the predicted level can be expected every $20 \cdot 1$ days. That is, roughly once a month we can suffer a loss that is heavier than the VaR level.[1]

Another important issue is the different type of risks taken by hedgers and speculators. Here is one example. Consider two American firms both having occasionally the same position: £1 M in cash and a future contract to exchange £1 M to $1.6 M three months from now. The first institution is a pure speculator and occasionally has an almost offsetting position. In one day's time there will be a new round of trade and there are almost no chances that this parity will remain. The second institution is a pure hedger and tries to prevent losses in the current position by a simple hedge. This strategy is precommitted and will be kept until maturity with daily readjustments. When working with a 10-day time horizon, how can we compare the riskiness of these firms? Intuitively we would like to say that the hedger is less risky. However, if we use the standard frozen approach we assume that the current position is unchanged during the whole period, and we get the same results. This clearly is not an accurate interpretation of the available information about the two very different companies.

Note that the frozen assumption is invalid for both companies. However, we know that the speculator will change positions according to his strategy and the hedger will always readjust his position according to changes in exchange rates and $/£ interest rates. The possible solution can be based on Dynamic VaR—a modification of the standard VaR, which takes into account some precommitted hedging strategies. This approach should be used when dealing with a pure speculator who uses stop-loss orders to prevent big losses. Here again, one should take into account the precommitted strategy of position change.

4. METHODS FOR VAR MEASUREMENT

We will discuss several widely used methods to calculate VaR. Typically this is not a precise type of calculation. There is a need to rely on many different parameters, and each one has a small error. As a result the raw data already has a lot of noise. It does not make sense to perform all of the calculations very precisely once we know that the initial data is not precise. Typically for bank supervision and for internal control it is enough only to estimate VaR from above, but the problem is more subtle when VaR is used for distribution of resources between trading desks. In this situation one should perform a deeper analysis to decide how much risk each separate division should be allowed to have. The common policy of central banks is to set capital requirements as a function of the VaR as specified by the Basle committee. In many cases an upper bound is sufficient when the bank capital is above the required level (a common situation) and there is no requirement for additional capital.

We discuss later the two basic types of methods: parametric and non-parametric. Parametric methods will include the variance-covariance approach and some analytical methods. The nonparametric model includes historical simulation and the Monte-Carlo approach. All VaR measurement approaches use a similar scheme:

1. Selection of basic parameters (time horizon, confidence level, time of measurement)
2. Selection of relevant market factors
3. Risk mapping
4. VaR calculation

For step 1, we define the relevant parameters according to our goals and resources. The next two steps, 2 and 3, assume some kind of model, either just a set of relevant factors or a completely specified pricing model. In any case the relatively small set of relevant parameters should be defined, and some method for portfolio valuation based on this set should be established. Step 4 includes the calculation itself. This step can be very time consuming, especially when Monte-Carlo methods are used. There are numerous techniques for speeding the calculations.

The following are the different types of techniques to calculate VaR.

Historical simulations

This is probably the simplest nonparametric method. There is no assumption of a complex structure of the markets. Instead we observe the historical behavior of our current portfolio over the last few years. We begin by measuring the daily percentage changes in the market parameters. Then we apply these changes to our current portfolio and measure the corresponding profits and losses. The most useful version of this approach is when the risk mapping procedure defines the price of the whole portfolio as a deterministic function of the market parameters P(p). Here P is the pricing function and p is the vector of all relevant market parameters. Then today's (day t) price is $P(p_t)$. The market parameters at some day j were p_j and on day j + 1 the parameters were p_{j+1}. Then we can model the possible changes in today's parameters in the following ways. We can use the relative change, where each market parameter is multiplied by the ratio of the same parameter at day j + 1 and day j. Another approach is when we add to today's value the difference between the values at day j + 1 and day j for each parameter. The multiplicative method is applicable when the volatility increases with the level of the parameter. This method is useful for stock indexes, exchange rates, etc. The additive approach assumes that the volatility is level independent. For example, for the additive approach we would take as a possible price tomorrow $P(p_t + (p_{j+1} - p_j))$. More complex combinations of both methods can be used as well. For example when modeling exchange rates in a band or interest rates.

Using a moving window, we calculate the profits and losses for each ten day period. After ordering all the resulting data, we set the level of VaR at the 5 percent quantile of worst outcomes (assuming that we are working with a 95 percent confidence interval). An alternative method is to calculate the profits and losses for each one day period, proceed as above, and multiply the result by $\sqrt{10}$. Both methods are applicable as per the Basle regulations.

This approach is relatively simple and it does not require simulations or the development of an analytical model. Moreover it can easily incorporate nonlinear instruments such as options.

A typical problem with this approach is that there is not enough data. The further we go into the past for data, the less relevant this information is to today's market. This is not a simple tradeoff. On the one hand, we would like to have more data in order to observe the rare events, especially the heavy losses. On the other hand, we do not want to build our current risk estimates on very old market data. Let's assume that we have agreed to take the last five years of data for our VaR estimate. If there was a big loss on a particular day, then exactly five years later the big market jump will disappear from the set of data we use. This will lead to a jump in our VaR estimate from one day to the next. This demonstrates that the results are not stable when using the historical simulations approach.

One important situation in which the historical simulation approach can not be used is for technical trading strategies developed on the basis of historical data. Technical trading strategies are generally conceived on the basis of historical data, and produce the best results on this data (i.e., most of big losses are a posteriori excluded). In such a case, one can certainly not use the data which was already used for calibration as the data set for the VaR estimate.

Variance covariance

This is a parametric method, based on the assumption that the returns are normally distributed. Historical data is used to measure the major parameters: means, standard deviations, correlations. The overall distribution of the market parameters is constructed from this data. Using the risk mapping technique, the distribution of the profits and losses over the time horizon (typically one day) can be found. When the market value of the portfolio is a linear function of the underlying parameters, the distribution of the profits is normal as well. Therefore, the 5 percent quantile

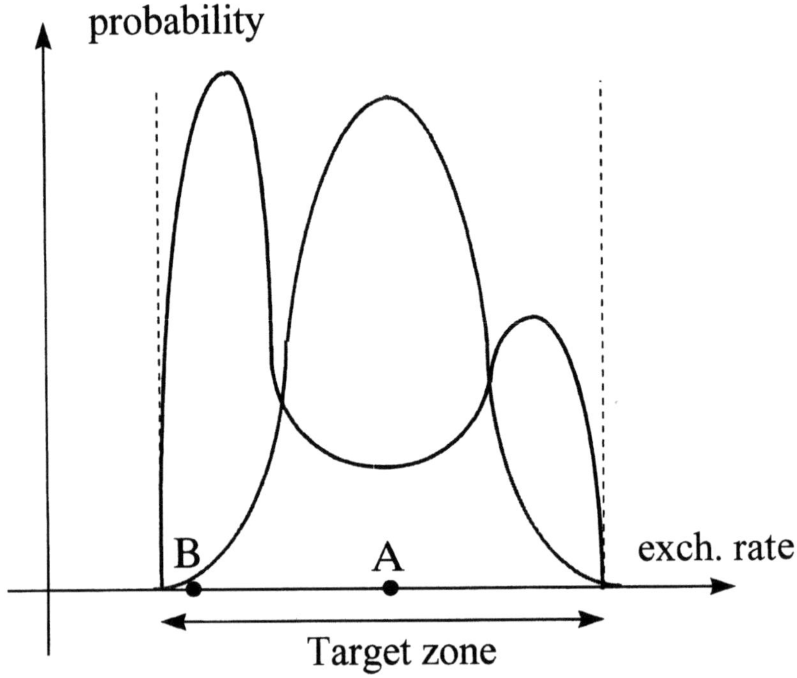

Figure 4. Probability density of the exchange rate under a credible target zone regime. The normality assumption is reasonable when the current exchange rate is close to the middle of the zone. When the exchange rate is close to the boundary the probability distribution is very far from being normal.

corresponding to VaR can be calculated at $1.65 \cdot \sigma$ below the mean ($2.33 \cdot \sigma$ will give the 1% level). One significant advantage of this scheme is that for many market parameters all of the relevant data is well known. The J.P. Morgan's RiskMetrics™ is probably the best source for this type of data in many markets. It is free and easily accessible at http://www.jpmorgan.com.[2]

The strong side of this approach is that it is flexible, simple, and widely used. It also enables the addition of specific scenarios and enables the analysis of the sensitivity of the results with respect of the parameters. However, it relies heavily on the important assumption that all of the major market parameters are normally distributed. Therefore when a significant portion of the portfolio is not linear (options for example) this method can not be used directly.

Another field of limited usage is foreign exchange, especially with European currencies. Whenever a target zone is used one can rely on this approach only when the exchange rate is in the middle of the band. This method becomes very problematic when the rate is close to the boundaries because in this situation the distribution of changes is far from normal. Figure 4 demonstrates that whenever the exchange rate is close to the middle of the target zone (point A), the next day's distribution of the exchange rate is practically normal. However, when the current exchange rate is at point B, the distribution has a completely different shape. Moreover, as some models of exchange rates show (see Ingersoll, 1996), as soon as the time horizon increases, the future distribution of the exchange rate becomes dumodal, even when the rate is currently in the middle of the band.

An additional problem with this approach is that historical distributions of market returns are far from being normal. This problem is well known and is related to fat tails (kurtosis). One can find several techniques of how to deal with these tails in the paper by Duffie and Pan (1997).

All of the problems above must be taken into account when using this approach. Even having solved them, one must remember that the direct usage of the variance covariance method for wide portfolios is restricted to simple linear instruments.

The major market information used in this approach is in the variance covariance matrix (and means). All of these parameters are typically extracted from historical data. The question of which time interval to use for historical correlations immediately arises. The proposed alternative Basle approach requires an estimation of the variances from at least the last year. A naive formula of covariances based on historical observations has two major drawbacks (both are described in details in Alexander, Leigh, 1997).

First, an important property of the variance covariance matrix is that it must be positive definite. However, because of the very high degree of correlation, even a small error in the data can easily lead to loss of this property. The standard procedure applied in this case is to decompose the matrix either to eigenvalues or to singular values and to replace small negative values (arising from numerical errors in data) by zeroes.

A second difficulty is related to the fixed rolling time window. The problem here is exactly the same as the one we have mentioned when discussing the historical simulations approach. Any big market move creates an abrupt change in all major parameters when the window moves.

The solution can be found with an appropriate weighting scheme. More weight is given to the recent past and less weight to the older events. One specific realization of this method is described in Alexander, Leigh (1997). Many similar versions of the weighting scheme can be used depending on the situation.

Monte Carlo simulations

This is another nonparametric method. It is probably one of the most popular methods among sophisticated users. It does not assume a specific form of the distributions. The first step is to identify the important market factors. Next, one should build a joint distribution of these factors based on one of the following: historical data; data implicitly implied by observed prices; data based on specific economic scenarios. Finally, the simulation is performed, typically with a large number of scenarios. The profit and losses at the end of the period are measured for each scenario. As in the other methods, these numbers should be ordered and the 5 percent quantile of the worst results is the VaR estimate.

This method has several important advantages. First, it does not assume a specific model and can be easily adjusted to economic forecasts. The results can be improved by taking a larger number of simulated scenarios. Options and other nonlinear instruments can be easily included in a portfolio. In addition, one can track path-dependence because the whole market process is simulated rather then the final result alone.

One important disadvantage is very slow convergence. Any Monte Carlo type simulation converges to the true value as $\frac{1}{\sqrt{N}}$, where N is the total number of simulated trajectories. This means that in order to increase the precision by a factor of 10 one must perform 100 times more simulations. This problem is the most serious disadvantage of this method. However in many cases there are well developed techniques of variance reduction. They are typically based on known properties of the portfolio, such as correlations between some markets and securities, or known analytical approximations to options and fixed income instruments.

Another class of useful techniques for speeding the standard Monte Carlo approach is portfolio compression, by which one can represent a large portfolio of similar instruments as a single artificial instrument with risk characteristics similar to the original portfolio. One important requirement for this bunching is that all of the instruments that we wish to unify have very similar risk characteristics.

When using the Monte Carlo simulations one should generate a large number of trajectories for all of the major parameters and then price every single instrument along these trajectories. The pricing of all of the instruments is very time consuming, however it can be reduced significantly when one divides all of the instruments into similar groups. This method of variance reduction is based on the knowledge that the instruments that we want to group have similar risk characteristics.

For example, consider a large portfolio of similar bonds. Each one has the current value of $\sum_{j=1}^{T_i} C_{ij} e^{-r(t_{ij})t_{ij}}$, assuming a bond with an index i and coupons C_{ij} paid at time t_{ij}. One can replace the whole portfolio with one artificial bond with the coupon rate C, and time to maturity T, such that its price is equal to the price of the whole portfolio and its duration is the same as the portfolio's duration. Thus the risk characteristics of this bond are similar to the properties of the whole portfolio. Now, instead of mapping the risk for each individual instrument we can consider the influence of market moves on the two parameters C and T. This can save a significant amount of computational time while keeping high accuracy. With this method there is no need to price every single bond along every path when running many simulations. Instead, one can use the artificial bond as a good approximation to the whole portfolio.

An additional problem with Monte Carlo simulations is that one needs to know the joint distribution of many market parameters. When there are more than 3–4 important parameters it is not easy to clean all the data and to build this multidimensional distribution. This is especially true in cases in which the variables are strongly correlated. Imagine a set of bonds with different maturities and different credit ratings. Together they form a very complex random structure, with different variables which are interconnected and which can not be measured easily.

An advantage of the Monte Carlo method is that it allows the use of the preliminary results of all of the methods mentioned above. The historical simulations can give a first approximation to the distribution functions. The variance covariance shows which connections between variables are important and which can be neglected.

In addition, one can easily perform stress testing on the Monte Carlo simulation or perform a more detailed analysis of a specific set of scenarios, including dynamic strategies, such as prepayments or partial recoveries.

Analytical methods

This set of methods is based on a specific parameterization of the market behavior. Typically these methods can not lead to a precise evaluation of VaR, however the upper and lower bounds can be found. These bounds are very useful in many situations in which there is no immediate need to raise additional capital. The analytical methods for VaR evaluation can be used in the several fields. For example, analytical methods can be used to measure the VaR of a portfolio of options in a Black-Scholes setting. In addition, an analytical estimate of VaR is applicable to some fixed income instruments with an underlying term structure model. Exchange rates in a target zone can provide another framework in which an analytical solution for VaR can be found. In most of the cases above the analytical approach is only when we have a dynamic model of the market leading to some bounds on the probability distribution of market parameters.

Let's consider an example of a simple stochastic model of market prices. Assume that s is market index and its dynamic is approximated by

$$ds = v(s,t)dt + z(s,t)dB_t.$$

Here v is a drift, and z—the diffusion parameter equal to the volatility times the current price $z(s,t) = \sigma(s,t)s$. B_t indicates the standard Brownian motion representing the market noise. The standard Black-Scholes option pricing model is a specific case of this approach. Among different methods we will describe briefly the change of variables methods which leads to a tight lower and upper bound for a portfolio of derivatives. A detailed description of the method can be found in Grundy, Wiener (1996).

Assuming the above the major problem is in modeling the behavior of such a diffusion process with non constant volatility. One can use the following monotonic change of variables:

$$F(s,t)=\int_{A(t)}^{s\alpha(t)}\frac{a(t)}{\sigma\left(\frac{x}{\alpha(t)},t\right)x}dx$$

Here $A(t)$, $a(t)$ and $\alpha(t)$ are free parameters, which can be used to simplify the new equation. They have the following meanings: $A(t)$ sets the zero level of the new variable, $a(t)$ gives the new diffusion parameter (in most cases the simplest choice for $a(t)$ is to be a constant), $\alpha(t)$ represents the predictable component of price changes (like inflation). The new variable F gives the generalization of returns for the original variable s, as one can see from the example below.

To demonstrate the method we consider the simple Black-Scholes type of dynamics. In this case there is no real need to apply the change of variables, however we use it to demonstrate the method. Let the price of the underlying asset follow the geometric Brownian motion with a drift:

$$ds=\mu(s,t)sdt+\sigma sdB_t$$

Applying the change of variables suggested above with $A(t) = K$ (typically set at the strike price), $a(t) = 1$, $\alpha(t) = 1$, we get

$$F(s)=\int_{K}^{x}\frac{dx}{\sigma x}=\frac{1}{\sigma}\ln\frac{s}{K}$$

The new variable F is the return of the underlying asset measured relatively to the price to strike ratio. Whenever the diffusion parameter $z(s,t)$ has a more complex form, the new variable F is a generalization of returns.

Substituting the new variable F and applying the Ito's lemma we immediately obtain

$$dF=\left(\frac{\mu(s,t)}{\sigma}-\frac{\sigma}{2}\right)dt+dB_t,$$

which in the case of a risk-neutral process (μ = r) has the familiar form

$$dF=\left(\frac{r-0.5\sigma^2}{\sigma}\right)dt+dB_t$$

This process has a known drift and a random component arising from the standard Brownian motion. Thus its density function can be calculated easily (a Normal distribution with variance t and mean $t\cdot(r-0.5\sigma^2)/\sigma)$. Therefore, it is easy to find any quantile and the corresponding VaR, first in the new variable F and then in the original variable s.

This approach is based on a monotonic change of variables. It leads to bounds on almost all of the quantitative characteristics of the stochastic process. Numerous examples of bounds on probabilities, deltas, and VaRs can be found in Grundy, Wiener (1996). Here we give without a proof only one result related to VaR (Lemma 4).

Suppose that the true process for the underlying asset starts at level s at time t and follows the diffusion $ds = \mu(s,t)sdt + \sigma(s,t)sdB_t$, *with the following bounds on its major parameters:* $\underline{\mu} \leq \mu(s,t) \leq \bar{\mu}$ *and* $\underline{\sigma} \leq \sigma(s,t) \leq \bar{\sigma}$. *Let the inflation to be i and denote by* $M = max\left[\frac{\bar{\mu}-i}{\underline{\sigma}}, \frac{\bar{\mu}-i}{\bar{\sigma}}\right]$ *and* $m = max\left[\frac{\underline{\mu}-i}{\underline{\sigma}}, \frac{\underline{\mu}-i}{\bar{\sigma}}\right]$. *Then using the standard inverse of the normal density* ($\Phi(k)$*—the* $1-k\%$ *quantile) we obtain:*

$if \dfrac{\partial z}{\partial s} \geq 0$ *for all s and then*

$$\text{VaR(k)} \geq \begin{cases} 1-\exp((i+M\underline{\sigma})(T-t)-\Phi(k)\underline{\sigma}\sqrt{T-t}) \text{ if } M\sqrt{T-t} \leq \Phi(k) \\ 1-\exp((i+M\bar{\sigma})(T-t)-\Phi(k)\bar{\sigma}\sqrt{T-t}) \text{ if } M\sqrt{T-t} > \Phi(k) \end{cases}.$$

$if \dfrac{\partial \sigma}{\partial s} \geq 0$ *for all s and then*

$$\text{VaR(k)} \geq \begin{cases} 1-\exp((i+(M-0.5\underline{\sigma})\underline{\sigma})(T-t)-\Phi(k)\underline{\sigma}\sqrt{T-t}) \text{ if } (M-0.5\underline{\sigma})\sqrt{T-t} \leq \Phi(k) \\ 1-\exp((i+(M-0.5\underline{\sigma})\bar{\sigma})(T-t)-\Phi(k)\bar{\sigma}\sqrt{T-t}) \text{ if } (M-0.5\underline{\sigma})\sqrt{T-t} > \Phi(k) \end{cases}.$$

$if \dfrac{\partial \sigma}{\partial s} \leq 0$ *for all s and then*

$$\text{VaR(k)} \leq \begin{cases} 1-\exp((i+(m-0.5\bar{\sigma})\bar{\sigma})(T-t)-\Phi(k)\bar{\sigma}\sqrt{T-t}) \text{ if } (m-0.5\bar{\sigma})\sqrt{T-t} \leq \Phi(k) \\ 1-\exp((i+(m-0.5\bar{\sigma})\underline{\sigma})(T-t)-\Phi(k)\underline{\sigma}\sqrt{T-t}) \text{ if } (m-0.5\bar{\sigma})\sqrt{T-t} > \Phi(k) \end{cases}.$$

Various numerical results based on simulations and using this lemma are presented in Table 2 in Grundy, Wiener (1996).

This change of variables can be used for more than one variable. Let us demonstrate this in the case of two variables (the general approach is similar):

$$\begin{cases} ds = v(s,q,t)dt + z(s,q,t)dB_t \\ dq = v(s,q,t)dt + w(s,q,t)dB_t \end{cases}$$

Then one can perform the change of variables simplifying the volatility to a constant form. In other words we are looking for a new pair of variables $S(s,q,t)$ and $Q(s,q,t)$ such that the new dynamic has a simple form. Using the Ito's lemma one can write the new variables as

$$\begin{cases} dS = S_1 ds + S_2 dq + S_3 dt + 0.5S_{11}(ds)^2 + S_{12}(dq)^2 + 0.5S_{22}(dq)^2 \\ dQ = Q_1 ds + Q_2 dq + Q_3 dt + 0.5Q_{11}(ds)^2 + Q_{12}(dq)^2 + 0.5S_{22}(dq)^2 \end{cases}$$

Thus, in order to get a simple form the random part of the new dynamic, we have to check

$$\begin{cases} dS = \cdots dt + (S_1(s,q,t)z(s,q,t) + S_2(s,q,t)w(s,q,t))dB_t \\ dQ = \cdots dt + (Q_1(s,q,t)z(s,q,t) + Q_2(s,q,t)w(s,q,t))dB_t \end{cases}$$

We have to solve separately the two (independent) partial differential equations of the first order (of Pfaff type) where the $a(t)$ and $b(t)$ are the new deterministic diffusion parameters:

$$S_1(s,q,t)z(s,q,t)+S_2(s,q,t)w(s,q,t)=a(t)$$
$$Q_1(s,q,t)z(s,q,t)+Q_2(s,q,t)w(s,q,t)=b(t)$$

The solution is based on a general solution of a system of ordinary differential equations:

$$\begin{cases} \dfrac{ds}{dt}=z(s,q,t) \\ \dfrac{dq}{dt}=w(s,q,t) \\ \dfrac{dS}{dt}=a(t) \end{cases}$$

There are many ways to solve such a system and we will not investigate it here further.

Another example of the analytical approach to VaR is through the delta or delta-gamma approach. This method is useful when there is an analytic formula (like Black-Scholes or the CEV model for options). In this case in order to measure a risk associated with a complex derivative (an option in this case) one can use a linear (delta approach) or a quadratic (delta-gamma approach) to measure the price distribution density of the derivative. For a detailed discussion and some implementations see Schaefer (1997) and Duffie and Pan (1997).

5. BACKTESTING

The Basle standard requires backtesting—a procedure in which one checks (a posteriori) how often the actual losses have exceeded the level predicted by VaR. As soon as a 99 percent confidence interval and the 10-day time horizon are used, there should not be too many cases in when the actual losses are greater than the predicted ones.

There are three zones. If during the last year (approximately 250 business days) there are four or less exceptions (losses that exceed the VaR level), the model is said to be in a green zone and it is acceptable. If there are five to nine exceptions it is in the yellow zone and certain actions (such as increase of the safety multiplier from 3 to 4) are recommended.[3] When there are ten or more exceptions the whole model should be revised.

This mechanism prevents banks from setting the VaR too low. However when current capital reserves are high the bank can safely set an upper bound of VaR instead of trying to calculate a precise value.

ACKNOWLEDGMENT

The author wishes to thank David Ruthenberg and Ben Schreiber, the organizers of the conference. The author gratefully acknowledge financial support from the Krueger and Eshkol Centers, the Israel Foundations Trustees, the Israel Science Foundation, and the Alon Fellowship.

NOTES

1. We learned this explanation from D. Pyle on the "Risk Management and Regulation in Banking" conference, Jerusalem 1997.

2. After July 17, 1997, the data set is available through Reuters WEB page: http://www.riskmetrics.reuters.com.

3. An interesting explanation of this multiplier and the assumptions about the probability distribution can be found in Stahl (1997).

REFERENCES

Alexander, Carol, and C. Leigh (1997). "On the Covariance Matrices Used In VaR Models," *Journal of Derivatives* 4 (Spring), 50–62.

Amendment to the Capital Accord to Incorporate Market Risks (1996). Bank for International Settlements.

Basel Committee on Banking Supervision (1995). An Internal Model-Based Approach to Market Risk Capital Requirements.

Duffie, D, and J. Pan (1997). "An Overview of Value at Risk," *Journal of Derivatives* 4 (Spring), 7–49.

Grundy Bruce D, and Zvi Wiener (1996). "The Analysis of VAR, Deltas and State Prices: A New Approach," Working paper of The Rodney L. White Center for Financial Research, The Wharton School, 11.

Ingersoll Johnathan E., Jr. (1996). "Valuing Foreign Exchange Derivatives with a Bounded Exchange Rate Process," *Review of Derivatives Research*, vol. 1, 159–181.

Jackwerth Jens Carsten, Rubinstein Mark (1996). "Recovering Probability Distributions from Option Prices," *The Journal of Finance*, vol. 51, no. 5, December, 1611–1631.

Linsmeier, Thomas, and Neil Pearson (1996). "Risk Measurement: An Introduction to Value at Risk," Working paper of the University of Illinois.

Marshall, Chris, and Michael Siegel (1997). "Value at Risk: Implementing A Risk Management Standard," *Journal of Derivatives*, vol. 4 (Spring), 91–110.

Schaefer Stephen (1997). "Management of Non-Linear Market Risk," Working Paper, London Business School.

Stahl Gerhard (1997). "Three Cheers," *Risk* vol. 10, no. 5, May, 67–69.

4. A COMPARISON BETWEEN THE BIS STANDARDIZED APPROACH AND THE INTERNAL MODELS APPROACH

MICHEL CROUHY,[1] DAN GALAI, and ROBERT MARK

1. INTRODUCTION

In the past, capital regulation consisted only of uniform capital standards, regardless of the banks specific risk profiles. In addition, those capital standards took only into consideration on-balance sheet loans, ignoring completely off-balance sheet positions and commitments.

The increased international competition among banks during the 1980s emphasized the inconsistencies in regulation of capital standards across countries. Japanese banks had no formal capital adequacy requirement, while in the United States and England, banks were required to finance more than 5 percent of their total assets by equity. The 1980s also witnessed a major increase in off-balance sheet activity by banks. This has changed the risk profile of banks while the regulatory requirements concerning equity ratios stayed the same.

The 1988 Basle Accord established international minimum capital guidelines, linking banks' capital requirement to their credit exposure, both on- and off-balance sheet. The 1996 Amendment to the Accord extended the initial guidelines by considering market risks in the bank trading accounts in calculating the capital requirements.

The debt crisis of the 1980s reminds us that the distinction between general market risk, specific risk, and credit risk is indeed important to bear in mind, although we cannot ignore the potential impact of an abrupt change in market risk on credit risk exposure. In the 1970s commercial banks involved in lending to Latin American countries innovated by proposing syndicated Eurodollar loans denominated in U.S. dollars and therefore without currency exposure for the U.S. banks. These loans were payable on a floating-rate basis, thus without interest rate risk, and were made to governments that were thought, initially, free from any credit risk exposure. After U.S. interest rates skyrocketed in the early 1980s, countries like Mexico and Brazil went into default and were unable or unwilling to stand by their commitments.

This chapter discusses the new BIS framework to assess regulatory capital for banks, which became effective in January 1998. Banks are required to satisfy three capital adequacy standards: first, a maximum assets to capital multiple of 20; second, a 8 percent minimum ratio of eligible capital to risk-weighted assets; and third, a minimum capital charge to compensate for market risk of traded instruments on- and off-balance sheet. In addition to these capital adequacy requirements, BIS has set limits on concentration risks. Large risks that exceed 10 percent of the bank's capital must be reported, and positions that are greater than 25 percent of the bank's capital are forbidden. The new BIS proposal, which supplements the old risk-based capital standards, now incorporates market risk.

The risk-based capital adequacy standards rely on principles that are laid out in the "International Convergence of Capital Measurement and Capital Standards" document, published in July 1988 (cf. Basle, 1988), and referred to in the following as the Accord. This Accord was initially developed by the Basle Committee on Banking Supervision and later endorsed by the central bank governors of the Group of Ten (G-10) countries. The G-10 is composed of Belgium, Canada, France, Germany, Italy, Japan, The Netherlands, Sweden, the United Kingdom, and the United States. On the Basle Committee sit senior officials of the central banks and supervisory authorities from the G-10, as well as Switzerland and Luxembourg. The Accord was fully implemented in 1993 in the twelve ratifying countries. This Accord is also known as the BIS requirements since the Basle Committee meets under the patronage of the Bank for International Settlements (BIS), usually in Basle, Switzerland. BIS is used in the text as a generic term to represent indifferently the Basle Committee and the regulatory authorities that supervise the banks in the member countries.

The proposed approach is quite simple and somewhat arbitrary and has been subject to many criticisms. This Accord should be viewed as a first step in establishing a level playing field for banks across member countries. It defines two minimum standards for meeting acceptable capital ratio. The first standard is an overall measure of the bank's capital adequacy. The second measure focuses on the credit risk associated with specific on- and off-balance sheet asset categories. This second measure is a solvency ratio, known as the Cooke ratio, and is defined as the ratio of capital to risk-weighted, on-balance sheet assets plus off-balance sheet exposures, where the weights are assigned on the basis of counterparty credit risk.

In April 1995, the Basle Committee issued a consultative proposal to amend the Accord, and that is known as the 1996 Amendment. It now requires financial institutions to measure and hold capital to cover their exposure to market risk associated with debt and equity positions located in the trading book, and foreign exchange and commodity positions in both the trading and banking books.[2] These positions should include all financial instruments that are marked-to market, whether they are plain vanilla products like bonds or stocks, or complex derivative instruments like options, swaps, or credit derivatives. Marking financial instruments to market must be done for both accounting and management purposes.

The most significant risk for the nontrading activities of financial institutions is credit risk associated with default. The Accord treated all instruments equivalently, whether in the trading or in the banking book. The 1996 Amendment has introduced the requirement of measuring market risk in addition to credit risk. The initial Accord still applies in-extenso to the nontrading items both on-balance sheet and off-balance sheet, as well as off-balance sheet over-the-counter (OTC) derivatives. Market risk must now be measured for both on- and off-balance sheet traded instruments. However, on-balance sheet assets are subject to market risk capital charge only, while off-balance sheet derivatives, like swaps and options, are subject to both market risk and credit risk capital charges according to the 1988 Accord. To summarize, the bank's overall capital requirement is now the sum of

- *credit risk capital charge,* as proposed in the initial 1988 Accord, which applies to all positions in the trading and banking books, as well as OTC derivatives and off-balance sheet commitments, *but excluding debt and equity traded securities in the trading book, and all positions in commodities and foreign exchange*
- market risk capital charge for the instruments of the trading book on-, as well as off-balance sheet

The authorities have recognized the complexity of correctly assessing market risk exposure, especially for derivative products. Flexibility in the modeling of the many components of market risk is thus allowed. The most sophisticated institutions, which already have an independent risk management division in place with sound risk management practices, will have the choice between their own internal VaR model, referred to as the *internal models approach,* and the standard model proposed by BIS, referred to as the *standardized approach,* to determine market risk related regulatory capital.

The new capital requirement related to market risks should largely be offset by the fact that the capital charge calculated under the 1988 Accord to cover credit risk, will no longer need to be held for on-balance sheet securities in the trading portfolio. The capital charge for general market risk and specific risk should be, on aggregate, much smaller than the credit risk capital charge for large investment grade trading books. Then, banks adopting the internal models approach should realize substantial capital savings, probably in the order of 20 to 50 percent, depending of the size of their trading operations and the type of instruments they trade.

In this chapter we compare the two alternatives to assess market risk as proposed by BIS 1998. The first one consists in using the standardized approach with set factors as determined by the BIS for various instruments. This approach is detailed in Section 2. The alternative approach, the internal model approach, is based on the proprietary models of individual banks to value securities and the probability distributions for changes in the values of claims. The BIS set rules and guidelines for central banks in the process of approving banks that opt to use internal models. These guidelines are detailed in Section 3. In Section 4, the pros and cons of the two approaches are discussed and a new approach, the precommitment approach is proposed. Finally, in Section 5, a numerical example is presented in order to illustrate the savings in capital requirement due to the use of internal models rather than the standardized approach.

The capital requirements for credit risk as set by BIS 1988 Accord and the 1996 Amendment are not presented in this paper. A discussion of the credit risk capital requirements appears in Crouhy, Galai, and Mark (1998).

2. THE STANDARDIZED APPROACH

The standardized model uses a building block type of approach, where the capital charge for each risk category (i.e., interest rate, equity, foreign exchange, and commodities) is first determined separately. Then, the four measures are simply added together to obtain the global capital charge related to market risk. In this section we present, and illustrate with simple examples, the main thrust of the method for the four risk categories.

2.1. Interest rate risk

The model encompasses all fixed-rate and floating rate debt securities, zero-coupon instruments, interest rate derivatives, hybrid products like convertible bonds, although they are treated like debt securities only when they trade like debt securities (i.e., when their price is below par) and are treated like equities otherwise. Simple interest rate derivatives like futures and forward contracts, including FRAs and swaps, are treated like a combination of short and long positions in debt contracts. Options are treated separately and will be covered later in this section.

The interest risk capital charge is the sum of the two components separately calculated, one related to specific risk, which applies to the net holdings for each instrument, the other related to the general market risk, where long and short positions in different securities or derivatives can be partially offset.

2.1.1. Specific risk

The capital charge for specific risk is designed to protect the bank against an adverse price movement in the price of an individual security due to idiosyncratic factors related to the individual issuer. Offsetting is thus restricted to matched positions in the same issue, including derivatives. The capital charge applies whether it is a net long, or net short position. Even if the issuer is the same, but there are differences in maturity, coupon rates, call features, etc., no offsetting is allowed since a change in the credit quality of the issuer may have a different effect on the market value of each instrument.

Table 1. Specific risk charge factor for net debt positions.

Debt Category	Remaining Maturity	Capital charge (%)
Government	N/A	0.00
Qualifying	6 months or less	0.25
	6 to 24 months[3]	1.00
	over 2 years	1.60
Other	N/A	8.00

Table 1 shows the specific risk charge for various types of debt positions. The weighting factors apply to the market value of the debt instruments and not their notional amount.

Government debt includes all form of debt instruments issued by OECD central governments, as well as non-OECD central governments provided some conditions are satisfied. The qualifying category includes debt securities issued by OECD public sector entities, regulated securities firms of the G-10 countries plus Switzerland and Luxembourg, and other rated investment grade bonds. The other category receives the same specific risk capital charge as a private sector borrower under the credit risk requirements of the 1988 Accord, i.e., 8 percent.

A specific risk charge also applies to derivative contracts in the trading book only when the underlying is subject to specific risk. For example, an interest rate swap based on LIBOR won't be subject to specific risk charge, while an option on a corporate bonds will. All over-the-counter derivative contracts are subject to coutnerparty credit risk charge according to guidelines of the 1988 Accord, even where a specific risk charge is required.

2.1.2. General market risk

Capital requirements for general market risk are designed to capture the risk of loss arising from changes in market interest rates. Banks have the choice between two methods, the maturity method and the duration method. The duration method is just a variant of the maturity method.[4]

The maturity method uses a maturity ladder, i.e., a series of maturity bands that are divided into maturity zones according to the rule given in Table 2. These maturity bands and zones are chosen to take into account differences in price sensitivities and interest rate volatilities across different maturities. A separate maturity ladder must be constructed for each currency in which the bank has a significant trading position. No offsetting is allowed among maturity ladders of different currencies. As illustrated in the previous section, the disallowance of offsetting between currencies greatly impacts financial institutions that trade in one currency and hedge in another currency due to the high correlation between them. For instance, if one did a swap in USD and performed an exactly offsetting swap in CAD, then the institutions should be exposed to some FX risk and to cross-currency basis risk. The BIS methodology will impose an onerous amount of capital

Table 2. Maturity bands and risk weights.

Zone	Coupon 3% or more	Coupon less than 3%	Risk weights (sensitivities)	Assumed changes in yield (%)
1	1 month or less	1 month or less	0.00%	1.00
	1 to 3 months	1 to 3 months	0.20%	1.00
	3 to 6 months	3 to 6 months	0.40%	1.00
	6 to 12 months	6 to 12 months	0.70%	1.00
2	1 to 2 years	to 1.9 years	1.25%	0.90
	2 to 3 years	to 2.8 years	1.75%	0.80
	3 to 4 years	2.8 to 3.6 years	2.25%	0.75
3	4 to 5 years	to 4.3 years	2.75%	0.75
	5 to 7 years	to 5.7 years	3.25%	0.70
	7 to 10 years	5.7 to 7.3 years	3.75%	0.65
	10 to 15 years	7.3 to 9.3 years	4.50%	0.60
	15 to 20 years	9.3 to 10.6 years	5.25%	0.60
	over 20 years	10.6 to 12 years	6.00%	0.60
		12 to 20 years	8.00%	0.60
		over 20 years	12.50%	0.60

for this trade and its hedge, while this institution is only exposed to little residual risk.

The first step in the maturity method consists of allocating the marked-to-market value of the positions to each maturity band. Fixed rate instruments are allocated to the residual term to maturity, and floating-rate instruments according to the residual term to the next repricing date.

Derivatives, like forwards, futures, and swaps, should be converted into long and short positions in the underlying positions. Options are treated separately. For example, a long one-year forward contract on a two-year bond is equivalent to a short position in the 6–12 month maturity band for an amount equal to the discounted value of the forward price of the bond, and a long position in the 1–2 year maturity band for the same market value. For swaps, the paying side is treated as a short position and the receiving side as a long position on the relevant underlying instruments. Offsetting is only allowed for matched positions in identical instruments with exactly the same issuer.

In the second step the positions in each maturity band are risk weighted according to the sensitivities given in Table 2. The third step consists of calculating capital requirements for general market risk according to the following principles:

1. Vertical disallowance to account for basis risk. In each maturity band the matched weighted position is imposed a capital charge of 10 percent. Then, only the unmatched positions in each maturity band are considered in the rest.
2. Horizontal disallowance to account for the risk related to twists in the yield curve. The matched weighted positions in each zone (zone 1, 2, and 3, respectively), between adjacent zones (between zones 1 and 2, then between zones 2 and 3), and between the two extreme zones (between zones 1 and 3) are allo-

Table 3. Horizontal disallowances for the risk related to twists in the yield curve.

Zones	Time-band	Within the zone	Between Adjacent Zones	Between Zones 1 and 3
Zone 1	0–1 month			
	1–3 months	40%		
	3–6 months			
	6–12 months		40%	
Zone 2	1–3 years			
	2–3 years	30%		100%
	3–4 years			
Zone 3	4–5 years		40%	
	5–7 years			
	7–10 years			
	10–15 years	30%		
	15–20 years			
	over 20 years			

cated a capital charge given in Table 3. Again, only the unmatched positions at each step are considered in the remaining calculations.

3. To account for the risk associated with a parallel shift in the yield curve, the residual unmatched weighted positions are given a capital charge of 100 percent.

The example presented in Table 4 illustrates the allocation process to each maturity band, and the calculation of the capital charge for general market risk.

PORTFOLIO:

A. Qualifying bond with a $13.33 million market value, a residual maturity of 8 years, and a coupon of 8 percent.

B. Government bond with a market value of $75 million, a residual maturity of 2 months and a coupon of 7 percent.

C. Interest rate swap at par-value, i.e. with a zero net market value, with a notional amount of $150 million, where the bank receives floating and pays fixed, with the next fixing in 9 months, and a residual life of 8 years.

D. Long position in interest rate futures contract with 6 month delivery date, for which the underlying instrument is a government bond with a 3.5 year maturity and a market value of $50 million.

Note that there is vertical disallowance only in zone 3 for the 7–10 year timeband. There is no horizontal disallowance within zones 2 and 3, since there is no offsetting positions between timebands within each of these two zones. However, there is horizontal disallowance within zone 1, and between zones 1 and 3. The short risk-weighted position in the 3–6 month timeband partially offsets the long positions in the adjacent timebands in zone 1. Then, after vertical disallowance in the 7–10 year timeband for $0.5 million, the net unmatched position in zone 3 becomes

Table 4. Illustration of the calculation of the capital charge to cover general market risk for interest rate instruments (except options).

	Zone 1				Zone 2			Zone 3							
Time-band															
Coupon >3%	0–1	1–3	3–6	6–12	1–2	2–3	3–4	4–5	5–7	7–10	10–15	15–20	>20		
Coupon <3%	0–1	1–3	3–6	6–12	1–1.9	1.9–2.8	2.8–3.6	3.6–4.3	4.3–5.7	5.7–7.3	7.3–9.3	9.3–10.6	10.6–12	12–20	>20
	Months				Years										
Positions															
A										+13.33 Qual.					
B		+75 Gov.													
C				+150						−150					
D			−50 Fut.	Swap			+50 Fut.			Swap					
Weight (%)	0.00	0.20	0.40	0.70	1.25	1.75	2.25	2.75	3.25	3.75	4.50	5.25	6.00	8.00	12.5
Position × Weight		+0.15	−0.20	+1.05			+1.125			+0.5 −5.625					
Vertical Disallowance										0.5 × 10% =0.05					
Horizontal Disallowance 1		0.20 × 40% = 0.08													
Horizontal Disallowance 2										1.125 × 40% = 0.45					
Horizontal Disallowance 3								1.0 × 100% = 1.0							

net short \$5.125 million. Given the net long position for \$1.125 million in zone 2, there is partial offsetting for this amount between zones 2 and 3, which leaves a net unmatched position of 0 in zone 2 and of net short \$4 million in zone 3. After horizontal disallowance in zone 1, the net unmatched position becomes net long \$1 million in this zone. Finally, there is partial offsetting for \$1 million between zones 1 and 3, which leaves an overall net unmatched position of \$3 million.

The total capital charge is (in \$ million):

• for the vertical disallowance (basis risk)	\$0.050
• for the horizontal disallowance in zone 1 (curve risk)	\$0.080
• for the horizontal disallowance between adjacent zones (curve risk)	\$0.450
• for the horizontal disallowance between zone 1 and 3 (steepening of the curve risk)	\$1.000
• for the overall net open position (parallel shift risk)	\$3.000
Total	**\$4.580**

2.1.3. Treatment of Options

There are three different approaches. The simplified approach applies to banks that only buy options, while the delta-plus method or the scenario approach should be used by banks that also write options.

SIMPLIFIED APPROACH. Table 5 shows the capital charge according to the simplified approach. As an example, suppose the bank is long 100 shares currently valued at \$10, and has a put on these shares with a strike price of \$11. The capital charge would be

+\$1,000 * 16% (8% for specific risk plus 8% for general market risk)	= \$160
−the amount the option is in the money, i.e. (\$11 − \$10) * 100	= \$100
Total:	**\$60**

Table 5. Capital charge for options according to the simplified approach.

Position	Treatment
Long cash and long put or Short cash and long call	The capital charge is the market value of the underlying security multiplied by the sum of specific and general market risk charges for the underlying, less the amount the option is in the money (if any), bounded at zero.
Long call or Long put	The capital charge will be the lesser of • the market value of the underlying security multiplied by the sum of specific and general market risk charges for the underlying, and • the market value of the option.

DELTA-PLUS APPROACH. For the purpose of capital charge calculation related to general market risk, the option is first considered as its delta equivalent in the underlying instrument, which is then allocated into the time-band corresponding to the maturity of the option (Table 4).

Then, two additional capital charges are added. The first one adjusts the capital charge for gamma risk or convexity risk, i.e.,

$$\text{Gamma capital charge} = \frac{1}{2}\text{Gamma} * \Delta V^2$$

It is simply the second order term in the Taylor expansion of the option price formula, where ΔV denotes the change in the value of the underlying. For interest rate products it is calculated according to the assumed changes in yield in the maturity band, as given in Table 2. For equities and foreign exchange and gold the price change is taken as 8%, while for commodities it is taken as 15 percent.

The second one compensates for vega risk, i.e.,

$$\text{Vega capital charge} = \text{vega} * 25\%\sigma,$$

where vega is the sensitivity of the option price to one unit of volatility, σ.

This vega term is the absolute value of the impact of a 25% increase or decrease in volatility.

SCENARIO MATRIX APPROACH. The scenario matrix approach adopts as capital charge the worst loss for all the scenari generated by a grid that allows for a combination of possible values of the underlying price, the volatility, and the cost of carry. The range of values being considered is the same as for the delta-plus approach.

2.2. Equity risk

General market risk charge is 8 percent of each net position. Capital charge for specific risk is 8 percent, unless the portfolio is both liquid and well diversified, in which case the charge is 4 percent.

Equity derivatives are treated the same way as interest rate derivatives. While there is no specific charge when the underlying is a government security or a market rate like LIBOR, for diversified broad market indices there is a specific risk charge of 2 percent of the underlying market value. The example given below illustrates the delta-plus approach.

Consider a short position in a European one-year call option on a stock with a striking price of \$490. The underlying spot price is \$500, the risk-free rate is 8% per annum, and the annualized volatility is 20%. The option value is \$65.48, with a delta and gamma of −0.721 and −0.0034, respectively, corresponding to a \$1 change in the underlying price; its vega is 1.68 associated with a change in volatility of 1 percentage point.

The three components of the capital charge are

delta equivalent: $\$500 * 0.721 * 8\% =$	\$28.84
gamma adjustment: $\frac{1}{2} * 0.0034 * (\$500 * 8\%)^2 =$	\$2.72
vega adjustment: $1.68 * (25\% * 20) =$	\$8.40
Total	**\$39.96**

Note that the gamma adjustment is based on an 8 percent move in the stock price. If the underlying were a commodity it would be 15 percent, and then the delta-equivalent would have been allocated to the time-band corresponding to the maturity of the option. (Table 8).

2.3. Foreign exchange risk, including gold price risk

There are two steps in the calculation of the capital charge. First, the exposure in each currency is measured, and second, the net long and net short exposures in all currencies are translated into an overall capital charge according to a rule called the shorthand method.

The measurement of the exposures is straightforward. It consists of the net spot position, the net forward position,[5] the delta-equivalent for options as discussed in Section 2.1.3, accrued interest and expenses, and other future income and expenses which are already fully hedged.

The capital charge is the absolute value of 8 percent of the greater of the net open long positions and the net open short positions in all currencies, plus 8 percent of the absolute value of the net open position in gold plus the gamma and vega adjustments for options. The example below illustrates the application of the rule.

Assume the net positions in each currency, expressed in the reporting currency i.e., \$, are as follows:

Long			**Short**		
Yen	DM	GB	FFR	US\$	Gold
+50	**+100**	**+150**	**−20**	**−180**	−35
	+300			−200	−35

Capital charge = 8% * 300 + 8% * 35 = \$26.80

2.4. Commodities risk

Commodities are broadly defined as physical products, which can be traded on an organized market, like agricultural products, oil, gas, electricity, and precious metals (except gold, which is treated as a foreign currency). Commodities' risks are often more complex to measure than for other financial instruments as markets are less liquid, prices are affected by seasonal patterns in supply and demand, and inventories play a critical role in the determination of the equilibrium price.

The main components of market risk are

- outright price risk, i.e., the risk of price movements in the spot prices
- basis risk, i.e., the risk of a movement in the price differential between different related commodity prices, as it is inherent for energy products whose prices are quoted as a spread over a benchmark index
- interest rate risk, i.e., the risk of a change in the cost of carry
- time spread risk or forward gap risk, i.e., the risk of movements in the forward commodity prices for other reasons than a change in interest rates; the shape of the forward curve is a function of supply and demand in the short run, and fundamental factors in the longer run
- options risk, i.e., delta, gamma, and vega risk as already discussed for other classes of products

The standardized model for commodities is somewhat similar to the maturity ladder approach for interest rate products. The idea being to design a simple framework that captures directional, curve risk as well as time spread risk.

First, positions are converted at current spot rates into the reporting currency, and located into the relevant timeband. Forwards, futures and swaps are decomposed as a combination of long and short positions like for interest rate products. The delta equivalent of options is placed in the timeband corresponding to the maturity of the option.

In order to capture spread risk and some of the forward gap risk the matched position in a timeband is allocated a capital charge of 3 percent. The unmatched position is carried forward into the nearest available timeband at a cost of 0.6 percent per time band. For example, if it is moved forward two time bands it is charged $2 * 0.6\% = 1.2\%$. At the end of the process, the net unmatched position is given a capital charge of 15%.

The following example, given in Table 6, illustrates the principle of the maturity ladder for commodities.

3. THE INTERNAL MODELS APPROACH

The 1996 Amendment of the BIS Accord, which became mandatory as of January 1, 1998, allows banks to assess market risk using their own internal models. The capital charge for market risk applies to all instruments on the trading book, on- as well as off-balance sheet.

The trading book means the bank's proprietary positions in financial instruments, whether on- or off-balance sheet, which are intentionally held for short-term trading, or that are taken on by the bank with the intention of making profit from short-term changes in prices, rates, and volatilities. All trading book positions must be marked-to-market or marked-to-model every day. For market risk capital purposes, an institution may include in its measure of general market risk certain nontrading book instruments that it deliberately uses to hedge trading positions.

According to BIS, market risk encompasses both general market risk and specific risk. General market risk refers to changes in market value of on-balance sheet assets

Table 6. Maturity ladder approach for commodities.

Time-band	Spread capital charge	Position	Capital charge	
0–1 m	1.5%	—		
1–3 m	1.5%	—		
3–6 m	1.5%	long $600 short $1,000	matched position: $600 × 3% = $400 carried forward 2 time-bands: $400 × 2 × 0.6% =	 $18 $4.8
6–12 m	1.5%	—		
1–2 y	1.5%	long $500	matched position: $400 × 3% = $100 carried forward 1 time-bind: $100 × 0.6 =	 $12 $0.6
2–3 y	1.5%	short $300	matched position: $100 × 3% =	 $3
over 3 y	1.5%	—		
			net unmatched position: $200 × 15% =	 $30
			Total	**$68.4**

and liabilities, and off-balance sheet instruments, resulting from broad market movements, such as changes in the level of interest rates, equity prices, exchange rates, and commodity prices. Specific risk refers to changes in the market value of individual positions due to factors other than broad market movements like liquidity, exceptional events, and credit quality.

While the regulators are not too specific about modeling requirements and the choice of the relevant risk, banks will have to satisfy some minimum qualitative requirements before they can envisage adopting the internal model approach, as presented below.

3.1. Issues regarding the adoption of the internal models approach

The regulators accept that institutions will use different assumptions and modeling techniques, simply because trading financial products relies on proprietary expertise both in trading and modeling markets. Modeling market risk is thus an issue, and will stay an issue since it is inherent to the trading of derivatives. Indeed, the ability of a trading institution to stay profitable, relies in part on the skill of its financial engineers and traders to build the appropriate pricing and hedging models. State of the art modeling provides institutions with a unique competitive edge. These models are kept relatively secret, although most of them are based on published papers in academic journals. However, the implementation and calibration of these models require a lot of ingenuity, strong numerical and computer skills, a good understanding of the products, and the markets. Very few bartenders are able to produce this elaborate cocktail. The same proprietary models are used in risk management to derive risk exposures, like deltas, gammas, vegas, and other "Greeks." However, the wrong model may lead to large trading losses as has been reported in the financial press. It can also lead to a poor assessment of market risk exposure. Financial institutions learn the hard way how to correct the limitations of their models. Recently, in the *Wall Street Journal* (March 28, 1997) it was reported that Bank of Tokyo-Mitsubishi had to write off $83 million on its U.S. interest rate derivatives book, because of the use of the wrong interest rate pricing model, which lead to systematic overvaluation of the position.

The regulator recognizes this unique feature of investment banking activity and requires institutions to scale up their VaR number derived from their internal model by a factor of three, referred to in the following as the ***multiplier***. This multiplier should be viewed as an insurance against model risk, imperfect assessment of specific risks, and other operational risks, although, as we discuss later on, the application of such a multiplier has been widely criticized. Another view on this multiplier is a safety factor against nonnormal market moves.

3.2. Qualitative requirements

Before an institution can expect to be eligible to use its own internal model to assess regulatory capital related to market risk, it should have sound risk management practices already in place. The institution should have a strong risk management group which is independent from the business units it monitors, and which reports directly to the senior executive management of the institution.

The internal models should not be used only for calculating regulatory capital, it should be fully integrated in the daily risk management of the institution. In addition the regulators requires that systematic backtesting and stress testing be conducted on a regular basis, in order to test the robustness of the internal model to various market conditions and crises. Improvements should be implemented in the case the model fails to pass the tests, e.g., when backtesting exhibits too many days where the trading losses are greater than VaR.

Implementing a VaR model is a massive and intensive system endeavor. The aim is to build a truly integrated, global, real time system which records all positions centrally in a data-warehouse, and map them to the risk factors tracked by the VaR model. Part of the challenge of implementing such a system, is a need to have in place controls to ensure that the model inputs, and therefore the risk measures, are reliable and accurate:

- A formal vetting system is needed to approve the models, their modifications assumptions, and calibration.
- Model parameters should be estimated independently of the trading desks to avoid the temptation by the traders to "fudge" volatility numbers and other key parameters to make their position smaller.
- The financial rates and prices which feed the risk management system should come from sources independent of the front office, and be located in a financial rates database (FRD) independently controlled by risk management.

3.3. Quantitative and modeling requirements

The internal model approach should capture the materiality of all market risks of the trading positions. Although each institution has some discretion in the choice of the risk factors, these risk factors should be selected with great care to guarantee the robustness of the VaR model. Oversimplification and failure to select the right risk factors inherent in the trading positions may have serious consequences, as the VaR model may miss components of basis risk, curve risk, or spread risk. These shortcomings should be revealed when backtesting the model, and may lead to penalties in the form of a multiplier greater than three.

Market risk can be broken down into four categories: interest rate risk, equity risk, exchange rate risk, and commodity price risk as follows:

- Interest rate risk applies only to the trading book. The base yield curve in each currency (government curve or swap curve) should be modeled with a minimum of 6 risk points. The other relevant yield curves, i.e., corporate curves and provincial curves for Canada, are defined with regard to the base curve by the addition of a spread (positive or negative). The model should also incorporate separate risk factors to capture spread risk.
- Equity price risk should incorporate risk factors corresponding to each of the equity markets in which the trading book holds significant positions. At a minimum, there should be a risk factor designed to capture market wide movements in equity prices, e.g., the broad market index in each national equity market to assess both, market risk and idiosyncratic risk, according to the Capital Asset Pricing Model (CAPM). The most extensive approach would have risk factors corresponding to each asset.
- Exchange rate risk should include risk factors corresponding to the individual currencies in which the trading and banking books have positions.
- Commodity price risk should incorporate risk factors corresponding to each of the commodity markets in which the trading and banking books have significant positions. The model should account for variations in the convenience yield.[6] It should also encompass **directional risk** to capture exposure from changes in spot prices, **forward gap and interest rate risk** to capture exposure to changes in forward prices arising from maturity mismatches, and **basis risk** to capture the exposure to changes in price relationship between similar commodities such as energy products which are defined relative to WTI crude oil.

The 1996 Amendment requires VaR to be derived at the 99 percent (one-tailed) confidence level, with a ten day horizon, i.e., with ten-day movements in rates and prices. However, in the initial phase of implementation of the internal model, the BIS allows the ten day VaR to be proxied by multiplying the one day VaR by the square root of ten, i.e., 3.16.[7]

The effective daily regulatory capital requirements corresponds to the maximum of previous day's VaR (VaR_{t-1}) and the average of daily VaR over the preceding 60 business days

$$\left(\overline{VaR} = \frac{1}{60}\sum_{i=t-1}^{t-60} VaR_i\right)$$

scaled up by the multiplier k, which normally should be equal to 3:

$$\text{Market risk capital charge (t)} = \text{Max}\left\{\text{VaR}_{t-1}, \text{k}\overline{\text{VaR}}\right\} \qquad (1)$$

As we discussed in Section 2.1, this arbitrary multiplicative factor is adopted to compensate for model errors, and imperfect assessment of specific risks and operational risks. This multiplicative factor can be increased, up to 4, by the regulators if the models do not meet backtesting requirements. (See Table 7.)

Institutions are allowed to take into account correlations among risk categories. Volatilities and correlations should be estimated based on past historical data with a minimum history of 250 days[8], i.e., approximately one year. Market parameters should be updated at least once every three months, or more frequently if market conditions warrant. If empirical correlations between risk categories are unavailable, then the aggregate VaR is calculated as the simple arithmetic sum of the VaR for each block, i.e., equity, interest rate, FX, and commodities. In that case, the aggregate VaR doesn't benefit from the risk reduction which results from diversification across risk classes.

The internal model should capture not only linear risks, known as delta risks, but also nonlinear risks, like convexity risk (gamma) and volatility risk (vega) inherent in options positions. The choice of the method is left to the institution, whether it chooses to implement full Monte-Carlo simulation or other pseudoanalytic methods based on the Greeks.

Banks that won't be able to meet all the requirements for the internal models will be allowed to use a combination of standard models and internal models, although they are expected to move towards an all internal models framework. Each risk category, however, must be measured according to only one approach. If a combination of approaches is used, then the total capital charge is determined by a simple arithmetic sum, without accounting for a possible correlation effect between risk categories.

Table 7. Multiplier based on the number of exceptions in backtesting.

Number of Exceptions	Multiplier
4 or fewer	3.00
5	3.40
6	3.50
7	3.65
8	3.75
9	3.85
10 or more	4.00

3.4. Specific risk

According to the 1996 Amendment, institutions are required to hold capital in support of specific risk associated with debt and equity positions in the trading books. In return, no more credit capital charge is allocated to them. In other words, specific risk is just a substitute for credit risk for traded on-balance sheet products.

Derivative instruments will have specific risk capital charge when the underlying is subject to specific risk. Thus, there will be no specific risk charge on interest rate and currency swaps, FRAs, forward FX contracts, interest rate futures, and futures on an interest rate index. However, when not traded on an exchange, i.e., when they are traded over-the-counter (OTC), these instruments have counterparty risk and they will be charged a capital amount to cover their credit risk exposure according to rules of the 1988 Accord.

Specific risk relates to the risk that the price of an individual debt or equity security moves by more or less than what is expected from general market movements, due to specific credit and/or liquidity events related to individual issuers. The capital charge for specific risk can be determined either using the internal models, still scaled up by a multiplier of 4, or the standardized approach.

Under the standardized approach, specific risk charges vary across debt and equity instruments, with individual equities receiving 8 percent charges, while those held in well diversified and liquid portfolios being charged 4 percent. Major stock indices are subject to 2 percent charges and certain arbitrage positions receiving lower requirements. For bonds, specific risk charges vary between 0 percent and 8 percent depending on the issuer, the maturity of the instrument, but no diversification is recognized.[9]

The new 1998 regulatory framework views specific risk, and consequently credit risk, as an outgrowth of market risk. As such it should be modeled with assumptions which are consistent with the market risk model. This is a significant improvement with respect to the 1988 Accord, where credit risk capital charge was calculated according to somewhat arbitrary ratios which didn't correctly account for the specificity of the instrument.[10]

At CIBC, the internal model for bonds captures both spread risk, and credit risk which comes from the event of default as well as credit migration, whether it is an upgrade or a downgrade. An approach based on credit migration analysis like CreditMetrics, proposed by J.P. Morgan (1997), is a good candidate for the internal model related to specific risk for bonds.

For equities, the approach is different since market risk, measured by the volatility of stock returns, already captures both general market risk and specific risk. Market risk and default risk for stocks are already fully accounted in the current spot price. The problem is now to break the total risk for a stock into general market risk and specific risk. For this purpose we rely on the statistical properties of a single index model, known also as the market model.[11] The basic idea is that the rate of return on any stock i is related to some common index I by a linear equation of the form:

$$R_i = \alpha_i + \beta_i I + u_i \tag{2}$$

where

R_i is the rate of return on stock i,

α_i is the constant component of the return of stock i,

I is the value of the index,

β_i is a measure of the average change in R_i as a result of a given change in the index I,

u_i is a deviation of the actual observed return from the regression line $\alpha_i + \beta_i R_m$ i.e., the error term, which is assumed to be normally distributed $\boldsymbol{N(0,\sigma_{u_i})}$.

The index we generally used for this model is the rate of return on the market portfolio, which we denote R_m. The crucial assumption is that for every pair of stocks (i,j) the error terms are uncorrelated, i.e., Cov $(u_i,u_j) = 0$. The error term is also assumed to be uncorrelated with the market portfolio i.e., Cov $\boldsymbol{(u_i,R_m) = 0}$. The parameters of (2) are estimated in practice by using the ex-post historical rates of return, and running a time series regression. It follows that

$$\beta_i = \frac{Cov(R_i, R_m)}{Var(R_m)}$$

Taking the variance of both sides of equation (2) we obtain:

$$\sigma_i^2 = \beta_i^2\sigma_m^2 + \sigma_{ui}^2$$

The total risk of a security as measured by its variance can be divided into components:

(i) $\beta_i^2\sigma_m^2$—systematic risk, or general market risk, which is nondiversifiable and associated with market fluctuations, where $\boldsymbol{\sigma_m}$ denotes the variance of the market return

(ii) σ_{ui}^2—idiosyncratic risk, or specific risk, which can be eliminated through diversification.

(iii) Given a stock, or a portfolio, whose price is denoted S_i, the general market risk (GMR) of the position is, according to the market model:
$\boldsymbol{GMR_i = S_i \times \beta_i \times \sigma_m}$

and its specific risk (SR) is:

$$SR_i = S_i\sigma_u = S_i\sqrt{\sigma_i^2 - \beta_i^2\sigma_m^2}$$

These risks can be easily aggregated. For a portfolio, with a total value of P, composed of n securities S_i, $i = 1, \ldots, n$, the general market risk for the portfolio is

$$GMR_P = \sum_{i=1}^{n} S_i\beta_i\sigma_m = P\sum_{i=1}^{n}\frac{S_i}{P}\beta_i\sigma_m = P\beta_P\sigma_m$$

where $\beta_P = \sum_{i=1}^{m} \frac{S_i}{P}\beta_i$ represents the beta of the portfolio P, which is the weighted average of the betas of the individual stocks, with the individual weight, $x_i = \frac{S_i}{P}$, being the proportion of stock i in the portfolio.

Under the assumption that the error terms are uncorrelated, the specific risk for the portfolio is simply:

$$SR_P = P\sqrt{\sum_{i=1}^{n} x_i^2 \sigma_{u_i}^2}$$

3.5. New capital requirements

Banks will now be allowed, under the 1996 Amendment, to add a new category of capital, tier 3 capital, which mainly consists of short-term subordinated debt subject to certain conditions, but only to meet on a daily basis market risk capital requirement as defined in (1).

Banks should first allocate tier 1 and tier 2 capital to meet credit risk capital requirements according to the 1988 Accord, so that together they represent 8 percent of the risk weighted assets. The risk weighted assets should be adjusted for the positions that are no longer subject to the 1988 credit risk rules, i.e., the traded instruments on-balance sheet like bonds and equities which are already subject to specific risk.

Then, the bank should satisfy a second ratio of eligible capital to the risk weighted asset equivalent. The risk weighted asset equivalent is simply the sum of the risk weighted on-balance sheet assets, the risk weighted off-balance sheet items, and 12.5 times the market risk capital charge, where 12.5 is the reciprocal of the minimum capital ratio of 8 percent.

Eligible capital is the sum of first, the whole bank's tier 1 capital, second, all of its tier 2 capital under the limit imposed by the 1988 Accord, i.e., tier 2 capital may not exceed 50 percent of tier 1 capital, and third, some of its tier 3 capital. Banks will be entitled to use tier 3 capital solely to satisfy market risk capital charge, but under some limiting conditions. The market risk capital charge should be met with tier 3 capital, and additional tier 1 and tier 2 capital not allocated to credit risk. Tier 1 capital should constitute the most substantial portion of the bank's capital, with the final rule imposing that:

- at least 50 percent of a bank's qualifying capital must be tier 1 capital, with term subordinated debt not exceeding 50 percent of tier 1 capital,
- the sum of tier 2 and tier 3 capital allocated for market risk must not exceed 250 percent of tier 1 capital allocated for market risk, i.e., 28.57 percent of market risk capital charge should be met with tier 1 capital.[12]

The following example illustrates the calculation of the capital ratio. Suppose the bank has

- risk weighted assets which amount to 7,500
- a market risk capital charge of 350.

The bank capital is assumed to be constituted of tier 1 capital for 700, tier 2 capital for 100, and tier 3 capital for 600.

Question: Does the bank meet the BIS capital ratio requirements?

Table 8 shows a possible allocation of capital.

Since after allocating tier 1 and tier 2 capital to credit risk, there is left 200 of unused tier 1 capital available to support market risk, then the maximum eligible tier 3 capital is only 500 according to the 250 percent rule. After the full allocation for credit risk there is left 250 of tier 3 capital which is still unused but eligible, and 100 unused tier 3 capital but not eligible. In this example the capital ratio is greater than the minimum of 8 percent, since we added 100 unused tier 1 capital in the numerator of the capital ratio.

3.6. Backtesting

Backtesting consists in company VaR measures calibrated to a one-day movement in rates and prices and a 99 percent (one-tailed) confidence level, against two measures of the profit & loss (P&L):

- the actual net trading P&L for the next day
- the theoretical, or static P&L, which would have occurred would the position at the close of the previous day had been carried forward the next day[13]

Assuming that the risk factors are correctly modeled and that markets behave accordingly, then we expect the absolute value of static P&L over the last 250 days to be greater than VaR only five days, on average.[14]

Backtesting should be performed daily.[15] In addition, institutions must identify the number of times when its net trading losses, if any, for a particular day exceeds the corresponding daily VaR. This BIS multiplicative factor can become higher than three if the number of exceptions during the previous 250 days is greater than five, and can rise up to four if the number of exceptions reaches ten or more during the period, as shown in Table 7.

However, there is some doubt on how seriously this rule will be enforced since exceptions to the rule are already envisaged when abnormal situations occur, like a market crash, a major political event, or a natural disaster. In addition, the regulators should acknowledge the fact that all the financial institutions, including the regulators, are learning by doing. It may thus not be appropriate to penalize an institution by applying a higher multiplier if the institution reacts quickly, and subsequently implements improvements to its VaR model after it has recognized its weaknesses.

The ISDA/LIBA Joint Models Task Force (see ISDA (1996)) has criticized the nondiscriminatory imposition of this scaling factor of three, and simply suggests to repeal this rule. Although it recognizes the benefits associated with backtesting in

Table 8. Calculation of the capital ratio under the 1996 Amendment.

Risk weightd assets	Minimum capital charge (8%)	Available capital	Minimum capital for meeting requirement	Eligible capital (excluding unused tier 3)	Unused but eligible tier 3	Unused but not eligible tier 3
Credit risk 7,500	600	tier 1 700	tier 1 500	tier 1 700		
		tier 2 100	tier 2 100	tier 2 100		
Market risk 4,375	350	tier 3 600	tier 1 100	tier 3 250	tier 3 250	tier 3 100
(i.e., 350 × 12.5)			tier 3 250			
				Capital ratio: 1,050/11,875 = 8.8%	Excess tier 3 Capital ratio: 250/11,875 = 2.1%	

assessing the accuracy of the internal model, it considers this multiplier of 3 as an unfair penalty on banks which are already sophisticated in the design of their risk management system, and the modeling of general as well as specific risks. Instead they should be rewarded. Backtesting is a powerful process to validate the predictive power of a VaR model, without requiring the use of a benchmark model. It is a self-assessment mechanism that allows a bank to check the validity of its internal model on an ongoing basis, and challenge its key assumptions whenever the bank's actual trading results become inconsistent with the VaR numbers. It provides a natural incentive framework to continuously improve and refine the risk modeling techniques.

The regulators should develop the right incentives for banks to implement best practices, and only banks, which fail to take the appropriate actions should be applied a scaling factor greater than one. An arbitrary high scaling factor may even provide perverse incentives to abandon initiatives to implement prudent modifications of the internal model.

3.7. Stress testing

In developing the VaR model many assumptions have to be made to make it practical. In particular, most market parameters are set to match normal market conditions. It should be noted that this is somewhat contradictory with the concept of maximum loss at the 99 percent confidence level. How robust is the VaR model? How sensitive are the VaR numbers to key assumptions? These are questions that stress testing aims to address.

Stress testing is the process that consists in generating market extreme scenari, although plausible, for which key assumptions in the VaR model may be violated. Stress testing should assess the impact on VaR of the breakdown of some, otherwise stable, relationship, like relative prices, correlations and volatilities. Stress testing should also investigate some causal relationships between market factors, between market and credit risks, and other exceptional relationships which may be triggered by abnormal events, i.e., low probability events.

Scenario which may require simulations are, e.g., the oil shocks of the 1970s, recent crises like the October 1987 and October 1989 market crashes, the ERM crises of 1992 and 1993, credit spreads widening, and the fall in the bond markets in May 1994 consecutive to the Fed tightening. For Canada we would also include a yes scenario to the next Quebec referendum.[16] These stress scenario should simulate large price movements, combined with a sharp reduction in market liquidity for several consecutive days, and a dramatic change in instantaneous volatilities and correlations. In market anomalies, it is the correlation structure that breaks down with correlations tending to the extremes, either +1 or −1.

Obviously, the impact of these stress tests will vary greatly depending on the bank's positions in the markets affected by the simulated crises. Accordingly, additional stress scenario may be run to reflect specific concentration risk in one geographic region or in one market. In some ways, stress testing allows the bank to derive some kind of confidence interval on its VaR numbers.

4. THE PROS AND CONS OF THE STANDARDIZED APPROACH AND THE INTERNAL MODELS: A NEW PROPOSAL—THE PRECOMMITMENT APPROACH

The standardized approach has been criticized for the reasons that it applies the same capital charge to vastly different financial instruments, e.g., to plain vanilla swaps and highly levered transactions. It also fails to account for portfolio effects for both credit risk and market risk.

The internal models approach obviously remedies many of these criticisms, and is an attempt to improve the accuracy of the standardized approach. However, some regulators question the banks ability to properly capture the key risks imbedded in their portfolios, i.e., directional, spread, curve, volatility, liquidity risks, and are still skeptical in the capacity of many banks to correctly model these risk factors.[17] Even if banks have the knowledge to develop the analytics, do they have the resources to implement the right infrastructure, especially the transactions database and the financial rates database. Without the necessary infrastructure the best VaR software is as useful as a Ferrari on a sandy trail in the middle of the Sahara desert. The proper infrastructure is key to success in risk management. Regulators bought an insurance policy by imposing safety factors like the multiplier of 3 to translate VaR into capital charge, and a multiplier of 4 to the capital charge related to specific risk. These conservative measures are not a panacea, since they may discourage the most sophisticated banks to improve their internal model, at least for regulatory capital purpose, and they may also induce a distorted allocation of capital.

Rating institutions like Standard & Poors have also expressed their concern that the new 1998 regulatory framework may substantially reduce the amount of regulatory capital. For on-balance sheet traded products like bonds and stocks, the expensive credit risk capital charge according to the initial 1988 Accord will be replaced by the less onerous capital charge associated with specific risk. The net effect as we discussed earlier should be an average net capital savings of 20 to 50 percent for the largest trading banks. Standard & Poors (1996) argues that market risks in a trading operation are largely overshadowed by other risks which are difficult to quantify such as operational risks related to employee fraud and systems failure, legal risk related to the potential for lawsuits from frustrated clients, reputation risk, liquidity risk, operating leverage. For example, Bankers Trust lost $200 million on legal settlements when its regulatory capital according to the internal models approach would have been $285 million at the end of 1995. Apparently, it is not enough to be considered a credible counterparty by rating institutions.

In recognition of the weaknesses inherent in both the standardized approach and the internal models, two senior economists at the Board of Governors of the Federal Reserve Board, P. Kupiec and J. O'Brien (1995b, 1995c, 1995d, 1996) have proposed an alternative approach, the so-called Precommitment Approach (PCA). The PCA would require a bank to precommit to a maximum loss exposure for its trading account positions over a fixed subsequent period. This maximum loss precommitment would be the bank's market risk capital charge. Should the bank incur trading losses that exceed its capital commitment, it would be subject to penalties. Violation of the limit would also bring public scrutiny to the bank, which also would provide a further feedback mechanism for sound management.

Under the PCA, the bank's maximum loss precommitment can reflect the bank's internal assessment of risks, including formal model estimates as well as management's subjective judgments. The PCA approach is an interesting initiative since it aims at replacing regulatory capital requirements based on ex-ante estimates of the bank's risks, with a capital charge that is set endogenously through the optimal resolution of an incentive contract between the bank and its regulators. Indeed, it can be shown that the PCA takes the form of a put option written on the bank's assets and issued to the regulators. The value of this liability for the bank increases with the penalty rate, set by the regulator, and the riskiness of the bank's assets, while it decreases with the striking price of the put, i.e., the precommitment level. When the bank increases the risk of its assets it increases the value of its precommitment liability, which is more or less than offset by the increase in the value of the fixed-rate deposit insurance. The optimal design of the incentive contract becomes bank specific and should be such that the bank finds itself the right tradeoff between the riskiness of its trading book and the level of precommitted capital. The objective would be to maximize the shareholder value and to minimize the exposure of the deposit insurance institution.[18]

The PCA has been criticized by Gumerlock (1996) who uses a metaphor comparing the PCA to speed limits and fines for reckless driving, while he compares the internal models approach to inspections to guarantee that vehicles are roadworthy at all speeds and on all types of roads and weather conditions.

The issue debated here is that risk management consists of more than internal models. They are only one important element of risk measurement. In practice, risk managers should rely on their experience, judgment and controls, and not just on formulas to translate models' results into actual capital. Precommitment attempts to take these multiple factors into account.

5. COMPARISONS OF THE CAPITAL CHARGES FOR VARIOUS PORTFOLIOS ACCORDING TO THE STANDARDIZED AND THE INTERNAL MODELS APPROACHES

The standardized approach will in general produce a much larger capital charge than any reasonable VaR based model. At CIBC we have compared the capital charges attributed to general market risk, on actual positions over a six-month period. The capital savings, i.e., the reduction in capital charge realized by adopting our internal model instead of the standardized approach, varies between a low of 60 percent to a high of 85 percent. The capital savings is higher when the portfolio is highly diversified across maturities and across countries, and when the portfolio is relatively well hedged in a VaR sense, i.e., its VaR exposure is small. The multiplier of 3 makes the capital charge according to the internal model quite sensitive to the market risk exposure.

To gain a better understanding of the extent of the capital charge differences between the standardized method and CIBC's internal method, four basic portfolios and a relatively well diversified cross-currency portfolio were investigated (Table 9). The cross-currency portfolio has products in both Canadian and US dollars covering a wide range of maturities. These portfolios are limited to linear interest rate products. All bonds are considered to be government issue to avoid the calculation of a specific risk capital charge. The model that CIBC is adopting for the purpose of specific risk will result in the 50 percent link being enforced, i.e., the capital charge for specific risk will be arbitrarily set to 50 percent of that required by the standardized approach. Therefore, there is no new insight to be gained from the inclusion of specific risk. The following examples all concentrate only on general market risk.

To illustrate the differences between the two methods in capturing the portfolio effects, we consider portfolios with short and long positions, first in a single currency, and then in two different currencies, namely the U.S. and the Canadian dollars. The interest rate curves that we used to perform the computations are given in Table 10 and correspond to market data as of April 5, 1997.

The first portfolio is simply a plain vanilla swap where the bank receives the fixed rate, the counterparty being a corporate. The internal model is a simple VaR model where the risk factors are the zero-coupon rates for the maturities shown in Table 10. The changes in those rates are supposed to follow a multivariate-normal dis-

Table 9. Portfolios of fixed income instruments.

	Portfolios
1	100 million USD 10 year swap, receive fixed against 3-month LIBOR; counterparty is a corporate
2	Portfolio 1
	+100 million USD 5 year swap, pay fixed against 3-month LIBOR; counterparty is a corporate
3	Long a 100 million USD 10 year Government bond with a 6.50% semi-annual coupon
	100 million USD 10 year swap, pay fixed against 3-month LIBOR; counterparty is a corporate
4	100 million USD 10 year swap, pay fixed against 3-mongh LIBOR; counterparty is a corporate
	140 million CAD 10 year swap, receive fixed against 3-month LIBOR; counterparty is a corporate
5	*CAD*
	long 100 million 3-month T-bill
	long 75 million 8% Government bond maturing in 20 years
	long 25 million 8% Government bond maturing in 3 years
	short 25 million 8% Government bond maturing in 12 years
	100 million 5 year swap, receive fixed against 3-month LIBOR
	100 million 20 year swap, pay fixed against 3-month LIBOR
	USD
	short 300 million 3-month T-bill
	long 100 million 6-month T-bill
	short 200 million 9-month T-bill
	long 100 mllion 6.5% Government bond maturing in 4 years
	long 200 million 6.7% Government bond maturing in 5 years
	long 100 million 7% Government bond maturing in 12 years
	100 million 2 year swap, pay fixed against 3-month LIBOR
	100 million 10 year swap, pay fixed against 3-month LIBOR
	100 million 20 year swap, pay fixed against 3-month LIBOR

Table 10. Interest rate curves zero-coupon curves with continuously compounded rates (April 5, 1997).

	U.S. (USD)		Canada (CAD)	
TERM	Treasuries	Swaps	Treasuries	Swaps
on	5.31%	3.04%	3.00%	3.00%
1 m	5.32%	5.50%	2.92%	3.10%
2 m	5.31%	5.55%	3.05%	3.18%
3 m	5.39%	5.56%	3.15%	3.25%
6 m	5.44%	5.62%	3.46%	4.70%
9 m	5.45%	5.70%	3.75%	5.09%
1 y	5.46%	5.79%	3.89%	5.34%
1.25 y	5.73%	5.88%	4.28%	5.50%
1.5 y	5.94%	5.96%	4.57%	5.64%
1.75 y	6.12%	6.03%	4.92%	5.75%
2 y	6.24%	6.10%	5.17%	5.85%
3 y	6.41%	6.41%	5.72%	6.59%
4 y	6.47%	6.56%	6.06%	6.62%
5 y	6.54%	6.66%	6.27%	6.58%
7 y	6.56%	6.66%	6.55%	7.13%
10 y	6.61%	6.66%	6.96%	7.73%

tribution with the volatilities given in Table 11 for the U.S. swap curve.[19] The VaR for this swap is 927,000 USD, while the sum of the VaR for each risk point on the curve is 962,549 USD (Table 11). The changes in the rates being highly correlated the risk reduction due to the portfolio effect is relatively modest, i.e., 3.7% in this example.

The application of the standardized approach for general market risk, already presented in Section 3.1.2, is shown in Table 12 for portfolios 1. It produces a capital charge of 3,750,000 USD. The capital charges calculated according to the standardized and the internal model approaches are summarized in Table 14. For the first portfolio (ten year swap), the adoption of the internal model does not allow to realize any capital saving, but on the contrary generates a capital surcharge of 132 percent.

There is also a capital surcharge of 103 percent for the second portfolio, which consists of a long and short positions in two plain vanilla swaps of different maturities, but in the same currency, the USD. The bank receives fixed on the ten-year swap, and pays fixed on the five-year swap. Since there is partial offsetting of cash flows up to five years, the portfolio effect is expected to be more substantial than for the first portfolio (Table 11). The standardized approach for general market risk is detailed in Table 13 and shows a capital charge of 1,845,000 USD, with one million related to parallel shift in the yield curve, and 845,000 to compensate for curve risk. In this case the cash flows are not well distributed among the various buckets. As a consequence there is little capital charge for basis risk, and curve risk among the different zones of the interest rate curve.

Table 11. Internal model for Portfolios 1 and 2.

	DV01 (USD)		Volatility (bp)	VaR/risk point (USD)	
Term	Portfolio 1	Portfolio 2	(σ)	Portfolio 1	Portfolio 2
3 m	(2,459)		3.59	20,588	
6 m	28		3.35	215	
9 m	123		3.46	988	
1 y	162		3.58	1,350	
1.25 y	195		3.95	1,794	
1.5 y	230		4.33	2.319	
1.75 y	264		4.70	2,894	
2 y	746	2	5.08	8.824	27
3 y	1,681	5	5.29	20,742	63
4 y	2,092	6	5.50	26,808	81
5 y	3,579	(34,320)	5.50	45,897	440,110
7 y	7,308	7,308	5.63	95,878	95,878
10 y	58,138	58,128	5.42	734,252	734,252

Notes:
DV01, denotes the sensitivity of the position to a decrease of 1 bp in the corresponding zero-coupon rate, and is expressed in currency units.
σ, denotes the daily volatility of the zero-coupon rate and is expressed in bp.
VaR/risk point denotes the VaR for the corresponding zero-coupon rate, at the 99% confidence level (one-tailed) and for a one-day horizon, i.e. 2.33 σ [DV01], assuming that interest rate changes are normally distributed.

	Portfolio 1	Portfolio 2
(1) Sum of the VaR/risk point	= 962,549 USD	= 1,270,411 USD
(2) VaR	= 927,000 USD	= 407,532 USD
Portfolio effect: (1)–(2)	= 35,549 USD	= 862,879 USD

The third portfolio consists of a long government bond position, which is hedged by a swap of the same tenor, 10 year in our example, and in the same currency. The capital saving is substantial, 62% as shown in Table 15. In that case the position is relatively well hedged in a VaR sense, since its VaR exposure is only 19,068 USD. The internal model benefits, with its multiplier of 3, greatly benefits from this situation.

The fourth portfolio is constituted of two 10 year swaps, a long and a short position, but in two different currencies, the U.S. dollar and the Canadian dollar. In this instance the capital saving is 11.5 percent. The calculations are detailed in Tables 15 and 16. For this portfolio the internal model benefits from the diversification across two different currencies. The standardized approach treats each currency independently, adding the capital charges without any benefit from diversification and hedging across the two countries.

Finally, Portfolio 5 shows the full benefit of the internal model when the position is well diversified across maturities and countries. We obtain a capital savings of 51 percent, which is comparable to the actual savings that we expect to achieve (Table 17).

Table 12. BIS standardized approach for general market risk: Portfolio 1.

	Zone 1				Zone 2			Zone 3							
Time-band															
Coupon > 3%	0–1	1–3	3–6	6–12	1–2	2–3	3–4	4–5	5–7	7–10	10–15	15–20	>20		
Coupon < 3%	0–1	1–3	3–6	6–12	1–1.9	1.9–2.8	2.8–3.6	3.6–4.3	4.3–5.7	5.7–7.3	7.3–9.3	9.3–10.6	10.6–12	12–20	>20
	Months				Years										
USD															
10 yr swap		(100)								100					
fixed receiver															
Weight (%)	0.00	0.20	0.40	0.70	1.25	1.75	2.25	2.75	3.25	3.75	4.50	5.25	6.00	8.00	12.5
Position × weight															
long										3.75					
short		(0.20)													
Vertical Disallowance															
Horizontal Disallowance 1		0 × 40% = 0				0 × 30% = 0						0 × 30% = 0			
Horizontal Disallowance 2						0 × 40% = 0						0 × 40% = 0			
Horizontal Disallowance 3								0.2 × 100% = 0.2							
Overall net position								3.55 × 100% = 3.55							
					Total capital charge for general market risk = 3.75										

Table 13. BIS standardized approach for general market risk: Portfolio 2.

	Zone 1				Zone 2			Zone 3							
Time- band															
Coupon > 3%	0–1	1–3	3–6	6–12	1–2	2–3	3–4	4–5	5–7	7–10	10–15	15–20	>20		
Coupon < 3%	0–1	1–3	3–6	6–12	1–1.9	1.9–2.8	2.8–3.6	3.6–4.3	4.3–5.7	5.7–7.3	7.3–9.3	9.3–10.6	10.6–12	12–20	>20
	Months				Years										
Positions															
A		(100)								100					
B		100						(100)							
Weight (%)	0.00	0.20	0.40	0.70	1.25	1.75	2.25	2.75	3.25	3.75	4.50	5.25	6.00	8.00	12.5
Position × weight															
long		0.20								3.75					
short		(0.20)						(2.75)							
Vertical Disallowance		0.20 × 10% = 0.02													
Horizontal Disallowance 1		0 × 40% = 0				0 × 30% = 0					2.75 × 30% = 0.825				
Horizontal Disallowance 2						0 × 40% = 0					0 × 40% = 0				
Horizontal Disallowance 3								0 × 100% = 0							
Overall net position								1 × 100% = 1							
					Total capital charge for general market risk = 1.845										

Table 14. Standardized versus Internal Models: Capital charge for Portfolios 1 & 2.

Internal model	Portfolio 1	Portfolio 2
(1) VaR	= 927,000 USD	407,532 USD
(2) general market risk: $3 \times \text{VaR} \times \sqrt{10}$	= 8,794,294 USD	3,866,188 USD
(3) counterparty risk* (1988 Accord)	= 60,000 USD	120,000 USD
Capital charge: (2) + (3)	= 8,854,294 USD	3,986,188 USD
Standardized approach		
(4) general market risk (cf. Table 14 and 14 bis)	= 3,750,000 USD	1,845,000 USD
(5) counterparty risk* (1988 Accord)	= 60,000 USD	120,000 USD
Capital charge: (4) + (5)	= 3,810,000 USD	1,965,000 USD
Capital addition**	= **132%**	**103%**

*Details for the calculation of the capital charge for counterparty risk:
- replacement cost = 0 (at-the-money swap)
- add-on = 100m USD × 1.5% = 1,500,000 USD
- risk-weighted amount = 1,500,000 USD × 50% = 750,000 USD
- capital charge = 750,000 USD × 8% = 60,000 USD

**Capital addition (saving) is the addition (saving) of capital realized by the bank by adopting the internal models instead of the standardized approach.

Table 15. Standardized versus Internal models: Capital charge for Portfolios 3 & 4.

Internal model	Portfolio 3	Portfolio 4
(1) VaR	= 19,068 USD	970,330 CAD
(2) general market risk: $3 \times \text{VaR} \times \sqrt{10}$	= 180,898 USD	9,205,390 CAD
(3) counterparty risk (swap) (1988 Accord)	= 60,000 USD	166,800 CAD***
Capital charge: (2) + (3)	= 240,898 USD	9,372,190 CAD
Standardized approach		
(4) general market risk*	= 575,000 USD*	10,425,000 CAD**
(5) counterparty risk (1988 Accord)	= 60,000 USD	166,800 CAD
Capital charge: (4) + (5)	= 635,000 USD	10,591,800 CAD
Capital saving	= **62%**	**11.5%**

*The derivation is left to the reader. The capital charge is made of 375,000 USD for basis risk and 200,000 USD for the overall net outright position. Obviously, for this portfolio the standardized approach appears to be excessively onerous, while the VaR is small as the portfolio is relatively hedged.

**According to the standardized approach the CAD swap has a capital charge of 5,250,000 CAD while it is 3,750,000 USD for the US swap, i.e., 5,175,500 CAD.

***The capital charge for the US swap is 60,000 USD, i.e. 82,800 CAD assuming an exchange rate of 1 USD = 1.38 CAD. The capital charge for the CAD swap is 84,000 CAD.

6. CONCLUSIONS

The primary purpose of the 1988 BIS Accord, and later of the 1996 Amendment, was to set international capital guidelines that link banks' capital requirements to both market risk and credit risk. The objective was to avoid the possibility of a meltdown in the banking industry and, at the same time, to establish a level playing field among international banks.

Table 16. Internal model for Portfolio 4.

	CAD-SWAP			USD-SWAP		
Term	DV01 (CAD)	Volatility (bp) (σ)	VaR (CAD)	DV01 (USD)	Volatility (bp) (σ)	VaR (USD)
on	0	10.40	0	0	30.23	0
1 m	0	4.63	0	0	6.30	0
2 m	(161)	4.07	1,523	0	3.91	0
3 m	(3,300)	5.09	39,150	2,459	3.59	20,588
6 m	131	6.67	2,042	(28)	3.35	215
9 m	196	7.16	3,264	(123)	3.46	988
1 y	250	7.64	4,446	(162)	3.58	1,350
1.25 y	307	8.11	5,796	(195)	3.95	1,794
1.5 y	362	8.58	7,230	(230)	4.33	2,319
1.75 y	433	9.05	9,124	(264)	4.70	2,894
2 y	1,152	9.51	25,541	(746)	5.08	8,824
3 y	2,614	9.13	55,584	(1,681)	5.29	20,742
4 y	3,253	8.63	65,407	(2,092)	5.50	26,808
5 y	5,551	8.14	105,280	(3,579)	5.50	45,897
7 y	11,049	7.55	194,397	(7,308)	5.63	95,878
10 y	73,161	7.00	1,193,291	(58,138)	5.42	734,252
15 y	0	6.39	0	0	5.44	0
20 y	0	6.07	0	0	5.07	0
30 y	0	5.79	0	0	5.18	0

Exchange rate
1 USD = 1.38 CAD
VaR USD-Swap = 1,279,000 CAD
VaR CAD-Swap = 1,626,000 CAD
VaR Portfolio 4 = 970,330 CAD

The rules to assess regulatory capital under the 1988 Accord are quite simple, and somewhat arbitrary, and have been subject to many criticisms. For example, the capital allocation for a bond issued by IBM is five times the capital charge for a similar facility issued by any OECD bank, such as Hokkaido Takushoku bank from Japan (before it recently failed). It also doesn't account for portfolio effect so that it treats equally concentrated as well as broadly diversified portfolios.

The 1988 Accord completely ignored market risk for marketable securities and derivatives, and only recognized credit risk for on-balance sheet assets and off-balance sheet products. With the 1996 Amendment, banks are now required to hold capital to cover market risk associated with their trading book, and foreign exchange and commodity positions in both the trading and the banking books. Table 18 summarizes the new BIS 1998 framework for capital requirement.

The 1996 Amendment represents a big leap forward in the risk management of financial institutions. Now there is a considerable incentive for banks to develop their own internal VaR model for both regulatory capital purposes, but also to closely monitor their risks, and actively manage the risk/return tradeoff and the pricing of new deals.

Since January 1998, leading banks have in place internal models for market risk.

Table 17. Standardized versus internal models for Portfolio 5 capital charges for general market risk

Internal model			
VaR for the CAD position			408,350 CAD
VaR for the US position			425,660 CAD
VaR for Portfolio 5			662,610 CAD
Capital charge	$3 \times \text{VaR} \times \sqrt{10}$	=	6,286,078 CAD
Standardized approach			
CAD position			3,570,000 CAD
US position			9,239,100 CAD
Total		=	12,809,100 CAD
Capital savings		=	51%

Table 18. New BIS 1998 framework for capital requirement.

Market Risk	Banking book (accrual accounting)	Trading book (positions marked-to-market)			
		Exchange Traded			
		FX	Commodities	Bonds/ Loans	Deivatives
General Market Risk		X	X	X	X
Specific Risk				X	X(*)
Credit risk (1988 Accord)	X				X

*Derivatives are subject to specific risk only if the underlying is itself subject to specific risk.

The next challenge is, for those banks, to develop appropriate internal models for credit risk, then to implement an integrated framework for market risk and credit risk to fully account for portfolio effect within, and across risk types.

With this capital attribution infrastructure and those risk measurement tools in place, the focus on performance measurement is gradually shifting. The board and top management of financial institutions are rapidly moving towards compensation system based on adjusted return on economic capital, also known as RAROC (Risk Adjusted Return on Capital). This new paradigm will spark further research in the integration of market risk, credit risk and other types of risks like operational risk. We can also expect the regulatory environment to evolve in the future toward a generalized use of internal models across all types of risks, provided data are available to support the models.

NOTES

1. Sanjiv Talwar deserves a special acknowledgment for his comments and suggestions.
2. Cf. Basle (1995).

3. For Canada, OSFI has set the horizon of the second bucket to 12 months instead of 24.
4. In Canada, only the maturity method is allowed by the regulator, OSFI. In this paper we just present the maturity approach. The duration approach differs only by its more accurate method of calculating the sensitivities, or risk weights (cf. Table 2).
5. It is valued at current spot exchange rates, since we are interested in the present value of the forward exposures.
6. The convenience yield for commodities, like energy products, reflects the benefits from direct ownership of the physical commodity, e.g., when there is a risk of shortage. It is affected by market conditions as well as specific conditions like the level of inventory and storage costs. Accordingly, the convenience yield may be positive or negative. When inventory is high, demand is low and marginal storage costs are high, the convenience yield is likely to be negative.
7. The square root of 10 rule is only valid when the changes in the portfolio values are not correlated and identically distributed.
8. If historical data are weighted to estimate volatilities and correlations, the average weighted average time lag of the individual observations should be at least half a year, which is what would be obtained if the observations were equally weighted.
9. See Section 2.1.1 for details.
10. Cf. ISDA (1996) and IIF (1996). ISDA (1996) sets out the conclusions of a Joint Task Force of members of the International Swaps and Derivatives Association (ISDA) and the London Investment Banking Association (LIBA) on aspects of the Basle Committee's standards for the use of the internal models to calculate market risk capital charge. IIF (1996) reports the conclusions on the specific risk issue of a task force composed of the representatives of 15 banks, which are members of the Institute of International Finance (IFF).
11. See Sharpe and Alexander (1990), chapter 8.
12. The limits on capital used vary slightly from one country to the other. For example, OSFI in Canada limits the use of tier 2 and tier 3 capital to meet market risk requirements, to 200% of tier 1 capital used to meet these requirements. In addition tier 1 and tier 2 capital cannot, in total, exceed 100% of tier 1 capital.
13. VaR is an assessment of the potential loss for a given, static portfolio, i.e., the closing position at the end of the day. Obviously the portfolio is traded all the time, and its actual composition keeps changing during the next trading day. Risk management is also active, and decisions to alter the risk exposure of the bank's position may be taken during the course of the day. This is why VaR should be compared ex-post to these two measures of P&L.
14. Indeed, 99% one-tail confidence level means that we expect losses, but also profits, to be greater than VaR in absolute value 2.5 days per year.
15. The obligation to backtest will be effective only after a year, i.e., in 1999, when institutions will have accumulated one year of historical market data to be used in backtesting. Initially, at least for 1998, the regulators will require only the comparison of VaR against actual P&L.
From our point of view, a better approach to backtesting would be historical simulation, where each day, the position would reevaluated based on the last 250 days closing market data. Then, the historical distribution of the changes in the position value would be compared with the theoretical distribution derived from the internal VaR model. This approach would permit over time to revisit some key assumptions made in the VaR model, which according to the historical simulation, are revealed to be inconsistent with market data and may produce a very biased picture of the bank's exposure.
16. For example, a Fed tightening scenario like in May 1994 could be characterized by a 100 bp upward shift in the overnight rate, and 30 bp increase for the 10 year yield for the U.S. curve. The yield curves for the other G-10 countries and Switzerland would also shift upward but by less than the U.S. curve. G-10 currencies would depreciate against the U.S. dollar. Equity markets would also react negatively, with at least a 2 percent downward move.
17. See Kupiec and O'Brien (1995c, 1995d, and 1996).
18. See Kupiec and O'Brien (1997).
19. To save space we don't show the correlation matrix.

REFERENCES

Basle (1995). *An Internal Model-Based Approach to Market Risk Capital Requirements.* Basel: Basle Committee on Banking Supervision, Bank of International Settlements.

Basle (1988). *International Convergence of Capital Measurement and Capital Standards.* Basle Committee on Banking Supervision, Bank of International Settlements, Basel, July.

Crouhy, M., D. Galai, and R. Mark (1998). "The New 1998 Regulatory Framework for Capital Adequacy: Standardized Approach versus Internal Models," in Risk Management and Analysis, vol 1, Measuring and Modelling Financial Risk, Editor: Carol Alexander, Ch. 1, John Wiley & Sons.

G-30 (1993). *Derivatives: Practices and Principles.* Global Derivatives Study Group. Washington, D.C.: Group of Thirty.

Gumerlock, R. (1996). "Lacking Commitment," *Risk* 9 (6), June, 36–39.

ISDA (1996). "Amendment to the Capital Accord to incorporate market risks: The use of internal models for supervisory purposes," *Comments of the ISDA/LIBA Joint Models Task Force,* October.

J.P. Morgan (1997). *CreditMetrics.*

Kupiec, P., and J. O'Brien (1995a). "The Use of Bank Trading Risk Measurement Models for Regulatory Capital Purposes," FEDS Working Paper 95–11. Washington D.C.: Federal Reserve Board.

Kupiec, P., and J. O'Brien (1995b). "A Pre-commitment Approach to Capital Requirements for Market Risk," FEDS Working Paper 95–34. Washington, D.C.: Federal Reserve Board.

Kupiec, P., and J. O'Brien (1995c). "Internal Affairs," *Risk,* May 8(5), 43–47.

Kupiec, P., and J. O'Brien (1995d). "Model Alternative," *Risk* 8(6), June, 37–40.

Kupiec, P., and J. O'Brien (1996). "Commitment Is the Key," *Risk* 9(9), September, 60–63.

Kupiec, P., and J. O'Brien (1997). "The Pre-Commitment Approach: Using Incentives to Set Market Risk Capital Requirements." Washington, D.C.: Board of Governors of the Federal System, 1997–14,

Sharpe, W., and G.J. Alexander (1990). *Investments.* Englewood Cliffs, New Jersey: Prentice-Hall.

Standard & Poors (1996). *Bank Ratings Comment: Market Capital Rules.* New York: November.

5. EVALUATING CREDIT RISK: AN OPTION PRICING APPROACH

MICHEL CROUHY, DAN GALAI, and ROBERT MARK

1. INTRODUCTION

A major problem facing banks is the evaluation of the capital risk of a potential client applying for credit. A similar problem is faced by an investor when evaluating the appropriate risk premium on a given corporate bond, above the yield on a government bond, due to credit risk.

The conventional approach is based on empirical experience or a statistical method, looking at the profile of the borrower and checking the past experience of borrowers with a similar profile. The credit premium is then based on the default rate of similar borrowers and the recovery rate of the loans.

In 1988, the Basle Committee came out with recommendations, known as the BIS Accord, for required minimal capital for banks against their exposure to credit risk. The BIS requirements are based on simplified principles, given in a set of tables based mainly on the loan's maturity and on broad classes of borrowers. The idea was to give up accuracy for the sake of easy application.

In this paper we propose an economic approach to evaluate credit risk. The economic value of default is presented as a put option on the value of the firm's assets. The merit of this approach is that each case can be analyzed individually based on its unique features. But this is also the drawback, since the information needed is rarely available to the bank or the investor.

Different approaches have been proposed in the literature, which are all consistent with the arbitrage free pricing methodology.[1] The option pricing model, with the seminal paper by Merton (1974)[2], builds on the limited liability rule, which allows shareholders to default on their obligations while they surrender the firm's assets to the various stockholders, according to prespecified priority rules. The firm's liabilities are thus, viewed as contingent claims issued against the firm's assets, with the payoffs to the various debtholders completely specified by seniority and safety covenants. Default occurs at debt maturity when the firm's assets value falls short of debt value at that time, and then, the loss distribution conditional on default is endogenously determined.

An alternative to this approach proposed by Hull and White (1995) and Longstaff and Schwartz (1995) allows bankruptcy to occur at a random default time. Bankruptcy is triggered the first time the value of the firm's assets reaches some prespecified default boundary, and it is also assumes exogenous the loss in the event of default. This approach simplifies the bankruptcy process by not relying explicitly on the priority structure of the debt instruments, but it loses its generality by assuming an exogenous recovery rate for each promised dollar in case of default. Stochastic interest rate are added to the Merton framework in these models.

The most recent approach developed independently by Duffie and Singleton (1994) and Jarrow and Turnbull (1995, 1997) characterizes bankruptcy as an exogenous process, e.g., a Markov process, in the firm's credit ratings, which does not explicitly depends on the firm's assets and the priority rules for the various debt instruments. However, they still need to assume the recovery factor as given in the event of default. Contrary to the previous approach the default event is not defined and occurs at a random time.[3] These models allow to derive the term structure of default probabilities from credit spreads, while assuming exogenous and somewhat arbitrary the recovery rate.[4]

In this chapter, we adopt the traditional option pricing framework to value corporate securities, and we show that it allows to retrieve results derived by Jarrow and Turnbull (1995), i.e., the credit spread on a corporate bond is the product of the probability of default and the loss rate. However, in our model the loss rate is endogenously determined and depends on the firm's assets value, volatility, and the default-free interest rate for the same maturity. In Section 2, we present the economic value of default as a put option. A numerical example is used to illustrate the application of option pricing theory to the assessment of credit risk. In Section 3, we analyze the probability of default and the conditional expected recovery value. In Section 4, it is shown how credit risk can be assessed based on share value rather than the firm's assets value. In many cases the results, which are based on mathematical approximations, are subject to small errors. The systematic risk of credit risk is derived in Section 5. Corporate taxation is incorporated in the model in Section 6, to show the impact of taxes on the risk-sharing rule between the bank, the borrower, and the government.

The model presented in this paper assumes a simple capital structure with one type of (zero-coupon) debt. It can be, however, easily extended to the case where the firm has issued senior and junior debts. Then the loss rates for each type of debt are endogenously derived, together with the default probability.[5]

2. ASSESSING CREDIT RISK AS A PUT OPTION

Consider the simple case of a firm with risky assets V, which is financed by equity, S, and by one debt obligation maturing at time T with face value (including accrued interest) of F and market value B. The loan to the firm is subject to credit risk, namely the risk that at time T the value of the firm's assets, V_T, will be below the obligation to the debt holders, F. Credit risk exists as long as the probability of default, Prob ($V_T < F$), is greater than zero, which implies that at time 0, $B_0 < Fe^{-rT}$, i.e., the yield to maturity on the debt, y_T, is higher than the risk free rate, r, where $\pi_T = y_T - r$ denotes the default spread which compensates the bond holders for the default risk they bear. If we assume that markets are frictionless, with no taxes, and there is no bankruptcy cost, then the value of the firm's assets is simply the sum of the firm's equity and debt, i.e.,

$$V_0 = S_0 + B_0 \tag{1}$$

From the viewpoint of a bank, which makes a loan to the firm, the questions are whether the bank can eliminate/reduce credit risk, and at what price? What is the economic cost of reducing credit risk? And, what are the factors affecting this cost?

In this simple framework credit risk is a function of the financial structure of the firm, i.e., its leverage ratio $LR \equiv Fe^{-rT}/V_0$ (where V_0 is the present value of the firm's assets, and Fe^{-rT} is the present value of the debt obligation at maturity), the volatility of the firm's assets, σ, and the time to maturity of the debt, T. The model was initially suggested by Merton (1974) and Galai and Masulis (1976).

The value of credit risk for the bank loan when this loan is the only debt instrument of the firm, and assuming that the only other source of financing is equity, is equal to the value of a put option on the value of assets of the firm, V, at a striking price of F, maturing at time T. If the bank purchases such a put option, it completely eliminates the credit risk associated with the loan. This is illustrated in Table 1.

By purchasing the put on V for the term of the debt, with a striking price equal to the face value of the loan, the bank can completely eliminate all the credit risk, and convert the risky corporate loan into a riskless loan with face value of F. If the riskless interest rate is r, than in equilibrium it should be that $B_0 + P = Fe^{-rT}$.

Table 1. Bank's pay-off matrix at times *0* and *T* for making a loan and buying a put.

Time	0	T	
Value of Assets	V_o	$V_T \leq F$	$V_T > F$
Bank's Position			
(a) make a loan	$-B_o$	V_T	F
(b) buy a put	$-P$	$F - V_T$	O
Total	$-B_o - P$	F	F

The conclusion is that the value of the put option is the cost of eliminating the credit risk associated with providing a loan to the firm. If we make the assumptions needed to apply Black and Scholes (BS) model to equity and debt instruments (see Galai and Masulis (1976) for a detailed discussion of the assumptions), we can write the value of the put as follows:

$$P = -N(-d_1)V_0 + Fe^{-rt}N(-d_2), \tag{2}$$

where P is the current value of the put, $N(.)$ is the cumulative standard normal distribution, and

$$d_1 = \frac{\ln(V_0/F) + (r + \frac{1}{2}\sigma^2)T}{\sigma\sqrt{T}} = \frac{\ln(V_0/Fe^{-rT}) + \frac{1}{2}\sigma^2 T}{\sigma\sqrt{T}}$$

$$d_2 = d_1 - \sigma\sqrt{T},$$

and σ is the standard deviation of the rate of return of the firm's assets.

The model illustrates that the credit risk, and its costs, is a function of the riskiness of the assets of the firm σ, and this risk is also a function of the time interval until debt is paid back, T. The cost is also affected by the risk-free interest rate r, and the higher is r the more costly it is to reduce credit risk. The cost is a homogeneous function of the leverage ratio, $LR = Fe^{-rT}/V_0$, which means it stays constant for a scale expansion of Fe^{-rT}/V_0.

We can now derive the yield to maturity for the corporate discount debt, y_T, as follows:

$$y_T = -\frac{\ln\frac{B_0}{F}}{T} = -\frac{\ln\frac{Fe^{-rT} - P}{F}}{T}$$

so that the default spread, π_T, defined as $\pi_T = y_T - r$, can be derived from (2):

$$\pi_T = y_T - r = -\frac{1}{T}\ln\left(N(d_2) + \frac{V_0}{Fe^{-rT}}N(-d_1)\right) \tag{3}$$

The default spread can be computed exactly as a function of the leverage ratio, $LR \equiv Fe^{-rT}/V_0$ the volatility of the underlying assets, σ, and the debt maturity, T. The following numerical examples in Table 2 show the default spread for various levels of volatility and different leverage ratios.

In Table 2, by using the BS model when $V_0 = 100$, $T = 1$, $r = 10\%$, and also $\sigma = 40\%$ with the leverage ration $LR = 70\%$,[7] we obtain the value of equity, $S_0 = 33.37$, and the value of the corporate risky debt, $B_0 = 66.63$. The yield on the loan is $77/66.63 - 1 = 0.156$, i.e., there is a 5.6 percent risk premium on the loan to reflect the credit risk.

Table 2. Default spread for corporate debt (For $V_o = 100$, $T = 1$, and $r = 10\%$[6]).

LR \ σ	0.05	0.10	0.20	0.40
0.5	0	0	0	1.0%
0.6	0	0	0.1%	2.5%
0.7	0	0	0.4%	5.6%
0.8	0	0.1%	1.5%	8.4%
0.9	0.1%	0.8%	4.1%	12.5%
1.0	2.1%	3.1%	8.3%	17.3%

The model also shows that the put value is $P = 3.37$. Hence the cost of eliminating the credit risk is 3.37 dollars for 100 dollars worth of firms assets, for the case the face value of the one-year debt is 77. This cost drops to 25 cents when volatility decreases to 20 percent and to 0 for ten-percent volatility. The riskiness of the assets as measured by the volatility σ, is a critical factor in determining credit risk.

In order to see that by purchasing the put the bank eliminates all its credit risk, we can compute the yield on the bank's position: $F/(B_0 + P) = 77/(66.63 + 3.37) = 1.10$, which translates to a riskless yield of 10% per annum.

In Appendix 1 we show how the conventional analysis, based on yield spreads, can be transformed to the options approach.

3. PROBABILITY OF DEFAULT, CONDITIONAL EXPECTED RECOVERY VALUE, AND DEFAULT SPREAD

From model (2), one can extract the probability of default for the loan. In a risk-neutral world $N(d_2)$ is the probability the firm's value at time T will be higher than F, and $1 - N(d_2) = N(-d_2)$ is the probability of default.

By purchasing the put, P, the bank buys an insurance policy whose premium is the discounted expected value of the expected shortfall in the event of default. Indeed, equation 2 can be rewritten as follows:

$$P = \left[-\frac{N(-d_1)}{N(-d_2)} V + Fe^{-rT} \right] N(-d_2) \tag{4}$$

Equation 4 decomposes the premium on the put into three factors. The absolute value of the first term inside the bracket is the expected discounted recovery value of the loan, conditional on $V_T \leq F$. It represents the risk-neutral expected payment to the bank in the case the firm is unable to pay the full obligation F at time T. The second term in the bracket is the current value of a riskless bond promising a payment of F at time T. Hence, the sum of the two terms inside the brackets yields the expected shortfall in present value terms, conditional on the firm being bankrupt at time T. The third factor, which determines P, is the probability of default, $N(-d_2)$. By multiplying the probability of default by the current value of the expected shortfall, we derive the premium for insurance against default.

Using the same numerical example as in the previous section (i.e., $V_0 = 100$, $T = 1$, $r = 10$ percent, $\sigma = 40$ percent, $F = 77$, and $LR = 0.7$), we obtain

$$\text{Discounted expected recovery value} = \frac{0.137}{0.244} \cdot 100 = 56.1$$

Value of Riskless Bond = $77.e^{-0.0953} = 70$

Expected Shortfall = 70 − 56.1 = 13.9

Probability of Default = 24.4%

Cost of Default[8] = 0.244 × 13.9 = 3.39

The previous results are based on risk-neutrality assumption. For the general case, when the assumption of a risk-neutral world is removed, the probability of default is given by $N(-d_2^1)$ where $d_2^1 = \dfrac{\ln(V_0/F) + (\bar{r}_V - \frac{1}{2}\sigma^2)T}{\sigma\sqrt{T}}$, and where $\bar{r}_v$ is the expected rate of return on asset V, and V is assumed to be log-normally distributed. (See Boness, 1964, and Galai, 1978, for a proof and an explanation of this result.) Referring to our numerical example, the risk-neutral probability of default is 24.4 percent. If we assume that the discrete time $\bar{r}_v$ is 16 percent, the probability of default is 20.5 percent. The expected recovery value is now given by

$$\frac{N(-d_1^1)}{N(-d_2^1)}V_0 = \frac{0.110}{0.205} \cdot 100 = 53.7.$$

From (4) we can compute the expected loss, EL_T, in the event of default, at maturity date:

$$EL_T = \text{probability of default x loss in case of default} = N(-d_2)F - N(-d_1)Ve^{rT}$$

$$= F - N(d_2)F - N(-d_1)V_0e^{rT} = F\left(1 - N(d_2) - N(-d_1)\frac{1}{LR}\right) \qquad (5)$$

Again, using our previous numerical example we obtain

$$EL_T = 0.244 \cdot 77 - 0.137 \cdot 100e^{0.0953} = 3.718.$$

This result is consistent with the definition of the default spread and its derivation in (3). Indeed, from (5) the expected payoff from the corporate debt at maturity is

$$F - EL_T = F\left(N(d_2) + N(-d_1)\frac{1}{LR}\right),$$

so that the expected cost of default, expressed in yield, is

$$-\frac{1}{T}\ln\left(\frac{F}{F-EL_T}\right)=-\frac{1}{T}\ln\left(\frac{F\left(N(d_2)+N(-d_1)\frac{V_0}{Fe^{-rT}}\right)}{F}\right)=\pi_T,$$

which is identical to (3).

The result (5) is similar to the conclusion derived from Jarrow and Turnbull's (1995) model, which is used to price credit derivatives, i.e., the credit spread is the product of the probability of default and the loss in the event of default. However, in their model they assume that the term structure of credit spread is known and can be derived from market data. The forward spread can then be easily derived. By assuming that the recovery factor is given and exogenous to the model, they can imply the forward probability of default.

In our model we reach the same conclusion, but both the probability of default and the recovery rate are simultaneously derived from equilibrium conditions. From equations 3 and 4, it is clear that the recovery rate cannot be assumed constant, it keeps varying as a function of time to maturity and the value of the firm's assets.

4. ESTIMATING CREDIT RISK AS A FUNCTION OF EQUITY VALUE

In Section 2, the cost of eliminating credit risk is derived based on the value of the firm's assets. A practical problem arises and that concerns the frequent unavailability of observations on V. In some cases, if both equity and debt are traded, V can be reconstructed by adding the market values of both equity and debt. However, more often corporate loans are not traded and the only observations we have are on equity. The question is whether the risk of default can be hedged with stocks and derivatives on the firm stock.

In our simple framework, equity itself is a contingent claim on the firm's assets. It's value can be expressed as follows:

$$S=VN(d_1)-Fe^{-rT}N(d_2) \tag{6}$$

Equity value is a function of the same parameters as the put calculated in (2).

A put can be created synthetically by selling short $N(-d_1)$ units of the firm's assets, and buying $FN(-d_2)$ units of government bond maturing at T, with face value of F. If one sells short $\frac{N(-d_1)}{N(d_1)}$ units of the stock, S, one creates effectively a short position in the firm's assets of $N(-d_1)$ units since

$$\frac{-N(-d_1)}{N(d_1)}S=-VN(-d_1)+Fe^{-rT}N(d_2)\frac{N(-d_1)}{N(d_1)}.$$

Therefore, if V is not directly traded or observed, one can create dynamically a put option by selling short the appropriate number of shares. The equivalence between the put and the synthetic put is valid over short time intervals, and must be readjusted frequently with changes in S and in time left to debt maturity.

We use the data from the previous numerical example

$$\frac{-N(-d_1)}{N(d_1)} = \frac{-0.110}{0.890} = -0.124.$$

In order to insure against default of one-year loan with maturity value of 77, for a firm with current market value of assets of 100, the bank should sell short 0.124 of the outstanding equity. (Note that the outstanding equity is equivalent to a short term holding of $N(d_1) = 0.89$ of the firm's assets. Shorting 0.124 of equity is equivalent to shorting 0.1 of the firm's assets.)

The question now is whether we can use a put option on equity in order to hedge the default risk. It should be remembered that equity itself reflects the default risk, and as a contingent claim its instantaneous volatility, σ_S, can be expressed as follows:

$$\sigma_S = \eta_{S,V}\sigma \tag{7}$$

Where $\eta_{S,V} = N(d_1)\frac{V}{S}$ is the instantaneous elasticity of equity with respect to the firm's value, and $\eta_{S,V} \geq 1$.

Since σ_S is stochastic, changing with V, the conventional *BS* model cannot be applied to the valuation of puts and calls on S. The *BS* model requires σ to be constant, or, to follow a deterministic path over the life of the option. However, it was shown by Bensoussan, Crouhy, and Galai (1994 and 1995) that a good approximation can be achieved by employing (7) in the *BS* model.

In practice, for long-term options, the estimated σ_S from (7) is not expected to change widely from day to day, Therefore, (7) can be used in the context of *BS* estimation of long-term options, even when the underlying instrument does not follow a stationary log-normal distribution.

5. THE SYSTEMATIC AND SPECIFIC RISK OF DEFAULT RISK

It should be noted that credit risk is closely related to the market risk of the firm, since the two major factors in determining the cost of default are the value of the firm, V, and its volatility, σ. We can add additional insight by relating V to the general market risk through the Capital Asset Pricing Model (CAPM). In the CAPM framework the current value of the firm is given by

$$V = \frac{E(V_T)}{1+\bar{r}_V},$$

where $E(V_T)$ is the expected value of the firm at time T, and $\bar{r}_V$ is the cost of capital of the firm. From the CAPM, $\bar{r}_V$ can be expressed as follows:

$$\bar{r}_V = r + \beta_V(\bar{r}_M - r),$$

where r is the riskless interest rate, $\bar{r}_M$ is the expected rate of return on the market portfolio of risky assets, and β_V is the systematic risk of the firm. The current value of the firm's assets is a function of the co-movements of the firm's value with the value of all risky assets in the economy

$$\beta_V = \frac{\mathrm{cov}(r_V, r_M)}{\sigma_M^2}$$

where cov is the covariance function and σ_M^2 is the variance of the rate of return on the market index of all risky assets.

In a continuous time framework it can be shown that credit risk has a systematic risk, which is related to market risk, as follows:

$$\beta_P \equiv \frac{\mathrm{cov}(r_P, r_M)}{\sigma_M^2} = \frac{\partial P}{\partial V} \cdot \frac{V}{P}\beta_V = -N(-d_1)\frac{V}{P}\beta_V \tag{8}$$

where r_P is the instantaneous rate of return on the cost of credit risk, P, as given by (2). The instantaneous beta risk of the cost of default is a factor of, first, the business risk of the firm (as measured by its relative co-movement with market risk, β_V), second, the probability term $N(-d_1)$, and third, the ratio of the firm's value to the cost of default $\frac{V}{P}$. The systematic risk of default risk in (7) is negative.

By giving a risky loan to the firm, the bank assumes positive beta risk of the firm $N(-d_1)V\beta_V/P$. Insuring against default risk by purchasing P, eliminates this beta risk.

In terms of our numerical example, adding the assumption that the firm's systematic risk is equal to 1 ($\beta_V = 1$), we get

$$\beta_P = -N(-d_1)\frac{V}{P}\beta_V = -0.137 \cdot \frac{100}{3.37} \cdot 1 = -4.065$$

The contract to eliminate the default has high negative beta risk. Its elasticity amplifies market movements by almost fourfold, over a short time interval.

In January 1988, the new BIS framework will come into force to assess regulatory capital. For on-balance sheet securities, like bonds and stocks, there is a capital charge for general market risk and for specific risk. Specific risk, according to BIS, relates to the risk that the price of an individual security moves by more or less than what is expected from general market movements, due to specific credit events related to individual issuers. The capital charge for specific risk can be determined either using the internal models or a somewhat arbitrary standardized approach. In that context, an internal measure of specific risk, SR, for one day, can be derived directly from (7), i.e.,

$$SR = N(-d_1)\frac{V}{B_o}\beta_v\sigma_m \sqrt{365} \tag{9}$$

and the capital charge, CC_{SR} for specific risk for the zero-coupon bond, is:[9]

$$CC_{SR} = B_o \cdot SR \cdot 2.33 \cdot \sqrt{10} \tag{10}$$

In our example, assuming σ_m = 20%, we find SR = 0.00216 and CC_{SR} = 3.178.

6. VALUATION OF THE CREDIT RISK PREMIUM FOR THE TAX CASE

In this section the model is extended by assuming that the borrowing corporation is paying taxes contingent on its net profits. More specifically, we assume corporations are subject to full-loss-offset tax at rate τ, and interest expenses, R, and depreciation expenses, D, are deducted from the future stochastic net operating income, $\tilde{X}$, to derive the taxable income. In this framework a distinction must be made between the interest component R, which is deductible for tax purposes, and the principal amount, K.

The maturity value of the one-period corporate debt B_1 is given by

$$\tilde{B}_1 = \begin{cases} \tau(R+D)+(1-\tau)\tilde{X}, & \tilde{X} \le M \\ R+K, & \tilde{X} > M \end{cases}, \tag{11}$$

where tilde denotes uncertain value, and M is defined as follows:

$$M = \frac{(R+M)-\tau(R+D)}{(1-\tau)}$$

The bank is fully paid in the event that future net operating income (NOI), $\tilde{X}$ is greater than M. If NOI is less than M, the firm is in bankruptcy, and its income, together with the tax shield of $\tau(R + D)$ is not sufficient to pay its debt obligation.

Let us define a new security Q with future contingent cash flow Q_1, as follows:

$$Q_1 = \begin{cases} (R+K)-[\tau(R+D)+(1-\tau)\tilde{X}] & \tilde{X} \le M \\ 0 & \tilde{X} > M \end{cases} \tag{12}$$

It is easy to see that

$$B_1 + \pi_1 = R + K$$

for all states of the world. Adding Q to the corporate loan turns it into a riskless portfolio. Therefore, Q_1 is the time 1 value of the credit risk of the bank vis a vis the firm. Its present value provides the current cost of the credit risk of the bank.

The framework suggested in Galai (1988) can be followed. It is assumed that the production model of the firm is a point input-point output model. *All* the inputs in capital, labor, raw materials, etc., are paid for at time zero. At time 1 all outputs are received. Hence, the value of the output at time 1 is the firm's operating income, denoted by $\tilde{X}$, and it must be nonnegative. Up to time 1, the firm does not experience any cash flows and pays no dividend to its shareholders. These assumptions actually exclude short-term liabilities (e.g., accounts payable) as well as future contingent liability (e.g., legal damages suites) from the capital structure. They also guarantee that the firm's value at 1 is nonnegative, which is a necessary condition for the assumption that the market value of $\tilde{X}$ during the period (0,1) follows a log-normal distribution.

The government is assumed to impose a full-loss-offset tax on the net income of the firm. The tax implies that when the net income at time 1, $\tilde{X} - R - D$ (where D is the depreciation), is positive the firm will pay a proportion τ to the government; however, if $\tilde{X} - R - D$ is negative, the government will have to pay back the proportion τ of the loss to the firm. All taxes are due at time 1.

Under the above assumptions and also denoting the present value of $\tilde{X}$ by V_0, the present value of Q_1 can be derived from the Black and Scholes option pricing model:

$$Q_0 = (1-\tau)[-V_0 N(-d_1) + Me^{-rT} N(-d_2)] \tag{13}$$

where $N(.)$ is the cumulative standard normal distribution, and

$$d_1 = \frac{\ln(V_0/M) + (r + \frac{1}{2}\sigma^2)T}{\sigma\sqrt{T}} = \frac{\ln(V_0/Me^{-rT}) + \frac{1}{2}\sigma^2 T}{\sigma\sqrt{T}}$$

$$d_2 = d_1 - \sigma\sqrt{T}$$

T is the time left to bond maturity, and σ is the standard deviation of the rate of return of the firm's NOI.

The model illustrates that the credit risk, and its costs, is a function of the riskiness of the assets of the firm σ, and this risk is also a function of the time interval until debt is paid back, T. The cost is also affected by the risk-free interest rate r, and the higher is r the less costly it is to reduce credit risk. This result is due to the fact that the present value of the future obligation to debt holders to pay them $R + K$, is reduced the higher is r. The cost is a homogeneous function of the leverage ratio, $LR = Me^{-rT}/V_0$, which means it stays constant for a scale expansion of Me^{-rT}/V_0. M measures the net leverage burden on shareholders: the debt-holders expect to receive $R + K$, however they are only guaranteed the riskless partial coverage through the tax shield $\tau(R + D)$, and the remaining part is contingent on net income after paying a proportion τ in taxes.[10]

The effect of the taxes is to lower the cost of credit risk. In our model

$$\frac{\partial Q_0}{\partial \tau} \leq 0$$

Table 3. Default Yields and Premier for Corporate Debt as a function of the Leverage Ratio $LR = Fe^{-rT}/V_0$.

LR	R	M	Q_0	B_0	y	π	π(no-tax)
0.5	5.25	42.39	0	50	0.100	0	0
0.6	6.31	57.74	0	60	0.100	0	0.001
0.7	7.36	73.07	0.08	69.92	0.101	0.001	0.004
0.8	8.41	88.41	0.87	79.13	0.111	0.011	0.015
0.9	9.47	103.76	3.66	86.34	0.142	0.042	0.041
1.0	10.52	119.09	9.15	90.85	0.196	0.096	0.083

and it reflects the governments partial participation in the credit risk through its tax shield and full-loss-offset tax mechanism. Consistent with this result is also the finding that the higher is the allowed depreciation D the lower is the probability of default, due to the higher tax shield, and therefore the cost of default, Q_0, decreases.

We can now derive the yield to maturity for the corporate discount debt, y, as follows:

$$y = -\frac{\ln\frac{B_0}{F}}{T} = -\frac{\ln\frac{Fe^{-rT} - Q_0}{F}}{T},$$

where $F = R + K$, so that the default spread, π, defined as $\pi = y - r$, can be derived from (13):

$$\pi = y - r = -\frac{1}{T}\ln\left(N(d_2) + (1-\tau)\frac{V_0}{Fe^{-rT}}N(-d_1) + \frac{\tau(R+D)}{F}N(-d_2)\right) \tag{14}$$

In Table 3 we present the results of a numerical example, showing the default premier for different levels of corporate debt. The risk premium is compared to the ones calculated in Section 2, for the no-tax case. Table 3 is based on the following assumptions:

$V_0 = 100$, $T = 1$, $r = 10\%$, $\sigma = 20\%$, $\tau = 30\%$, $D = 80$.

For high leverage ratio the default spread is lower for the no tax case than for the tax case.

APPENDIX 1: INTEGRATING YIELD SPREAD WITH OPTIONS APPROACH.

To show how the options approach can be employed given yield spreads, we use the following numerical example, which follows the conventional analysis. Next table presents the prevailing yields on treasury bonds and on corporate bonds:

The above data can be transformed to derive the zero coupon curves for the treasury notes and the corporate bonds.

Table 4. Prevailing Market Yields and Spreads.

Maturity (Years)	US Treasury Par Yields	Company X Par Yields	Credit Spread
1	5.60%	5.85%	0.25
2	5.99%	6.34%	0.35
3	6.15%	6.60%	0.45
4	6.27%	6.87%	0.60
5	6.34%	7.04%	0.70
6	6.42%	7.22%	0.80
7	6.48%	7.38%	0.90

Semi-annual 30/360 yields.

Table 5. Zero Coupon Curve.

Maturity (Years)	US Treasury Zeros	Company X Zeros
1	5.52%	5.76%
2	5.91%	6.25%
3	6.07%	6.51%
4	6.19%	6.80%
5	6.27%	7.18%
6	6.36%	7.37%
7	6.42%	7.54%

Continuously compounded 30/360 zero coupon rates.

Table 6. One Year Forward Rates N Years Forward.

Maturity (Years)	US Treasury Forwards	Company X Forwards	One Year Forward Credit Spreads N Years Forward
1	5.52%	5.76%	0.24
2	6.30%	6.74%	0.44
3	6.40%	7.05%	0.65
4	6.56%	7.64%	1.08
5	6.56%	7.71%	1.15
6	6.81%	8.21%	1.40
7	6.81%	8.47%	1.65

One year continuously compounded 30/360.

The zero-coupon table is used in order to derive the one year forward rates *N* year forward. This information is needed for credit matrix and other evaluation systems which are based on yield spreads.

For our purposes we use the data for the zero coupon curves to evaluate the implied parameter for a firm with T-year bond outstanding.

If company X has a two-year bond, it should have a yield consistent with 6.25 percent per annum for a zero-coupon bond. In other words, by converting the two-year corporate coupon bond into its two-year zero-coupon equivalent, its economic discrete time yield should be 6.25 percent. The risk-free yield on an equivalent two-year zero-coupon government bond is 5.91 percent.

If we also assume that the bond has a face value of F = 100 at T = 2, its present value, B_0, should be $B_0 = F/(1.0625)^2 = 88.58$. If the standard deviation of the rate of return on the firm's assets, σ, is equal to 20 percent we can calculate the equity value S_0 for any given firm's value, V_0. The problem is to find V_0 and hence S_0 such that $88.58 + S_0 = V_0$. This problem is equivalent to that of finding V_0 such that the put value is equal to $P = F/(1.0591)^2 - F/(1.0625)^2 = 0.57$.

By trial and error, given the above assumptions, we find that by introducing $V_0 = 144$ in the Black-Scholes model, the derived equity value is $S_0 = 55.44$ such that $88.58 + 55.44 = 144.02$ and also P = 0.58.

The cost of credit risk for the two-year corporate bond can be derived from the value of a put option on V_0 given F = 100, which is 0.58 for the above parameters. The present value of the recovery value of the loan is given by

$$\frac{N(-d_1)}{N(-d_2)} \cdot V_0 = -\frac{0.033}{0.060} \cdot 144 = 79.20.$$

By following the same procedure for $\sigma = 15\%$ we find that for $V_0 = 124$, the value of bond and equity are, respectively, 88.58 and 35.42. The cost of credit risk is P = 0.57 and the present value of the recovery value is 81.5. For $\sigma = 25\%$ the yield spread is consistent with a market value of $V_0 = 170$, which means a leverage ratio, LR, of only 0.524 and an equity value of 81.42.

NOTES

1. Cf., for example, Duffie (1992).
2. This contribution has been followed by Galai and Masulis (1976), Black and Cox (1976), Merton (1977), Lee (1981), Ho and Singer (1982), Pitts and Selby (1983), Johnson and Stulz (1987), Chance (1990), Cooper and Mello (1991), Shimko, Tejima, and van Deventer (1993), Leland (1994), and Kim, Ramaswamy, and Sundaresan (1996).
3. See also Litterman and Iben (1991) and Madan and Unal (1996). This approach is consistent with the "CreditMetrics" methodology suggested by J.P. Morgan (1997) to assess credit risk exposure for the banks' portfolio of fixed income instruments.
4. This approach is difficult to implement in practice, and in some instances the model calibration yields negative default probabilities. This inconsistent result comes from the fact that the recovery factors not only vary over time, but also should be endogenously determined in the model since the loss incurred by the debt holders should depend explicitly on the value of the firm's assets.
5. The model builds on Black and Cox's (1976) extension of Merton's (1974) model.
6. 10 percent is the annualized interest rate discreetly compounded, which is equivalent to 9.5 percent contiguously compounded.
7. A leverage factor equal to 0.7 can be presented by a face value F = 77.
8. The computed cost of default is slightly different from the put value due to rounding errors.
9. The capital charge corresponds to a maximum loss at the one-tailed 99 percent confidence interval over a 10-day horizon. Assuming normality of the price change variations, and serial independence, the instantaneous volatility needs to be scaled up by the factor $2.33\sqrt{10}$. There is an additional multiplier of 3 required by BIS to compensate for additional risks not captured by the model, like liquidity risk.

10. For the special case that $K = D$ then $M = R + K$ which means that the bankruptcy event is defined identically to the no-tax case. (Note, however, that the cost of credit risk will be lower by a factor of $(1 - \tau)$ for the tax-case compared to the no-tax case.)

REFERENCES

Anderson, R.W., and S.M. Sundaresan (1996). "Design and Valuation of Debt Contracts," *Review of Financial Studies* 9(1), 37–68.

Bensoussan, A., M. Crouhy, and D. Galai (1997). "Black-Scholes Approximation of Complex Option Values: The Cases of European Compound Call Options and Equity Warrants," *Option Embedded Bonds*, I. Nelken (ed.) Irwin Professional Publishing, 167–154.

Bensoussan, A., M. Crouhy, and D. Galai (1994). "Stochastic Volatility Related to Leverage Effect I: Equity Volatility Behavior," *Applied Mathematical Finance* Vol 1, No. 1, 63–85.

Black, F., and J.C. Cox (1976). "Valuing Corporate Securities: Some Effects of Bond Indenture Provisions," *Journal of Finance* 31, 351–67.

Black, F., and M. Scholes (1973). "The Pricing of Options and Corporate Liabilities," *Journal of Political Economy* 81, 637–54.

Brennan, M.J., and E.S. Schwartz (1977). "Convertible Bonds: Valuation and Optimal Strategies for Call and Conversion," *Journal of Finance* 32, 1699–1715.

Brennan, M.J., and E.S. Schwartz (1980). "Analyzing Convertible Bonds," *Journal of Financial and Quantitative Analysis* 15, 907–29.

Chance, D. (1990). "Default Risk and the Duration of Zero Coupon Bonds," *Journal of Finance* 45(1), 265–274.

Chen, A.H., and E. Han Kim (1979). "Theories of Corporate Debt Policy: A Synthesis," *Journal of Finance* 34, 371–84.

Constantinides, G.M. (1984). "Warrant Exercise and Bond Conversion in Competitive Markets," *Journal of Financial Economics* 13, 371–97.

Cooper, I., and M. Martin (1996). "Default Risk and Derivative Products," *Applied Mathematical Finance* 3, 53–74.

Cooper, I., and A. Mello (1991). "The Default Risk of Swaps," *Journal of Finance* 46(2), 597–620.

Cox, J.C., J.E. Ingersoll, Jr., and S.A. Ross (1980). "An Analysis of Variable Rate Loan Contracts," *Journal of Finance* 35, 389–403.

Crouhy, M., and Galai, D. (1995). "The Interaction between the Financial and Investment Decisions of the Firm: The Case of Issuing Warrants in a Levered Firm," *Journal of Banking and Finance*, Vol 18, 861–880.

Duffie, D. (1992). *Dynamic Asset Pricing Theory*. Princeton: Princeton University Press.

Duffie, D., and K.J. Singleton (1994). "Econometric Modeling of Term Structure of Defaultable Bonds," Working Paper, Graduate School of Business, Stanford University.

Dunn, K.B., and C.S. Spatt (1984). "A Strategic Analysis of Sinking Fund Bonds," *Journal of Financial Economics* 13, 399–423.

Galai, D. (1988). "Corporate Income Taxes and the Valuation of Claims on the Corporation," *Research in Finance*, Vol. 7, 75–90.

Galai, D., and R.W. Masulis (1976). "The Option Pricing Model and the Risk Factor of Stock," *Journal of Financial Economics* 3, 53–81.

Galai, D., and M.I. Schneller (1978). "Pricing of Warrants and the Value of the Firm," *Journal of Finance* 33, 1333–42.

Geske, R. (1977). "The Voluation of Corporate Liabilities as Compound Options," *Journal of Financial and Quantitative Analysis* 12, 541–52.

Geske, R., and H. Johnson (1984). "The Valuation of Corporate Liabilities as Compound Options: A Correction," *Journal of Financial and Quantitative Analysis* 19, 231–32.

Ho, T.S.Y., and R.F. Singer (1982). "Bond Indenture Provisions and the Risk of Corporate Debt," *Journal of Financial Economics* 10, 375–406.

Ho, T.S.Y., and R.F. Singer (1984). "The Value of Corporate Debt with a Sinking-Fund Provision," *Journal of Business* 57, 315–36.

Hull, J., and A. White (1991). "The Impact of Default Risk on the Prices of Options and Other Derivative Securities," *Journal of Banking and Finance* 19(2), 299–322.

Ingersoll, J.E. (1977). "A Contingent-Claims Valuation of Convertible Securities," *Journal of Financial Economics* 4, 289–321.

Ingersoll, J.E. (1977). "An Examination of Corporate Call Policies on Convertible Securities," *Journal of Finance* 32, 463–78.

Ingersoll, J.E. (1987). *Theory of Financial Decision Making*. Rowman and Littlefield Publishers.

Jarrow, R.A., and S.M. Turnbull (1995). "Pricing Derivatives on Financial Securities Subject to Credit Risk," *Journal of Finance* 50(1), 53–85.

Jarrow, R.A., D. Lando, and S.M. Turnbull (1997). "A Markov Model for the Term 'Structure of Credit Spreads'," *Review of Financial Studies*.

Johnson, H., and R. Stulz (1987). "The Pricing of Options with Default Risk," *Journal of Finance* 42(2), 267–280.

Morgan, J.P. (1997). *CreditMetrics*.

Kim, I.J., K. Ramaswamy, and S.M. Sundaresan (1993). "Valuation of Corporate Fixed-Income Securities," *Financial Management* 22(3), 60–78.

Lee, C.J. (1981). "The Pricing of Corporate Debt: A Note," *Journal of Finance* 36, 1187–1189.

Leland, H. (1994). "Risky Debt, Bond Covenants and Optimal Capital Structure," *Journal of Finance* 49, 1213–1252.

Litterman, R., and T. Iben (1991). "Corporate Bond Valuation and the Term Structure of Credit Spreads," *Financial Analysts Journal* (Spring), 52–64.

Longstaff, F., and E. Schwartz (1995). "A Simple Approach to Valuing Risky Fixed and Floating Rate Debt," *Journal of Finance* 50(3), 789–819.

Mason, S.P., and S. Bhattacharya (1981). "Risky Debt, Jump Processes, and Safety Covenants," *Journal of Financial Economics* 9, 281–307.

Merton, R.C. (1974). "On the Pricing of Corporate Debt: The Risk Structure of Interest Rates," *Journal of Finance* 29, 449–70.

Merton, R.C. (1977). "On the Pricing of Contingent Claims and the Modigliani-Miller Theorem," *Journal of Financial Economics* 5, 241–249.

Park, S.Y., and Subrahamanyam (1990). "Option Features of Corporate Securities," *Financial Options* edited by Figlewski, Silber and Subrahamnyam, 66–97.

Pitts, C.G.C., and M.J.P. Selby (1983). "The Pricing of Corporate Debt: A Further Note," *Journal of Finance* 38, 1311–1313.

Shimko, D., N. Tejima, and D. van Deventer (1993). "The Pricing of Risky Debt When Interest Rates Are Stochastic," *Journal of Fixed Income* (September), 58–66.

Warner, Jerold B. (1977). "Bankruptcy, Absolute Priority, and the Pricing of Risky Debt Claims," *Journal of Financial Economics* 4, 239–76.

Weinstein, Mark I. (1983). "Bond Systematic Risk and the Option Pricing Model," *Journal of Finance* 38, 1415–30.

6. NONLINEAR VALUE-AT-RISK[1]

MARK BRITTEN-JONES and STEPHEN M SCHAEFER

1. INTRODUCTION

Consider a portfolio consisting of quantities $\mathbf{x} = (x_1, x_2, \ldots, x_n)'$ of assets $1, 2, \ldots, n$ with time t values $\mathbf{v} = (v_1, v_2 \ldots v_n)'$.[2] Then the change in the price of the portfolio, V, over the next interval Δt is given by

$$\Delta V = \sum_{i=1}^{n} x_i \Delta v_i, \tag{1.1}$$

where Δv_i (ΔV) denotes the change in the value of asset i (the portfolio) over the interval t to $t + \Delta t$. The value-at-risk of the portfolio $\mathbf{x}$ for some defined probability level α, is defined as the level of loss, $\Delta V^\star(\alpha)$, such that the probability that $\Delta V \leq \Delta V^\star$ is equal to α. When the joint distribution of the change in asset values can be taken as multivariate normal with a known mean and variance, the calculation of $\Delta V^\star$ is straightforward. In many cases, however, and particularly when some of the assets are options, the assumption of multivariate normality will be inappropriate, even when appropriate for the underlying rates and prices.

In this case one of two approaches is typically employed. In the first, the so-called delta-only method, the nonlinear relation between asset values and the underlying rates and prices is replaced by a linear approximation based on each asset's delta. Assume that the value of each asset i depends on time and K "factors", $\mathbf{f} = \{f_1, f_2 \ldots f_K\}$. Then $\Delta^\delta V$, the first-order approximation to ΔV, is given by

$$\Delta^{\delta}V = \sum_{i=1}^{n} x_i \frac{\partial v_i(\mathbf{f},t)}{\partial t}\Delta t + \sum_{i=1}^{n} x_i \sum_{k=1}^{K} \frac{\partial v_i(\mathbf{f},t)}{\partial f_k}\Delta f_k \tag{1.2}$$

$$\equiv \mu_p + \sum_{k=1}^{K} \delta_k \Delta f_k, \tag{1.3}$$

where μ_p is the change in portfolio value resulting from the passage of time:

$$\mu_p = \sum_{i=1}^{n} x_i \frac{\partial v_i(f)}{\partial t}\Delta t, \tag{1.4}$$

and δ_k, the aggregate delta, is given by:

$$\delta_k = \sum_{i=1}^{n} x_i \frac{\partial v_i(f)}{\partial f_k}. \tag{1.5}$$

Assuming **f** has a multivariate normal distribution with known parameters, $\Delta^{\delta}V$ has a univariate normal distribution and the mean and variance of $\Delta^{\delta}V$, and from this the value at risk, are easily computed.

The most widely used alternative to the delta-only approach involves revaluing each contract for a large number of simulated values of the underlying factors. In a portfolio with many instruments, this procedure may be computationally expensive or even infeasible.

In this paper we propose an alternative approach in which the change in value of an asset is approximated, not as a *linear* function of the underlying factors but as a *linear-quadratic* function. In many cases this provides a better approximation to the true distribution than the delta-only approach while being substantially less resource intensive than full valuation. Including a quadratic term in the approximation to ΔV implies using the *gamma* of an option as well as the delta. This approach is also discussed in Wilson (1994), Fallon (1996), Rouvinez (1997), and Jahel, Perraudin, and Sellin (1997) as well as in previous work by the authors (Britten-Jones and Schaefer, 1995). Rouvinez uses Imhof's (1961) numerical technique to invert the characteristic function of the quadratic approximation and so recover the exact distribution. Jahel et al. also use characteristic functions to compute the moments of the approximation and then fit a parametric distribution to the moments. Fallon's approach, like ours, uses an approximation to the distribution derived from the moments. An extensive review of alternative approaches to the calculation of VaR is given in Duffie and Pan (1997).

Wilson (1994) also uses a linear-quadratic approximation but the statistic he derives—capital-at-risk [CAR]—differs significantly from the standard definition of VaR. In fact, Wilson's CAR is *always conservative* with respect to VaR. The relation between CAR and VaR is discussed in the Appendix.

The paper is organized as follows. In Section 2 we deal with the univariate case and show how, by completing the square, we may derive the exact distribution of a quadratic approximation to the relation between asset value and the underlying rates and prices. Section 2 also includes some examples comparing VaR calculated under linear and linear-quadratic approximations to VaR under full revaluation. Section 3 deals with a special case where the relation between VaR's under delta-only and delta-gamma approximations can be characterised in terms of a single parameter involving the delta and gamma of the position and the volatility of the underlying factor. Section 4 discusses the multivariate case and shows how the distribution of a quadratic approximation to portfolio value may be itself approximated. Section 5 gives an example which uses the approximation described in Section 4 to compute VaR in the multivariate case. Section 6 concludes.

2. THE UNIVARIATE CASE

Consider the portfolio $\mathbf{x} = (x_1, x_2, \ldots, x_n)'$ defined earlier and assume that the number of underlying prices or rates on which the values of the assets depend is unity ($K = 1$). We now introduce, $\Delta^\gamma v_i$, a quadratic approximation to Δv_i, the change in value of the ith asset:

$$\Delta^\gamma v_i = \frac{\partial v_i}{\partial t}\Delta t + \frac{\partial v_i}{\partial f}\Delta f + \frac{1}{2}\frac{\partial^2 v_i}{\partial f^2}(\Delta f)^2 \tag{2.1}$$

$$\equiv \mu_i + \delta_i \Delta f + \frac{1}{2}\gamma_i (\Delta f)^2, \tag{2.2}$$

where δ_i and γ_i are, respectively, the delta and gamma of asset i with respect to the factor f. As before, the term μ_i captures the first-order effect of the change in value due to the passage of time:

$$\mu_i = \frac{\partial v_i}{\partial t}\Delta t.$$

The corresponding delta-gamma approximation[3] to the change in value of the portfolio is given by:

$$\Delta^\gamma V = \sum_{i=1}^{n} x_i \mu_i + \left(\sum_{i=1}^{n} x_i \delta_i\right)\Delta f + \frac{1}{2}\left(\sum_{i=1}^{n} x_i \gamma_i\right)(\Delta f)^2 \tag{2.3}$$

$$\equiv \mu_p + \delta \Delta f + \frac{1}{2}\gamma(\Delta f)^2, \tag{2.4}$$

where $\mu_p = \Sigma_{i=1}^{n} x_i \mu_i$, $\delta = \Sigma_{i=1}^{n} x_i \delta_i$, and $\gamma = \Sigma_{i=1}^{n} x_i \gamma_i$. This is to be contrasted with the standard (delta-only) linear approximation:

$$\Delta^\delta V = \mu_p + \delta \Delta f. \tag{2.5}$$

We assume throughout that the underlying factors are normally distributed; thus here we assume:

$$\Delta f \sim N(\mu_f, \sigma_f^2),$$

where μ_f and σ_f are, respectively, the mean and standard deviation of Δf. Thus, in equation (2.3) the term which is linear in Δf is normally distributed and the quadratic term is distributed as a noncentral chi-squared. The problem of characterising the distribution of $\Delta^\gamma V$, the delta-gamma approximation to ΔV, is therefore that of characterising the distribution of a sum of a normal variate and a noncentral chi-squared variate. Fortunately, this problem is easily solved if we simply complete the square in eq. 2.3. Thus,

$$\Delta^\gamma V = \mu_p + \delta \Delta f + \frac{1}{2}\gamma(\Delta f)^2 = \mu_p^\star + \frac{1}{2}\gamma(e + \Delta f)^2, \tag{2.6}$$

where

$$e = \frac{\delta}{\gamma} \quad \text{and} \quad \mu_p^\star = \mu_p - \frac{1}{2}\frac{\delta^2}{\gamma}. \tag{2.7}$$

Since Δf is normally distributed, $(e + \Delta f)$ is also normal with mean $e + \mu_f$ and variance σ_f^2. It follows that

$$\frac{\Delta^\gamma V - \mu_p^\star}{\gamma\sigma_f^2/2} = \left(\frac{e + \Delta f}{\sigma_f}\right)^2 \equiv w \sim \text{non-central } \chi^2{:}v,\, d, \tag{2.8}$$

where

$$v = 1 \text{ and } d = \left(\frac{e + \mu_f}{\sigma_f}\right)^2.$$

Thus, under the delta-gamma approximation, the value-at-risk of the portfolio may be computed directly from the cdf. of the noncentral chi-squared distribution defined in eq. 2.8. For a given probability level, say α, let $w^\star(\alpha)$ be such that

$$\Pr(w \le w^\star(\alpha)) = \alpha.$$

Then the value at risk, for probability level α is $\Delta^\gamma V^\star(\alpha)$, where:

$$\Delta^\gamma V^\star(\alpha) = \mu_p^\star + \frac{1}{2}\gamma\sigma_f^2 w^\star(\alpha).$$

Including the gamma term in the approximation for the change in portfolio value, changes the form of the distribution from normal to a translated non-central chi-squared. The materiality of the difference in value-at-risk computed under these two approximations depends on the relation between the portfolio delta and gamma. If delta is large and gamma small then almost all the risk of the portfolio will be associated with directional, or delta, risk in the underlying. In this case the delta-only approximation will provide almost the same results as the delta-gamma. If delta is small and gamma large then little of the risk will be associated with directional changes in the underlying and the delta-only approximation will be poor.

The effect of the relative size of delta and gamma on the relation between VaR under the delta-only and delta-gamma approximations is discussed further in Section 3.

2.1. An example

Table 1 illustrates the effect on VaR of gamma and the time interval over which the distribution is assessed. The Table summarizes the positions of a number of hypothetical portfolios and their corresponding deltas and gammas.

Each portfolio combines a put and a call and thus has a lower delta and a higher gamma than a similar position in either one type of option or the other.

For portfolio 1, VaR is assessed over a short—one day—interval; here the gamma effect is relatively unimportant. Portfolio 2 has a lower delta and a higher gamma (both in absolute terms) and VaR is assessed over a longer period (one week). Thus we expect that a delta-only approach will perform relatively less well for portfolio 2 than portfolio 1. Finally, portfolio 3 is identical to portfolio 1 but here VaR is assessed over a 10-day interval, as the Basle Committee have recently proposed.[4] Even though gamma and delta in this case are the same as those for portfolio 1, the effect of gamma will be greater as a result of the longer interval over which VaR is assessed.

The calculations described below show that, particularly for portfolios 2 and 3, VaR calculated using a delta-gamma approach is significantly more accurate than a delta-only approach. But first it is useful to compare the linear and quadratic approximations (equations 1.2 and 2.3 respectively) to the true (Black-Scholes) relation between portfolio value and the underlying.

Table 1. Portfolio positions used in Example.

Price of the underlying asset is 100 with assumed volatility level of 30% p.a. The (annually compounded) riskless interest rate is 10% and the strike price for each option is 101. We assume a zero dividend yield.

Portfolio	1	2	3
Maturity of options (days)	60	42	60
quantity of calls	−1.0	−1.0	−1.0
quantity of puts	−0.5	−0.6	−0.5
time horizon	1 day	1 week	10 days
aggregate delta	−0.314	−0.239	−0.314
aggregate gamma	−0.049	−0.063	−0.049

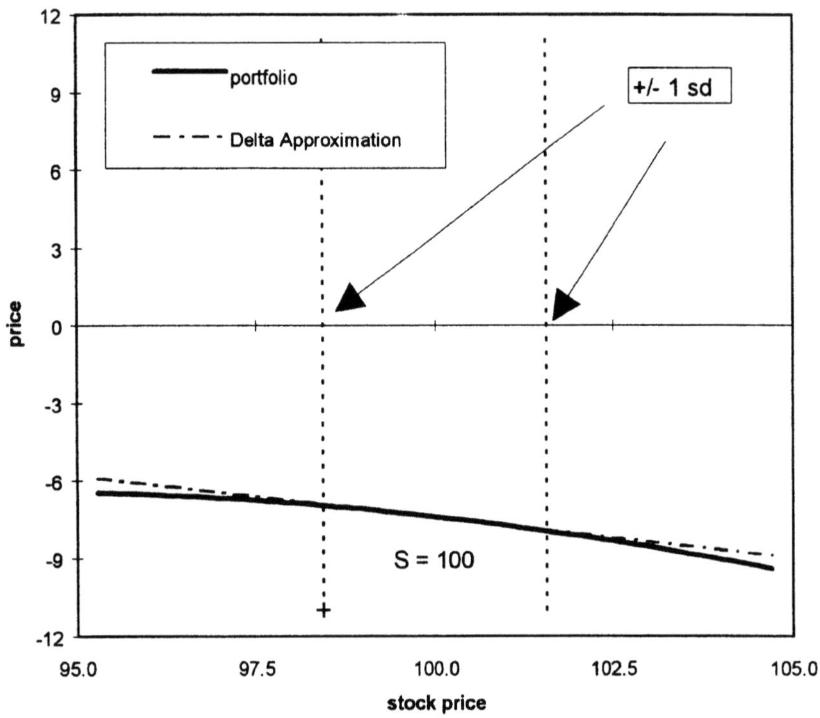

Figure 1. Relation between value of portfolio 1 and price of underlying stock using (i) "true" (Black-Scholes) value and (ii) delta-approximation.

Figure 1 shows the true value of portfolio 1 at the end of one day as a function of the underlying asset price and also the value under the linear approximation. The vertical dotted lines show ±1 standard deviation limits for the underlying asset price, S. We see that over the majority of the range of likely values for S the linear approximation is quite close to the true value. In this case, therefore, we would not expect to find that a VaR measure based on a quadratic approximation, performs much better than a linear approximation. In Figure 2 we see that this is not the case for portfolio 2, which has a higher gamma and a lower delta. Here, for a one week horizon, a quadratic relation provides a much better approximation to the true value. Thus we expect to find that, for portfolio 2, VaR based on a quadratic approximation performs better than a linear approximation.

Figure 3 shows the cumulative distribution of change in value for portfolio 1 using (a) complete revaluation under Black Scholes, (b) a linear (delta-only) approximation and (c) a quadratic (delta-gamma) approximation. In this case, for the reasons observed earlier, the difference between the alternative approaches is small. Figure

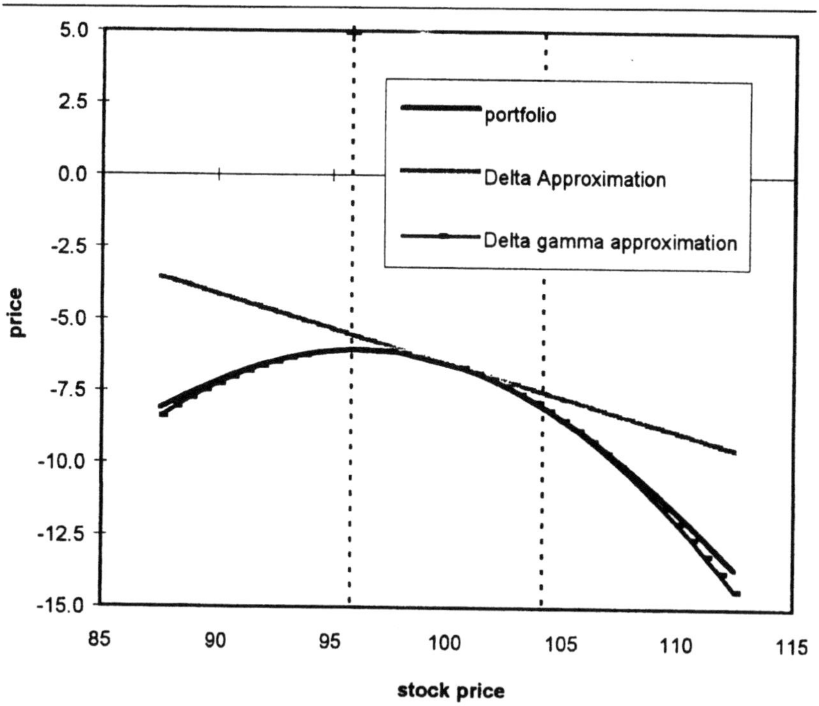

Figure 2. Relation between value of portfolio 2 and price of underlying stock using (i) "true" (Black-Scholes) value, (ii) delta-approximation and (iii) delta-gamma approximation.

4 shows the corresponding results for portfolio 2. Once again, the results correspond closely to those expected from Figure 2: the distribution of the quadratic approximation is much closer to that of the true value than the delta-only approximation. Figure 5 shows the results for example 3, which is identical to example 1 except that the distribution of value is assessed over 10 days rather than one. Here we find, as in example 2, that the quadratic approximation performs much better than the linear approximation.

These examples illustrate three main points. First, that when gamma is large relative to delta, the linear approximation may perform quite poorly. Second, in these cases the VaR based on a quadratic approximation may provide a much better estimate of the true value, and third, that even when a linear approximation works quite well over short periods, it may perform poorly over longer periods.

2.2. Positions that are both concave and convex in the underlying asset

Finally we give an example where the delta-gamma method does not perform well. In the examples discussed earlier the portfolio was convex or concave over the likely

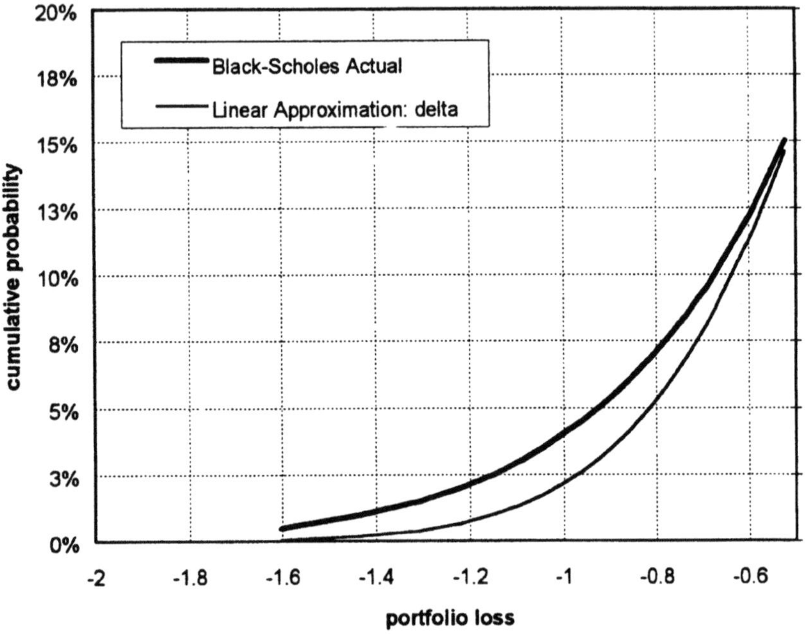

Figure 3. The distribution of value change for portfolio 1 (1 day horizon) under (i) "true" (Black-Scholes) value, (ii) delta-approximation and (iii) delta-gamma approximation.

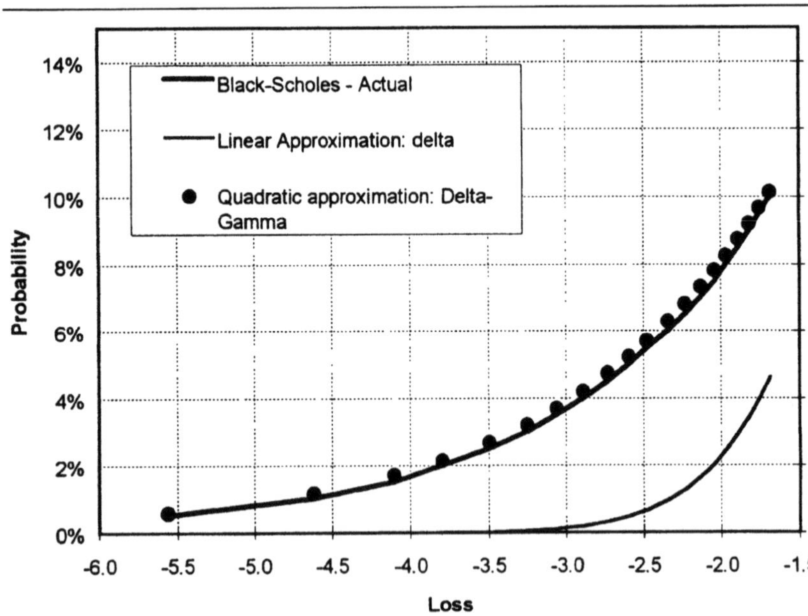

Figure 4. The distribution of value change for portfolio 2 (1 week horizon) under (i) "true" (Black-Scholes) value, (ii) delta-approximation and (iii) delta-gamma approximation.

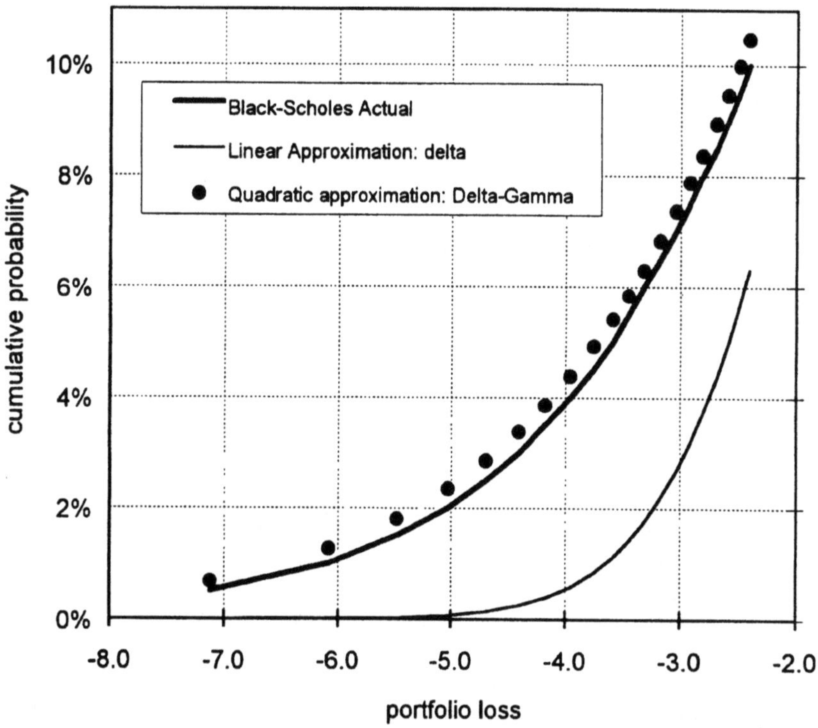

Figure 5. The distribution of value change for portfolio 3 (as portfolio 1 but with 10 day horizon) under (i) "true" (Black-Scholes) value, (ii) delta-approximation and (iii) delta-gamma approximation.

range of prices of the underlying. In these cases the portfolio value was quite well approximated by a quadratic function of the price of the underlying and, consequently, the delta-gamma performed well.

For many option positions, however, the portfolio value may have both convex and concave regions in the range of likely prices of the underlying. Here, a quadratic approximation may not provide a good fit and, in this event, the delta-gamma method is likely to be unreliable.

Table 2 shows a position in which a put and a call are sold with a strike price of 95 and a call is bought with a strike of 105. As Figure 6 shows, although the actual position experiences substantial losses when the stock price falls, the delta-gamma approximation is convex and the maximum loss in this case (approximately 0.6) occurs when the stock price rises. As a result, as Figure 7 shows, the distribution of losses under the delta-gamma approach provides a very poor approximation to the distribution of actual portfolio value. Indeed, in this particular case, the delta approach performs much better.

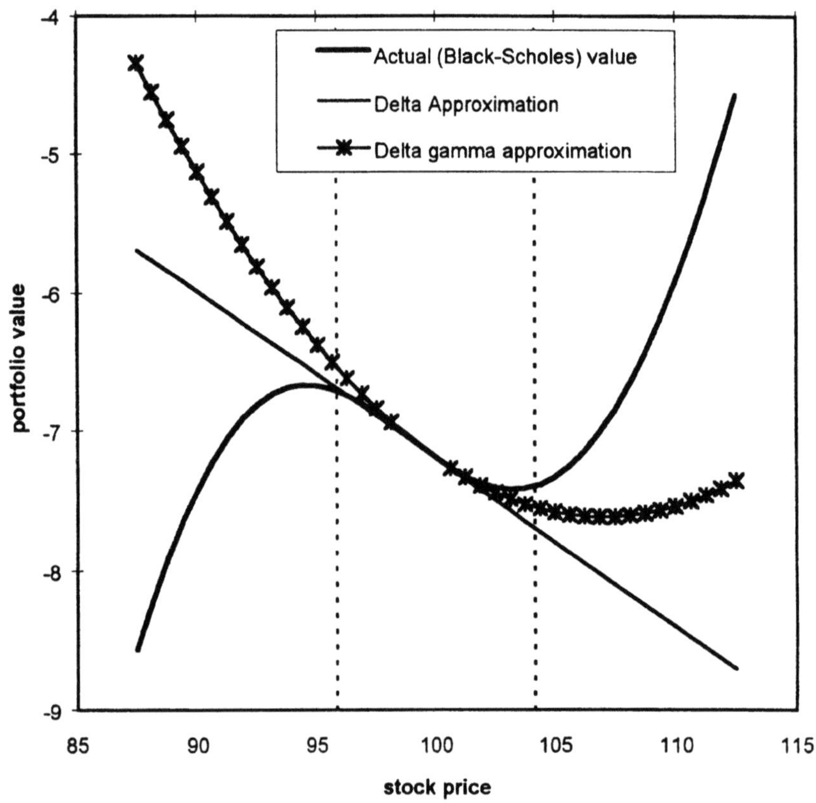

Figure 6. Portfolio value in the case where the relation between the portfolio value and the price of the underlying stock case is neither convex nor concave.

Table 2. Portfolio which is both convex and concave in the underlying.

Type	Put	Call	Call
Strike	95	95	105
Time to maturity (weeks)	4	4	4
Quantity	−1.0	−1.5	+2.5

3. THE RELATION BETWEEN VaR UNDER DELTA-ONLY AND DELTA-GAMMA APPROXIMATIONS: A SPECIAL CASE

In the special case where (i) the expected change in the underlying factor, μ_f, is zero and (ii) VaR is measured relative to the expected change in value of the portfolio, the ratio between VaR computed under the delta and delta-gamma approxi-

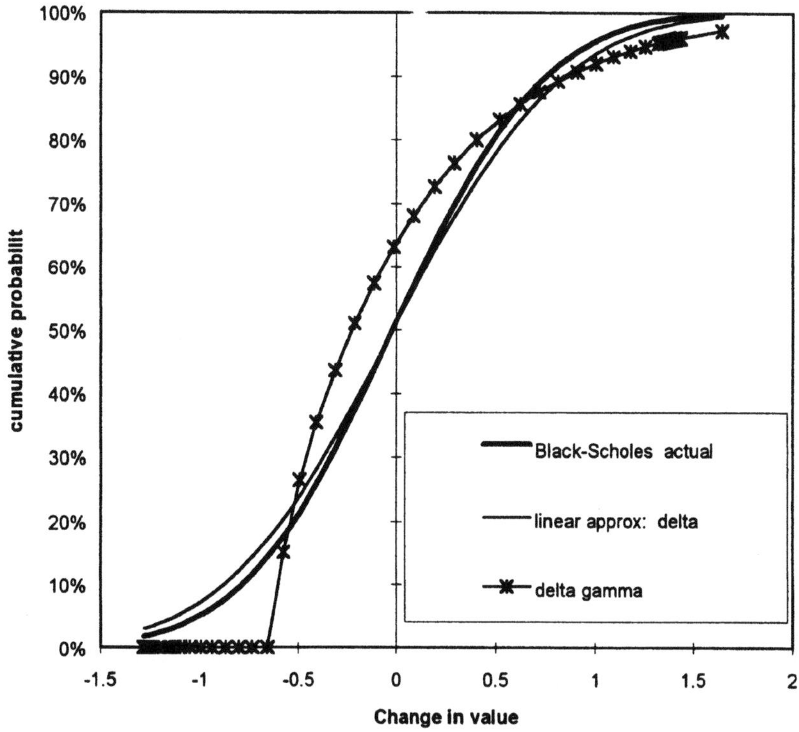

Figure 7. Distribution of portfolio value under (i) full revaluation, (ii) delta only approximation and (iii) delta-gamma approximation when the portfolio is neither convex nor concave in the value of the underlying.

mations depends on a single parameter, θ, which is a function of the portfolio delta and gamma and the volatility of the underlying asset.[5]

The delta-only approximation to value is given by equation 1.2:

$$\Delta^{\delta} V = \mu_{\delta} + \delta \Delta f,$$

and, under assumptions (i) and (ii) above, the corresponding delta-only VaR at probability level α, $\mathrm{VaR}_{\delta}(\alpha)$ is given by

$$\mathrm{VaR}_{\delta}(\alpha) = \phi^{-1}(\alpha)\delta\sigma_f, \tag{3.1}$$

where $\phi^{-1}(\alpha)$ is the αth quantile of the normal distribution and σ_f is the standard deviation of Δf over the interval t to $t + \Delta t$.

The change in value under the corresponding delta-gamma approximation is given by equation 2.6, which, using the values for e and $\mu^{\star}_{p\gamma}$ in equation (2.7), becomes

$$\Delta^{\gamma}V = \mu_{\gamma} + \delta\Delta f + \frac{1}{2}\gamma(\Delta f)^2 = \mu_{\gamma} - \frac{1}{2}\frac{\delta^2}{\gamma} + \frac{1}{2}\gamma\sigma^2\left(\frac{\delta}{\sigma\gamma} + z\right)^2, \tag{3.2}$$

where

$$z \equiv \frac{\Delta f}{\sigma} \sim N(0,1).$$

Setting $E(\Delta^{\gamma}V) = E(\Delta^{\delta}V)$ in equation 3.2 we have

$$\mu_{\gamma} = \mu_{\delta} - \frac{1}{2}\gamma\sigma^2,$$

and (3.2) therefore becomes

$$\Delta^{\gamma}V = \mu_{\delta} - \frac{1}{2}\gamma\sigma^2 - \frac{1}{2}\frac{\delta^2}{\gamma} + \frac{1}{2}\gamma\sigma^2\left(\frac{\delta}{\sigma\gamma} + z\right)^2,$$

We now compute the deviation of $\Delta^{\gamma}V$ from its mean, μ_{δ}, in units of the delta-only VaR. Defining:

$$\Delta V^{\star}_{\delta-g} \equiv \frac{\Delta^{g}V - \mu_{\delta}}{\mathrm{VaR}_{\delta}(\alpha)},$$

and using equation 3.1, we have

$$\Delta V^{\star}_{\delta-\gamma} = -\frac{1}{2}\frac{\gamma^{\sigma}}{\phi^{-1}(\alpha)\delta} - \frac{1}{2}\frac{\delta}{\gamma\phi^{-1}(\alpha)\sigma} + \frac{1}{2}\frac{\gamma^{\sigma}}{\phi^{-1}(\alpha)\delta}\left(\frac{\delta}{\sigma\gamma} + z\right)^2 \tag{3.3}$$

$$= \frac{1}{2\phi^{-1}(\alpha)}\left[-\frac{1}{\theta} - \theta + \frac{1}{\theta}(\theta + z)^2\right]. \tag{3.4}$$

where

$$\theta = \frac{\delta}{\sigma\gamma}. \tag{3.5}$$

From equation 3.4 we have

$$2\phi^{-1}(\alpha)\Delta V^{\star}_{\delta-\gamma}\theta + (1+\theta^2) = (\theta + z)^2 \equiv \tilde{w} \sim \chi^2_{nc}(1,d),$$

where

$d = \theta^2$.

Let $\bar{w}(\alpha)$ be such that

$\Pr(\tilde{w} \le \bar{w}(\alpha)) = \alpha$.

Then

$\Pr\left(2\phi^{-1}(\alpha)\Delta V^{\star}_{\delta-\gamma}\theta + (1+\theta^2) \le \bar{w}(\alpha)\right) = \alpha,$

or

$$\Pr\left(\Delta V^{\star}_{\delta-\gamma} \le \frac{\bar{w}(\alpha) - (1+\theta^2)}{2\phi^{-1}(\alpha)\theta}\right) = \alpha. \tag{3.6}$$

The right-hand side of the inequality in 3.3 is the ratio of the VaR under a delta-gamma approximation to the delta VaR and, as equation 3.7 shows, for a given probability level, α is a function of $\theta = \delta/\sigma\gamma$:

$$\frac{\Delta^{\gamma}V^{\star}(\alpha)}{\Delta^{\delta}V(\alpha)} = \frac{\bar{w}(\alpha) - (1+\theta^2)}{2\phi^{-1}(\alpha)\theta}. \tag{3.7}$$

Figure 8 shows the ratio of the delta VaR to the delta-gamma VaR, the *inverse* of the expression in 3.7, for values of α of 1%, 2.5%, 5% and 10% and for a range of values of θ. As θ tends to zero, delta risk constitutes a diminishing fraction of total portfolio risk and $\Delta^{\delta}V(\alpha)/\Delta^{\gamma}V^{\star}(\alpha)$ tends to zero. As θ increases $\Delta^{\delta}V(\alpha)/\Delta^{\gamma}V^{\star}(\alpha)$ increases although, at the 99th percentile, its value is less than 0.5 for values of θ less than 0.95[6].

3.1. The "gamma adjusted" delta method

One approach incorporating the effect of gamma risk is to use the delta method but to adjust the delta (or the standard deviation of the underlying factor) to reflect the increase in volatility created by exposure to gamma risk.[7] Using equations 2.4 and 3.5 we may show that the standard deviation of the delta-gamma approximation in the univariate case is:

$$\sigma(\Delta^{\gamma}V) = \delta\sigma_f\left(1+\frac{1}{2\theta^2}\right)^{1/2} \equiv \delta'\sigma_f,$$

where δ', the "adjusted delta" is given by:

$$\delta' \equiv \left(1+\frac{1}{2\theta^2}\right)^{1/2}.$$

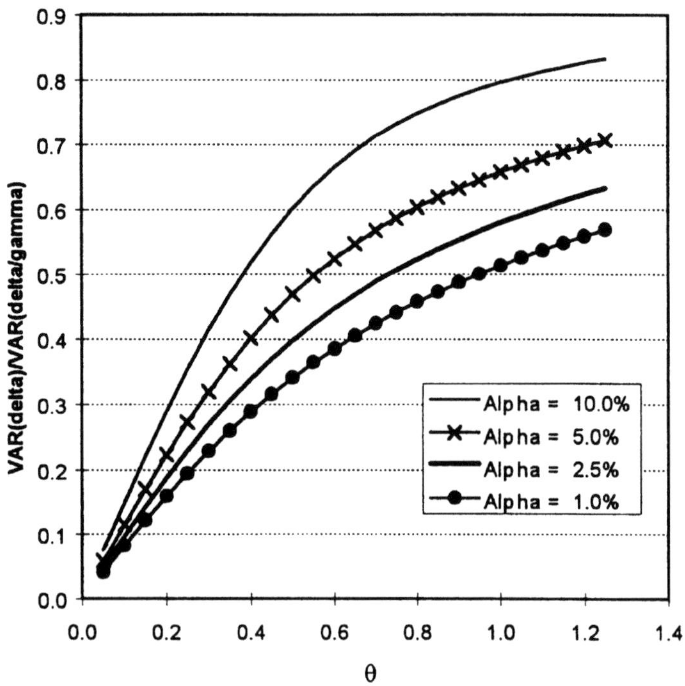

Figure 8. The figure shows the ratio of VAR under the delta-only approximation to VAR under the delta-gamma approximation as a function of θ, defined as $\theta = \dfrac{\delta}{\sigma\gamma}$.

Using this approach the gamma adjusted VaR for probability level α is therefore given by:

$$k(\alpha)\delta\sigma_f\left(1+\frac{1}{2\theta^2}\right)^{1/2},$$

where $k(\alpha)$ is as defined earlier. Now, following the analysis of the previous section we may now show that, $\mathrm{VaR}_\gamma(\alpha)/\mathrm{VaR}_\delta(\alpha)$, the VaR under the delta-gamma approximation *measured in units of the "gamma adjusted" delta VaR* is given by

$$\frac{\mathrm{VaR}_\gamma(\alpha)}{\mathrm{VaR}_\delta(\alpha)}=\frac{\overline{w}(\alpha)-(1+\theta^2)}{\sqrt{2}k(\alpha)(1+2\theta^2)^{1/2}}.$$

The inverse of this ratio is plotted against θ in Figure 7. Although the ratio is much closer to one for low values of θ than in the case of the delta-only approximation the deviations from unity remain significant. As in the case of the delta-

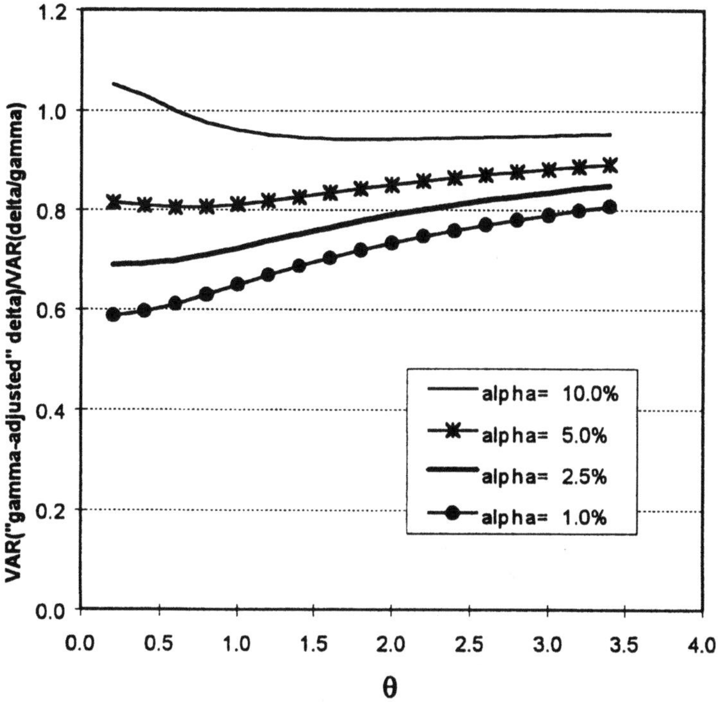

Figure 9. The figure shows the ratio of VAR under the "gamma adjusted" delta approach to VAR under the delta-gamma approximation as a function of θ, defined as $\delta/\sigma\gamma$.

only approximation, a major problem with the gamma adjusted delta approach is that the understatement of VaR (overstatement in some case) varies significantly with the probability level. Thus, for $\theta = 1$, for example, the ratio varies from 0.63 for $\alpha = 1\%$ to 0.98 for $\alpha = 10\%$. Thus it is not possible to find an "adjustment factor" that would correct the bias in the gamma adjusted VaR for different probability levels.

4. THE MULTIVARIATE CASE

The multivariate case is parallel to the univariate case considered earlier except that the distribution of the delta-gamma approximation now involves the sum of non-central chi-square variates. We assume that the vector of changes in the underlying factors follows a multivariate normal with mean $\boldsymbol{\mu}_f$ and covariance matrix $\boldsymbol{\Sigma}$:

$$\Delta \mathbf{f} \sim N_n(\mu_f, \Sigma). \tag{4.1}$$

The quadratic approximation to ΔV is obtained, as before, as a second-order Taylor series expansion of the portfolio value:

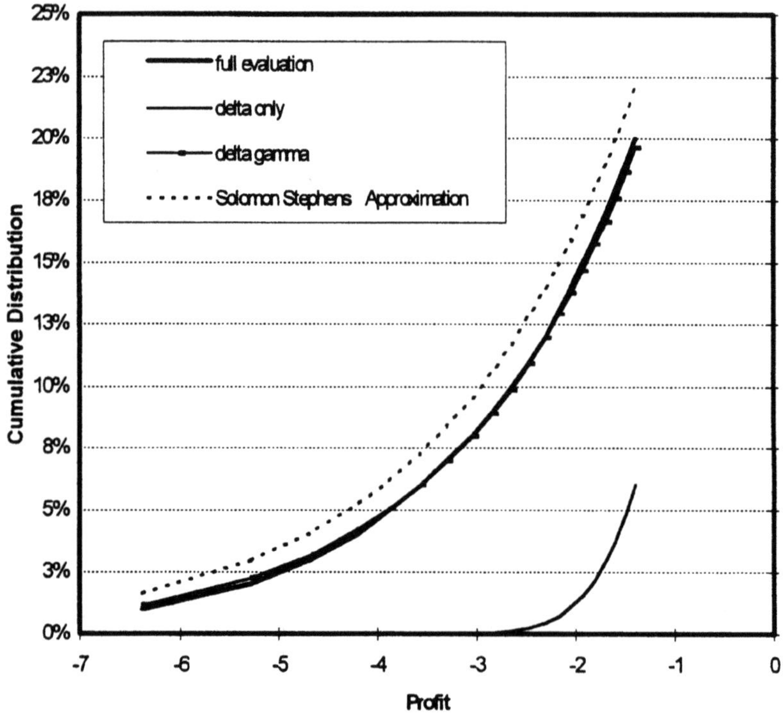

Figure 10. The lower tail of the distribution of portfolio value for the first multivariate example. The graph shows the cdf computed using (i) "true" (Black-Scholes) values, (ii) the delta-only approximation, (iii) the actual values of the delta-gamma approximation and (iv) the Solomon-Stephens approximation to the delta-gamma approximation.

$$\Delta V^{\gamma} \equiv \mu + \frac{\partial V'}{\partial f}\Delta \mathbf{f} + \frac{1}{2}\Delta \mathbf{f}'\frac{\partial^2 V}{\partial f \partial f'}\Delta \mathbf{f}, \tag{4.2}$$

where μ is the change in value resulting from the passage of time. Now we assume that the first and second derivatives of portfolio value with respect to stock prices have been calculated from the deltas and gammas of the individual instruments. We thus assume that aggregate delta:

$$\delta = \frac{\partial V}{\partial f} = \begin{pmatrix} \frac{\partial V}{\partial f_1} \\ \vdots \\ \frac{\partial V}{\partial f_K} \end{pmatrix} \tag{4.3}$$

and aggregate gamma,

$$\Gamma = \frac{\partial^2 V}{\partial f \partial f'} = \begin{pmatrix} \frac{\partial^2 V}{\partial f_1 \partial f_1} & \cdots & \frac{\partial^2 V}{\partial f_1 \partial f_K} \\ \vdots & \ddots & \vdots \\ \frac{\partial^2 V}{\partial f_K \partial f_1} & \cdots & \frac{\partial^2 V}{\partial f_K \partial f_K} \end{pmatrix} \tag{4.4}$$

can be calculated.

Portfolio value is thus approximated by a quadratic function of normally distributed variables. In matrix notation we write this as

$$\Delta V^{\Upsilon} \equiv \mu_{\Upsilon} + \delta'\Delta\mathbf{f} + \frac{1}{2}\Delta\mathbf{f}'\Gamma\Delta\mathbf{f}.$$

Before examining the complete probability distribution of this quadratic function, we first calculate its volatility.

4.1. Portfolio volatility

Portfolio value V has a variance approximately equal to the sum of the variances of the delta and gamma terms plus the covariance between the delta and gamma terms. In this section we assume that the factor changes have mean zero, i.e., $\mathbf{f} \sim N_n(\mathbf{0},\boldsymbol{\Sigma})$. The variance of portfolio value is given by

$$\begin{aligned} \mathrm{Var}[\Delta V^{\Upsilon}] &= \mathrm{Var}\left[\delta'\Delta\mathbf{f} + \frac{1}{2}\Delta\mathbf{f}'\Gamma\Delta\mathbf{f}\right] \\ &= \mathrm{Var}[\delta'\Delta\mathbf{f}] + \frac{1}{4}\mathrm{Var}[\Delta\mathbf{f}'\Gamma\Delta\mathbf{f}] + \mathrm{Cov}\left[\delta'\Delta\mathbf{f}, \frac{1}{2}\Delta\mathbf{f}'\Gamma\Delta\mathbf{f}\right]. \end{aligned} \tag{4.5}$$

Now the covariance term in (4.5) equals zero from Stein's (1981) lemma,[8] thus the variance of portfolio value is comprised of two parts, a delta or linear term and a gamma or quadratic term. Consider the gamma term $\Delta\mathbf{f}'\Gamma\Delta\mathbf{f}$. We first orthogonalize the factors and define a new random vector $\Delta\mathbf{y}$:

$$\Delta\mathbf{y} = \boldsymbol{\Sigma}^{-1/2}\Delta\mathbf{f}, \tag{4.6}$$

where $\boldsymbol{\Sigma}^{-1/2}$ is a symmetric matrix satisfying $\boldsymbol{\Sigma}^{-1/2}\boldsymbol{\Sigma}^{-1/2} = \boldsymbol{\Sigma}^{-1}$.[9] By construction $\Delta\mathbf{y}$ is multivariate normal, with a covariance matrix equal to the identity matrix:

$$\Delta\mathbf{y} \sim N_n(0, \mathbf{I}_n). \tag{4.7}$$

The gamma term can thus be written

$$\frac{1}{2}\Delta\mathbf{f}'\Gamma\Delta\mathbf{f} = \frac{1}{2}\Delta\mathbf{y}'\boldsymbol{\Sigma}^{1/2}\Gamma\boldsymbol{\Sigma}^{1/2}\Delta\mathbf{y} = \frac{1}{2}\Delta\mathbf{y}'\mathbf{A}\Delta\mathbf{y} \tag{4.8}$$

where $\mathbf{A} = \boldsymbol{\Sigma}^{1/2}\Gamma\boldsymbol{\Sigma}^{1/2}$. Now decompose the square matrix A using a spectral decomposition:

$$\mathbf{A} = \mathbf{C\Lambda C'}, \tag{4.9}$$

where $\mathbf{\Lambda}$ is a diagonal matrix containing the eigenvalues $(\lambda_1, \ldots, \lambda_n)$ of $\mathbf{A}$ and $\mathbf{C}$ is an orthogonal matrix containing the eigenvectors of $\mathbf{A}$. We see that the gamma term is a linear combination of independent χ_1^2 variables:

$$\frac{1}{2}\Delta\mathbf{f}'\Gamma\Delta\mathbf{f} = \frac{1}{2}\Delta\mathbf{y}'\mathbf{C\Lambda C'}\Delta\mathbf{y} = \frac{1}{2}\mathbf{x}'\mathbf{\Lambda x} = \frac{1}{2}\sum_{i=1}^{n}\lambda_i x_i^2, \tag{4.10}$$

where

$$\mathbf{x} \sim N_n(0, \mathbf{I}_n). \tag{4.11}$$

Since the variance of x_i^2 is 2, the variance of the gamma term is simply given by half the sum of the squared eigenvalues of $\mathbf{A}$:

$$\text{Var}\left(\frac{1}{2}\Delta\mathbf{f}'\Gamma\Delta\mathbf{f}\right) = \left(\frac{1}{2}\right)^2 \sum_{i=1}^{n}\lambda_i^2 \times 2 \tag{4.12}$$

$$= \frac{1}{2}\sum_{i=1}^{n}\lambda_i^2. \tag{4.13}$$

As the square of a matrix has eigenvalues that are squares of the eigenvalues of the original matrix, and because the sum of eigenvalues equals the trace of the matrix, the above expression simplifies to,

$$\text{Var}\left(\frac{1}{2}\Delta\mathbf{f}'\Gamma\Delta\mathbf{f}\right) = \frac{1}{2}\text{tr}\mathbf{A}^2 = \frac{1}{2}\text{tr}\left[(\Sigma\Gamma)^2\right]. \tag{4.14}$$

We can now write total portfolio variance as

$$\text{Var}(\Delta V^\gamma) = \delta'\Sigma\delta + \frac{1}{2}\text{tr}\left[(\Sigma\Gamma)^2\right]. \tag{4.15}$$

Thus portfolio volatility can easily be calculated from the portfolio's aggregate deltas and gammas and from the covariance matrix of factor innovations.

4.2. Skewness and other moments

Of course portfolio volatility by itself is less informative when gamma is significant as the resultant distribution of portfolio value is not normal. Higher order moments such as skewness are helpful in this case for two reasons. First it is interesting to know how the presence of derivatives may impart skewness to a portfolio's distribution; second, higher-order moments can be used to construct approximations to the complete probability distribution.

The completion-of-the-square approach used in the univariate case can also be used in the multivariate case so long as the gamma matrix is nonsingular (i.e. when Γ^{-1} exists). The technique is as follows:

$$\Delta V^{\gamma} \equiv \mu_{\gamma} + \delta'\Delta\mathbf{f} + \frac{1}{2}\Delta\mathbf{f}'\Gamma\Delta\mathbf{f} = \mu_c + \frac{1}{2}(\Delta\mathbf{f} + \Gamma^{-1}\delta)'\Gamma(\Delta\mathbf{f} + \Gamma^{-1}\delta),$$

where $\mu_c = \mu_{\gamma} - \frac{1}{2}\delta'\Gamma^{-1}\delta$. Now $\boldsymbol{\Delta}\mathbf{f} + \Gamma^{-1}\boldsymbol{\delta}$ is normally distributed with a mean $\boldsymbol{\mu} + \Gamma^{-1}\boldsymbol{\delta}$ and covariance $\boldsymbol{\Sigma}$. Redefining $\mathbf{y}$ as

$$\mathbf{y} = \Sigma^{-1/2}(\Delta\mathbf{f} + \Gamma^{-1}\delta),$$

where $\mathbf{A}$, as before, is given by

$$\mathbf{A} = \Sigma^{1/2}\Gamma\Sigma^{1/2},$$

we can express the change in portfolio value as

$$\Delta V^{\gamma} = \mu_c + \frac{1}{2}\mathbf{y}'\mathbf{A}\mathbf{y},$$

where $\mathbf{y}$ is normally distributed:

$$\mathbf{y} \sim N(\mu_f + \Gamma^{-1}\delta, \mathbf{I}).$$

As before we can decompose the square matrix A using a spectral decomposition:

$$\mathbf{A} = \mathbf{C}\Lambda\mathbf{C}', \tag{4.16}$$

where $\boldsymbol{\Lambda}$ is a diagonal vector containing the eigenvalues $(\lambda_1, \ldots, \lambda_n)$ of $\mathbf{A}$, and $\mathbf{C}$ is an orthogonal matrix containing the eigenvectors of A. We can then express the change in portfolio value as a linear combination of independent χ_1^2 variables:

$$\Delta V^{\gamma} \approx \mu_c + \frac{1}{2}\Delta\mathbf{y}'\mathbf{C}\Lambda\mathbf{C}'\Delta\mathbf{y} = \mu_c + \frac{1}{2}\mathbf{z}'\Lambda\mathbf{z} = \mu_c + \frac{1}{2}\sum_{i=1}^{n}\lambda_i z_i^2, \tag{4.17}$$

where

$$\mathbf{z} \sim N_n(\mathbf{C}'(\mu + \Gamma^{-1}\delta), \mathbf{I}_n). \tag{4.18}$$

This representation expresses the change in portfolio value as the sum of a set of noncentral chi-square variables. Mathai and Provost (1991, pp. 53–54) derive the integer moments for this distribution. In our notation the rth moment of the change in portfolio value $E(\Delta V^{\Upsilon})^r$ is given by

$$E(\Delta V^{\Upsilon})^r = \left\{ \sum_{r_i=0}^{r-1} \binom{r-1}{r_i} m(r-1-r_i) \sum_{r_j=0}^{r_i-1} \binom{r_i-1}{r_j} m(r_i-1-r_j) \cdots \right\}$$

where the function m is defined by,

$$m(0) = \mu_{\Upsilon} + \delta' \mu_f + \frac{1}{2} \mu_f' \Gamma \mu_f + \frac{1}{2} \mathrm{tr} \Gamma \Sigma$$

$$m(1) = \frac{1}{2} \mathrm{tr}(\Gamma \Sigma)^2 + \delta' \Sigma \delta$$

$$m(2) = \mathrm{tr}(\Gamma \Sigma)^3 + 3\delta' \Sigma \Gamma \Sigma \delta$$

$$m(k) = \frac{k!}{2} \mathrm{tr}(\Gamma \Sigma)^{k+1} + \frac{(k+1)!}{2} \delta' (\Sigma \Gamma)^{k-1} \Sigma \delta, \; k \geq 1,$$

and an empty product is assumed to have a value of unity. From this we can calculate any desired integer moments of the distribution of portfolio value. Expressions for the first three moments are shown below.

$$E(\Delta V^{\Upsilon}) = m(0) = \mu_{\Upsilon} + \delta' \mu_f + \frac{1}{2} \mu_f' \Gamma \mu_f + \frac{1}{2} \mathrm{tr} \Gamma \Sigma \tag{4.19}$$

$$E(\Delta V^{\Upsilon})^2 = m(1) + m(0)^2 = E[\Delta V^{\Upsilon}]^2 + \frac{1}{2} \mathrm{tr}(\Gamma \Sigma)^2 + \delta' \Sigma \delta \tag{4.20}$$

$$\begin{aligned} E(\Delta V^{\Upsilon})^3 &= m(2) + 3m(1)m(0) + m(0)^3 \\ &= E[\Delta V^{\Upsilon}]^3 + \mathrm{tr}(\Gamma \Sigma)^3 + 3\delta' \Sigma \Gamma \Sigma \delta + 3\left(\frac{1}{2} \mathrm{tr}(\Gamma \Sigma)^2 + \delta' \Sigma \delta \right) E[\Delta V^{\Upsilon}]. \end{aligned} \tag{4.21}$$

Solomon and Stephens (1977)[10] have suggested that the random number given by $K_1 \omega_p^{K_2}$, where ω_p has a χ^2 distribution with p degrees of freedom, and K_1, and K_2 are constants, can provide a good approximation to the density of a sum of noncentral chi-square variates, such as $\Delta V^{\Upsilon} - \mu_c$, when K_1, K_2 and p are chosen to match the first three moments of $\Delta V^{\Upsilon} - \mu_c$.[11]

Now the moments ($r = 1, 2, \ldots$) of the χ^2 distribution about zero are given by

$$E\omega_p^r = \frac{2^r \Gamma(r + p/2)}{\Gamma(p/2)}, r = 1, 2, \ldots$$

where $\Gamma(.)$ is the gamma function. The moments about zero of $K_1\omega_p^{K_2}$, $\mu_1', \mu_2', \mu_3', \ldots$, are given by

$$\mu_s' = (K_1)^s 2^{sK_2} \frac{\Gamma(sK_2 + p/2)}{\Gamma(p/2)}, \; s = 1, 2, 3 \ldots. \tag{4.22}$$

Let

$$R_2 = \frac{\mu_2'}{(\mu_1')^2} = \frac{\Gamma(p/2)\Gamma(2K_2 + p/2)}{(\Gamma(K_2 + p/2))^2}, \tag{4.23}$$

and

$$R_3 = \frac{\mu_3'}{(\mu_1')^3} = \frac{(\Gamma(p/2))^2\Gamma(3K_2 + p/2)}{(\Gamma(K_2 + p/2))^3}. \tag{4.24}$$

Using (4.19), (4.20) and (4.21), equations 4.23 and 4.24 may be solved for K_2 and p. Finally, K_1 may be obtained using (4.19) and the expression for μ_1'. Once the parameter values are found the probability of losses of greater than a certain magnitude can be read from a Table of χ^2.

5. MULTIVARIATE EXAMPLES

In this section we present two examples of the application of the delta-gamma approximation in the multivariate case. In the first we consider a portfolio consisting of puts and calls on three uncorrelated stocks; Table 3 gives the prices and volatilities of the underlying stocks and the strike prices, maturities and quantities of the options. In this example the position has negative gamma in all three of the underlying stocks; Table 4 gives the aggregate deltas and gammas.

We now proceed according to Sections 4.1 and 4.2 and compute the eigenvalues and noncentrality parameters of the quadratic approximation given in equation 4.16.

Table 3. Asset and Option Characterisitics for Multivariate Example.

	Asset 1	Asset 2	Asset 3
Price	100	50	80
Volatility (% p.a.)	0.30	0.40	0.20
Call			
Strike	100	50	80
Maturity (years)	0.1	0.1	0.1
Quantity	−100	−100	−30
Put			
Strike	100	50	80
Maturity (years)	0.1	0.1	0.1
Quantity	−100	−30	−100

Table 4. Portfolio Deltas and Gammas for Multivariate Example.

	Asset 1	Asset 2	Asset 3
Delta	−12.15	−42.35	−25.22
Gamma	−8.313	−8.12	−10.07

Table 5. Asset and Option Characterisitics for Multivariate Example with convexity in one asset and concavity in the other.

	Asset 1	Asset 2
Price	100	100
Volatility (p.a.)	30%	30%
Correlation between returns	0.7	
Call		
Strike	101	101
Maturity (weeks)	6	6
Quantity	−1.0	−0.6
Put		
Strike	101	101
Maturity (weeks)	6	6
Quantity	+1.0	+0.5
Delta	−0.2391	+0.2866
Gamma	−0.0625	+0.0586

From this we compute the three eigenvalues and noncentrality parameters in equation 4.17 and then compute the first three moments from equation 4.19, 4.20 and 4.21. Finally, we solve for the parameters K_1, K_2, and p as described above. Using these values we compute the cumulative density function (cdf) of the Solomon-Stephens approximation.

The results are shown in Figure 8, which shows the cdf computed using full evaluation (Black-Scholes), the delta approximation, the *actual* delta-gamma approximation (via simulation) and the Solomon-Stephens approximation to the delta-gamma approximation. While we cannot claim any generality for the results—the example is just an example—they are encouraging. Although the delta-only approximation performs poorly—as it was bound to do in this example—both the actual delta-gamma approximation and the Solomon-Stephens approximation are very close to the true values.

In the second example we consider a position involving two underlying assets where the portfolio is convex in the price of one underlying and concave in the other. Table 5 summaries the position and the relation between the portfolio value and the prices of the two underlying stocks is shown in Figure 11. As the figure shows, the position is concave with respect to the price of asset 1 and convex in the price of asset 2. Nonetheless, this relation is well approximated by a function

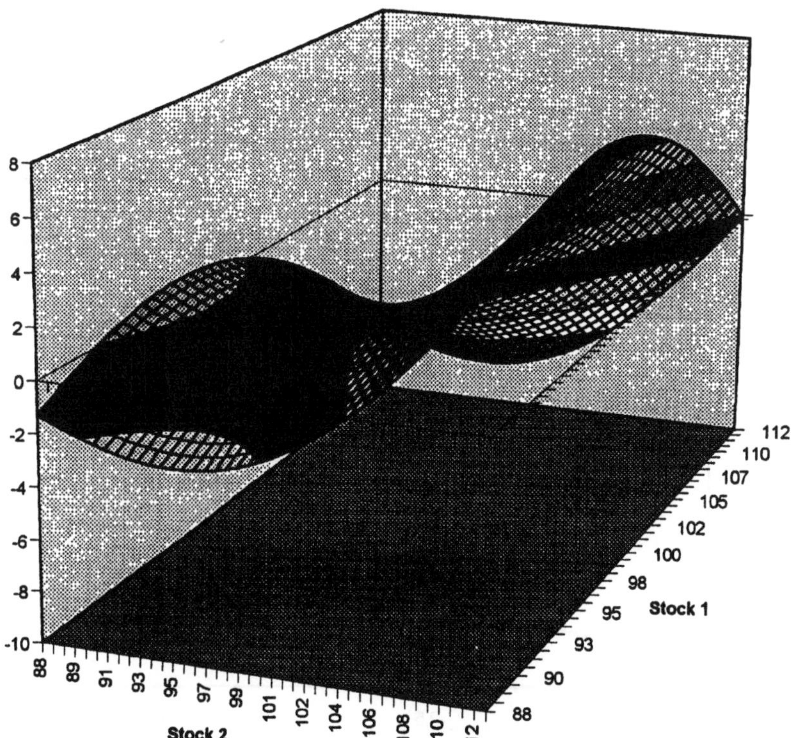

Figure 11. The relation between portfolio value and the prices of the two underlying assets for a portfolio containing options written on two assets whose value is convex with respect to one asset and concave with respect to the other.

which is quadratic in the two stock prices and, as a result, the distribution of a delta-gamma approximation to portfolio value is close to the distribution using full revaluation.

In this case, however, the Solomon-Stephens approach is not suitable since, as a result of the convexity with respect to one underlying and concavity with respect to the other, the eigenvalues of matrix A (see equation 4.10) have different signs. Thus the value of $\Delta V^{\Upsilon} - \mu_c$ in this case is unbounded both below and above. When all the eigenvalues are positive $\Delta V^{\Upsilon} - \mu_c$ is unbounded above and bounded below at zero just as the variate proposed by Solomon and Stephens. When the eigenvalues are not all of the same sign, therefore, the Solomon and Stephens approach is unlikely to perform well and, in the example under discussion here, we were unable to find admisable values of K_1, K_2, and p which matched the moments of $\Delta V^{\Upsilon} - \mu_c$.[12]

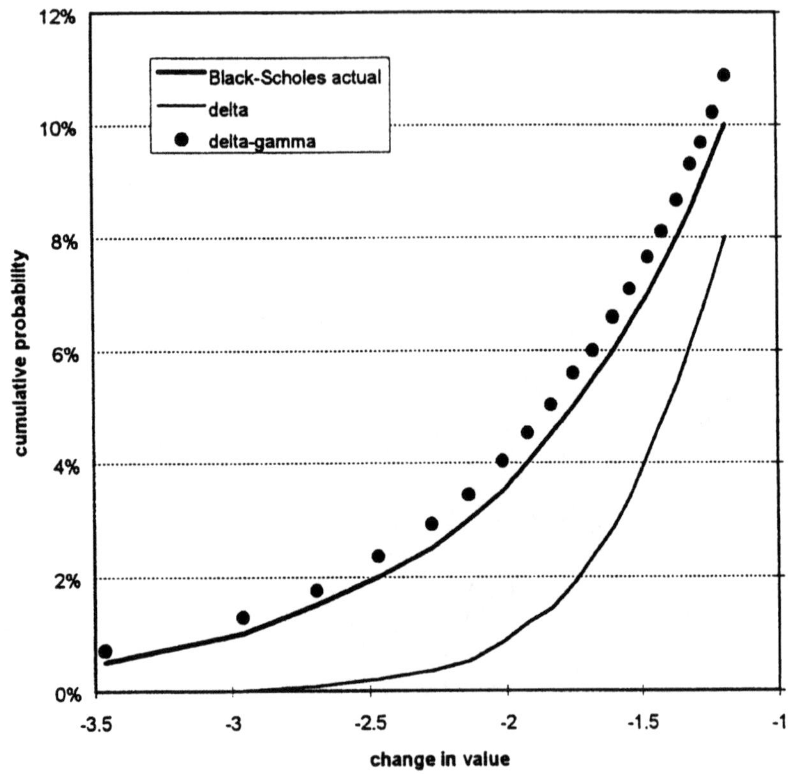

Figure 12. The figure shows the lower tail of the distribution of portfolio value under (i) full revaluation, (ii) delta approximation and (iii) delta-gamma approximation for the example in which the portfolio is concave in the value of one underlying and convex in the other.

6. CONCLUSION

Linear approximations to the relation between derivative values and the underlying price or rate are unlikely to be robust and risk assessment methods based on them will usually fare no better. In this paper we have proposed an approach to VaR which is based on a second-order delta-gamma approximation and recognises the impact that this will have, not only on variance, but on the form of the distribution.

For the case of portfolios of derivatives on a single underlying asset the paper derived the exact distribution of the delta-gamma approximation and, subject to some further mild assumptions, the relation between the delta-gamma and the delta-only VaR. For a given probability level. the latter depended on a single parameter, θ, which is a function of the portfolio delta and gamma and the volatility of the underlying instrument.

For the multivariate case the paper derived the moments of the delta-gamma approximation and showed that when the matrix of gammas and cross-gammas is invertible the delta-gamma approximation is distributed as the sum of independent noncentral chi-square variates. An approximation to this sum, due to Solomon and Stephens (1977) was described and an example of its application to a portfolio of put and call options presented.

ACKNOWLEDGMENT

This article was originally published in the *European Financial Review*, Volume 2, Issue 2 (1999) published by Kluwer Academic Publishers.

NOTES

1. We are grateful for comments and suggestions from participants at the 1997 EFA meetings in Vienna and at a conference, "Empirical Research in Finance," at the London School of Economics and also to Bill Farebrother, Steven Satchell, Caspar de Vries, and particularly, to Simon Benninga (the editor), Zvi Weiner (the referee), and Davide Menini.
2. All the analysis in this paper takes place over the interval t to $t + \Delta t$. We therefore dispense with a time subscript except where necessary.
3. The approximation is quadratic in the factors, but only linear in time, as we only include the first order effect of time. This is justifiable, since in most cases, the passage of time, by itself, does not result in large value changes.
4. See Basel Committee on Banking Supervision (1996).
5. In this section we suppress, for clarity, the subscript p denoting "portfolio."
6. The values of θ for the three portfolios analyzed earlier are, respectively, 3.42, 0.91 and 1.08.
7. See, e.g., Duffie and Pan (1997).
8. Stein's lemma states that the covariance between a normally distributed variable x, and a smooth function $f(y)$ of a normally distributed variable equals the covariance between x and y, multiplied by the expected value of the first derivative of the function

$$\text{cov}(x, f(y)) = E[f'(y)] \times \text{cov}(x, y).$$

9. The symmetric decomposition of a nonnegative definite matrix can be formed from its spectral decomposition. See Mardia, Kent, and Bibby (1994, p. 475) for details.
10. See Mathai and Provost (1992), pp. 172–173.
11. See also Johnson, Kotz, and Balakrishnan (1977), pp. 444–450.
12. In this case it is always possible to proceed by simulation. Alternatively, the expression $\Sigma_{i=1}^{n}\lambda_i x_i^2$ could be spilt into two. Without loss of generality, assume that the first m eigenvalues are positive and the remainder negative. We may therefore write $\Sigma_{i=1}^{n}\lambda_i x_i^2$ as the difference between two positively weighted sums of noncentral chi-squared variates:

$$\equiv \sum_{i=1}^{m} \lambda_i^{+} x_i^2 - \sum_{m+1}^{n} (-\lambda_i^{-}) x_i^2.$$

These two expressions may each be approximated using the Solomon-Stephens approach and the two distributions finally combined using Monte-Carlo.

REFERENCES

Basel Committee on Banking Supervision (1996). Amendment to the Capital Accord to Incorporate Market Risks, January.

Britten-Jones, Mark, and Stephen M. Schaefer (1995). "Practical Advances in Making Risk Assessment and Value-at-Risk Models Work," Presentation .. Ri$k'95 Conference, Paris, December.

Davis, R.B. (1980). "The Distribution of Linear Combination of Chi-Squared Variables," *Applied Statistics*, Vol. 29.

Duffie, Darrell, and Jan Pan (1997). "An Overview of Value at Risk," *The Journal of Derivatives*, Vol. 4, No. 3, Spring, 9–49.

Fallon, William (1996). "Calculating Value-at-Risk," Working Paper, Columbia University, January.

Farebrother, R.W. (1990). "The Distribution of a Quadratic Form in Normal Variables," *Applied Statistics*, Vol. 39, No. 2, 294–309.

Imhof, J.P. (1961). "Computing the Distribution of a Quadratic Form in Normal Variables," *Biometrika*, Vol. 48, 419–426.

Jahel, Lina El, William Perraudin, and Peter Sellin (1997). "Value at Risk for Derivatives," Working Paper, Birkbeck College, University of London, September.

Johnson, Norman L., Samuel Kotz, and N. Balakrishnan (1994). *Continuous Univariate Distributions*, Vol. 1. New York: Wiley.

Mathai, A.M., and Serge B. Provost (1992). *Quadratic Forms in Random Variables: Theory and Applications*. New York: Marcel Dekker.

Mardia, K.V., Kent J.T., and J.M. Bibby (1994). *Multivariate Analysis*. London, UK: Academic Press.

Rounvinez, Christophe (1997). "Going Greek with VaR," *Risk* 10(2) February. 57–65.

Solomon, H., and M.A. Stephens (1977). Distribution of a sum of weighted chi-square variables, *Journal of the American Statistical Association*, 72, 881–885.

Stein, Charles (••). "Estimation of the Mean of a Multivariate Normal Distribution," *The Annals of Statistics* 9(6), 1135–1151.

Wilson, Tom (1994). "Plugging the Gap," *Risk* October, 74–80.

APPENDIX

Capital-at-Risk vs. Value-at-Risk

One method of implementing the delta-gamma approach that avoids explicit calculation of the probability distribution of a quadratic form is the quadratic programming (QP) approach outlined by Wilson (1994) and Rouvinez (1997). The method is relatively simple and intuitively appealing. The starting point involves a redefinition of value at risk as *the maximum possible loss over a specific time horizon within a given confidence interval.* To the extent that this definition is meaningful, it means the level of loss, $\Delta V^{\star}(\alpha)$, such that the probability that $\Delta V \geq \Delta V^{\star}$ is equal to $1 - \alpha$. In other words, if α is 5% then the VaR under this approach is defined as the level of loss which 95% of the time will be worse than the actual outcome. The quadratic programming approach then seeks to *solve for the market event which maximizes potential losses subject to the constraint that the event and all events generating smaller losses are within a given confidence interval.*

The key step here is that we have gone from a confidence region defined over *portfolio value* changes (one-dimensional) to a confidence region defined over *factor realizations* which are (in general) multidimensional. A $1 - \alpha$ confidence region is a region within which realizations will fall $(1 - \alpha)$% of the time. In general, for any random variable or set of random variables, there is an infinite number of different confidence regions corresponding to any particular probability level $1 - \alpha$. To see this consider a random variable z distributed as a standard normal: $z \sim N(0, 1)$. A fifty percent confidence region is $(-0.68, +0.68)$; another is $(0, +\infty)$; still another is $(-\infty, 0)$. The reader can check that z has a 50% probability of falling into each of these regions.

The arbitrariness of confidence regions does not extend however to the calculation of VaR. The region in which all outcomes worse than a particular level fall with a particular probability is uniquely defined by the probability distribution and the chosen probability level α. For z the 5% VaR is simply −1.65, and this is unique since the region so defined has one end fixed implicitly at $+\infty$. The 95 percent confidence region corresponding to the VaR is $(-1.65, +\infty)$ and z has a 95 percent chance of falling into this region. Thus VaR has a natural way of uniquely determining the confidence region.

How can we determine a unique confidence region for a set of random variables? The method commonly employed is to focus on regions defined by *iso-density* lines. This is the approach used by Wilson. Viewing a density function as a hill, an iso-density line is a contour line at constant height. In the one dimensional case the iso-density region consists of two points at equal height, one on each side of the distribution. For the multiasset case the confidence region is defined by the region bounded by a multidimensional ellipse. Using the iso-density criterion for the previous univariate case of z results in a 50 percent confidence region defined by (−0.68, +0.68). The 95 percent confidence region is (−1.92, 1.92).

An inadequacy is now immediately apparent. The regions described by the VaR definition and the quadratic programming approach are different even in the simple one-dimensional case. The relevant confidence region (over a standard normal variable) for VaR was $(-1.65, +\infty)$. The QP approach uses the region (−1.92, 1.92). Consider the case where there is one factor determining portfolio value, and the change in portfolio value is simply equal to the change in this factor. Assume the factor is standard normal. The QP approach suggests that the 5 percent VaR is −1.92. The actual VaR at 5 percent is only −1.65.

In this case, it is fairly clear why the QP approach is not working—the tail areas are counted twice under QP but only on one side under VaR. This is easily fixed, but deeper problems remain.

Consider a more complex nonlinear case. To highlight the QP approach, we shall assume that the exact portfolio value is given by a quadratic function of a single factor z which is distributed standard normal. Assume the relation is as follows:

$$\Delta V = -10 + 25{,}000z^2.$$

The maximum loss of −10 occurs at $z = 0$ and, as this is within the 95 percent confidence region for z, the VaR(5%) under the QP approach is defined to be −10. However losses only occur for z in (−0.02, 0.02). The chance that any loss at all occurs is only 1.6 percent. So we can see that the true VaR at the 5 percent level must be a positive number.

The reason for the erroneous result, is that it simply is not possible to use a confidence region (defined over factors) to make inferences over a function of those factors. In fact, if it were possible to do so, much of the work in statistics involving distributions of functions of random variables would be unnecessary!

Simply because a point lies within a 95 percent confidence region does not mean that it has a 95 percent chance of occurrence. A point may lay within some 95 percent region, have a negligible chance of occurring and have a massive loss associated with it. The size of this loss does not give any indication of the true VaR. In short the QP approach is conceptually flawed and will give erroneous results under all but special situations where it will happen to coincide with the correct answer.

It is possible to say something more about the relation between the QP version of VaR and the VaR: the **true VaR is always greater than or equal to the QP VaR**, i.e., the true VaR will be a smaller loss, or a larger profit, than the QP VaR. Thus the QP VaR is conservative in that it predicts that a larger amount of capital is at risk.

To prove this statement, we need to set some notation. Define the true value at risk for a particular probability level α as $\Delta V^{\star}$ such that

$$\Pr(\Delta V < \Delta V^{\star}) = \alpha.$$

The QP version of value at risk is defined for a particular confidence region **C**. The confidence region **C** is defined in the space of factor realizations and must satisfy

$$\Pr(\mathbf{\Delta f} \in \mathbf{C}) = 1 - \alpha.$$

We noted before that confidence regions are not uniquely defined by the probability, but our results apply to **any** confidence region that satisfies the above criterion. The QP value at risk $Q^{\star}$ can now be defined simply as

$$Q^{\star} = \min_{\mathbf{\Delta f} \in \mathbf{C}} \Delta V(\mathbf{\Delta f}).$$

An immediate implication of the QP definition is that the probability of an outcome above (or equalling) $Q^{\star}$ must be at least as great as $1 - \alpha$:

$$\Pr(\Delta V \geq Q^{\star}) \geq 1 - \alpha.$$

This follows immediately since the set of all outcomes above (or equaling) $Q^{\star}$ includes **C**

$$\begin{aligned}\Pr(\Delta V \geq Q^{\star}) &= \Pr(\mathbf{\Delta f} \in \mathbf{C}) + \Pr(\text{those } \mathbf{\Delta f} \text{ outside of } \mathbf{C} \text{ and resulting in } V \text{ above } Q^{\star}) \\ &\geq 1 - \alpha.\end{aligned}$$

Thus the probability of an outcome *worse* than $Q^{\star}$ is lower than (at best equal to) α:

$$\Pr(\Delta V \leq Q^{\star}) \leq \alpha.$$

Since Pr $(\Delta V < \Delta V^\star) = \alpha$, it follows that $Q^\star \leq V^\star$ provides an overly conservative estimate of value at risk. The extent to which it is conservative requires evaluation of the actual probability distribution, and thus leads us back to the probabilistic approach, such as the approximations discussed above or full simulation.

IV. MARKET RISKS: THE 1996 BASEL ACCORD

7. A CRITIQUE OF THE BASEL REGULATIONS, OR HOW TO ENHANCE (IM) MORAL HAZARDS

GIORGIO SZEGO

1. PROLOGUE

In theory, banks, especially universal banks, are among the most useful manmade creations. In addition to their core operations, demand deposits and loans, they offer all kinds of financial services.

It is unfortunate that in the last decade the banking systems of many countries have been rocked by severe turbulence. More problems are looming in the background.

From 1991 to 1993, with a peak in 1992, the banks of all Nordic countries went practically bankrupt[1]. The total costs for the taxpayers ranged from 2 percent of GNP in Norway to 9 percent in Finland. In 1993–94 the floor fell under the largest local bank in France, Credit Lyonnais; the body count has not ended yet, but it may reach the 20 billion dollars, around 1.5 percent of GNP.

In 1994–95 to compete with its Latin neighbor, the seventh largest bank in Italy, the Bank of Naples, became technically insolvent. A special law had to be passed to keep it afloat. Its losses were considerable, about US$ 4 billion, but only sufficient to run for the bronze medal in the All Europe Bad-Bank Tournament.

In the 1980s the United States has witnessed the S&L crisis (estimated cost for the taxpayer, 160 billion dollars, 3 percent of GNP) and is currently living through a major consolidation drive within the banking industry initiated by the bad health of many banks[2]. Also in Japan, according to expert analysis, a major banking crisis is looming behind the scene[3].

Finally throughout the world, the return of banking shares is considerably smaller than that of other sectors[4]. This anomaly may imply both high bank inefficiency and high rent from control in banking.

We must ask ourselves what can be the causes of all these troubles. Scandinavian and Japanese banks have been destroyed by commercial real estate loan concentration. In the case of Credit Lyonnais and Banco di Napoli, both state-owned banks, while real estate losses were not negligible, the main cause seems to have been politically dictated credit allocation and forbearance policies. The underlying causes of the troubles may be different, but the triggering factors, forbearance and concentration, were always the same. Furthermore under all skies the crises had an identical consequence: zap the taxpayer. Believers in the solvency ratio creed will immediately say that these troubled banks obviously did not satisfy the prescribed capital requirements. I am sorry, but I have to disappoint these people.

For example in 1992, the average solvency ratio of Swedish banks was 9.3 percent and no bank was under the mythical 8 percent figure. The Bank of Naples in 1993, just before the troubles, presented a ratio of 9.98 percent. The shows that, even in the most benign analysis, solvency ratios do not have any effect in preventing banking crisis. We can say they are like using expensive umbrellas as parachutes. The events that I have described cast some doubts on

- the meaningfulness of prudential regulation
- the effectiveness of supervision
- the rationale of solvency ratio
- the survival of the costly and inefficient financial intermediaries, called banks

2. PRUDENTIAL SUPERVISION

One of the most interesting recent papers on bank regulation is a paper by Nichols devoted to the provisions contained in the innovative system recently adopted in New Zealand[5].

This paper begins by posing a very crucial preliminary question: Does the financial system, and in particular the banking sector, warrant a special regulation because it is not sufficiently protected by the Core of Law?

The main characteristic of the legal system is to try to control the behavior of people and organizations by means of the dissuasive power of ex-post punishment. The dream of prudential regulation is to prevent the occurrence of some unwanted events and to cut short the sequence of crime-punishment.

It is felt that in the case of financial intermediation, this traditional approach does not provide sufficient protection. For this reason financial markets, for example, derivatives markets, have installed self-controlling mechanisms in which no mishap, beside criminal acts, can create damage.

Going back to the relationship between the common law and prudential regulation, we reach the following conclusions:

- Prudential regulations are meaningful if the controlled subject behaves.
- Prudential regulation is fully dependent on respect of the core of law.

We can, therefore, define *prudential regulation* as "a set of rule of conduct aimed at minimizing public losses, when the controlled subject respects the core of law." Prudential regulation does not apply to the case in which the cashier runs away with the money in the till or in the case of creative accounting practices. It is also an illusion to rely on prudential regulation in the credit sector where it is almost impossible to distinguish between bad luck, incompetence, and fraudulent behavior and where the full discretion of the credit-forbearance decision makes theft very tempting.

The new regulatory system introduced in New Zealand[5] has greatly increased the personal responsibility of bank managers and board members. In view of the intrinsic difficulty to precisely identify these responsibilities and the possible danger of being wrongly penalized in case of an honest mistake, the only reasonable conduct for any manager would be to start filling his pockets. The New Zealand system has been tried about 150 years ago; it was called Suffolk system and it failed[6].

3. CONFLICT OF INTERESTS IN BANKING

The main cause of bank losses (say for more than 90 percent) lies in credit activity. The decisions connected with this specific activity cannot be objective but are discretionary. The decision to extend credit to somebody and then to monitor it is discretionary. Also discretionary is the decision of using forbearance to technically insolvent borrowers, choosing to downgrade a loan, and finally to start some recuperation procedure. In particular, my experience shows that bank managers have a monopoly on information and have the power to delay default by simply extending new credit to the borrower when his probability of insolvency increases. The procedure is identical to the case of sovereign debt in many developing countries, which went through a sequence of rescheduling and refinancing in the late 1980s and early 1990s. Clearly the credit-granting institutions that I have described, are just sitting on a pile of Ponzi's schemes that can be sustained only as long as deposits are growing. Notice that within a bank, the loan control is mostly performed by the same people who grant the loan in the first place. This introduces a strong bias in favor of forbearance. It is worthwhile to point out that there exists an almost complete identity between the forbearance decision problem and the management of a forward contract with a declining value. The dilemma between selling the contract and taking a loss or keeping it, hoping for a change of trend, is analogous to the decision that the bank must make to either renegotiate a loan, recall it, or provide a borrower with new financing.

Between the management of a forward contract and that of nontraded credit, there exists however an important difference: the value of the former can be continuously monitored, while the value of the latter, in spite of the important improvement in corporate distress prediction techniques, can still only be the object of an educated guess. In dealing with continuously traded assets, one can asses risk and, obviously without any guarantee of success, continuously modify the investment strategy. On the contrary, credits are intrinsically illiquid and the values of the parameters that influenced the original allocation change very slowly.

Financial market operators can continuously reverse their position, promptly correct a decision and implicitly discount the likelihood of a wrong choice. A loan officer cannot reverse his position; he is stuck with it and must live with it. If we cannot blame the dealers for increasing their positions in contracts of falling volume, hoping to recoup the losses, should we blame a forbearing loan officer? In most cases, the probability of reversal of economic situation of the borrower cannot be ruled out. I have never heard a loan officer admit a mistake: the cause of bad loans is always blamed on an unpredictable event. The defense of the original decision and covering-up its consequences is a very natural behavior. Indeed, particularly on large loans, the bank manager has a justifiable strong bias towards forbearance. The situation may improve with the growth of securitization and with the development of a secondary market for bank loans, following the example of the market for Third-World debt. The dematerialization of credit seems to be the only way to overcome the moral hazard that we have just described. Market risk control methods have reached a high degree of sophistication for tradable securities. Such operations have a minimum weight in the banking operation, but they might become more relevant in the future. This trend, and in particular securitization, is unfortunately not encouraged by the Basle rule that does not acknowledge any liquidity premium of a tradable security with respect to the underlying assets. To avoid this main cause of troubles, a regulation should be enacted to prevent banks from keeping in their portfolio the loans that they have granted. Banks should sell them to the market. This will introduce some market discipline, since the loan will have to be reevaluated by a different party.

We have argued that loan concentration is the other main cause of bank default. Concentration can take place in one borrower or in a group of connected borrowers and be caused by forbearance or by specialization in the same economic sector, for instance common real estate or Third World debt.

It can be shown that the lemming or herd behavior is the most rational decision that a bank manager can take. I have myself been a witness and an accomplice to this behavior. When a company asks for a large syndicated new loan or refinancing, the first and almost only question asked by bank managers is: Who else is in the group?

The rationale is that the bank cannot afford to be left out. In case of a borrower default, since by definition not all banks can be managed by fools, one can always lay the blame on an unpredictable change of fundamental economic conditions, or an act of God. Somebody, i.e., taxpayers, will then necessarily help. We must point out another difference between credit and security management. In the financial sector, there is no herd behavior but rather a strong tendency towards diversification. This main tenet of portfolio theory does not tun against managerial motivation but, in addition, fear of liquidity traps enhance the diversification strategy.

Notice that a credit decision is an asymmetrical operation between the lender and the borrower while any financial operation is completely symmetric: one can buy a security only if somebody else, with a different payoff, wants to sell[7].

If properly performed, any loan decision would be very costly and in most cases not justified by an expected return. This may be a reason for the perfunctory analysis actually performed and for the reliance on pro-facie real guaranties. In addition or alongside securitization, the moral hazard connected with credit operations could be curtailed by the introduction of mandatory use of internal credit worthiness and monitoring decision models. The introduction of these methods has so far been prevented by the bank managers who, quite rightly, see it as an attempt to curtail their absolute discretion over credit decisions on which their power lies. The use of models for the control of market risk was not resented for the reason that most top bank managers are not familiar with finance. The racist-motivated comments that this type of perverse behavior can take place only in state-owned southern banks can be easily repelled. One does not have to be a professor of geography to realize that Scandinavia is not located near Sicily and that most Nordic banks, before the crash, were privately owned.

4. THE INTERNAL CONTRADICTIONS OF SURVEILLANCE

We have previously pointed out that in the case of the most troubled institutions, the management was able to maintain a high solvency ratio until the sky fell. Only very seldom was the decision to see the cards taken by supervision agencies. On the other hand, these agencies had all possibilities of timely intervention. Loss of charter under regulatory-enforced closure is an attractive assumption in academic papers specialized in nowhere land, but it seems to be extinct, if it even existed! What went wrong? In addition to discretionality of credit, there is also a strong discretionality in bank supervision. Examination schedules, credit worthiness analysis, and acceptable degrees of forbearance are all decided on a purely discretionary basis. Even if such procedures were objective, it would be difficult to exactly assess credit risk without a complete, careful analysis of the economic situation of each borrower. Such analysis would be time-consuming and costly, since the supervision authority cannot rule out the possibility that the financial reports or budget presented by the borrower could be, let us say, imprecise. A proper credit supervision would therefore imply a complete duplication of the analysis made, or that should have been made, by the bank, albeit, in a completely objective form (i.e., according to some very specific criteria, which of course should be the same in all cases). The bank found guilty will be punished, according to the crime-punishment sequence, which we have rejected as inadequate in the financial sector.

Let us now assume that a certain supervision authority wants to set up a Structured Early Intervention and Resolution (SEIR) program in order to introduce a truly effective prudential regulatory system. In view of delaying loan downgrading, so well-known to banks, this procedure can perform a successful early intervention only if the examinations are frequent and thorough, the more frequent and thorough the better. Now either the banks will follow exactly the same rules adopted by the supervision authorities, or they will be forced to do so. In both cases the outcome will be the same: the whole system will behave as one bank, call it Gosbank, of Soviet memory, if you want. I do not recall that this system was very efficient!

5. REGULATORY CAPITAL REQUIREMENTS

A few days ago I had an interesting informal conversation with some top bank regulators. One of them told me, "The risk-adjusted Basel 8 percent rule may not be optimal, but its implementation had the positive effect of increasing the average bank capital." So what?

The only way of assessing the possible success of the Basel rule would be to show a decline in the number of bank defaults since its introduction. This has not been the case. On the contrary, it is a reasonable hypothesis that the introduction of a solvency ratio has been in itself a cause of bank defaults. I anticipate the objection of the Basel Fan Club members to this statement; they will argue that this is exactly what they wanted: to kick out the beggars. In my opinion this answer has the same rationality as proposing to enforce the closure of all banks in which the chairman of the board is unable to jump over 2 meters and 48 centimeters. I would like to propose the following thesis:

- The Basle solvency ratio is not risk-adjusted, but, at best, liquidity-adjusted.
- The solvency ratio completely ignores the main cause of bank failures: loan concentration.
- The urge to satisfy the ratio induces a high-risk (and high expected return) lending policy, since all credits have the same weight[8].
- Even if a bank has good reasons to collect new capital, by doing so it gives a bad signal to the market. Indeed the market will interpret this move, not as dictated by sensible industrial motivations but as imposed by the need to presatisfy the requirements in view of some forthcoming losses.
- The need to collect new capital in order to meet the requirements induces banks to expand their activities regardless of the related expected return. In this way banks masquerade their crucial capital needs of new capital as the outcome of a long-term growth plan. This is what happened with the Credit Lyonnais and the Bank of Naples.
- At the time of the original implementation of the capital accord, in order to squeeze the highest possible book value of their nontraded assets, notably real-estate investments, many banks bent all reasonable evaluation techniques. This fact made it impossible for them, when the need came, to sell these assets without showing large losses.

In view of these problems why did the twelve wise men from Basel[9] introduce this rule? In an interview given in 1996[10], Mr. Peter Cooke, the historical chairman of the Basel committee, stated, "Capital was a singularly convenient and useful element of banking business for regulators to seize upon and legislate over." Most views are not so benign. The capital rule has been interpreted not as economically motivated but as a weapon of the market share war[11].

6. SOME POSSIBLE FUTURE SCENARIOS

Before discussing some possible future scenarios, I would like to wrap up some conclusions from the previous analysis.

1. Credit activity is now poisoned by two intrinsic sources of damage: concentration and forbearance. Both are rational choices for the bank managers.
2. Bank supervision, even if performed in the most timely and objective way cannot eradicate these distortions without incurring very high costs and additional systemic risk.
3. The current system, based upon the defense of old banking practices and privileges is costing the taxpayers huge sums, and there is no hope for future improvements.
4. While it could be wise to impose internal risk control models on credits, similarly to what has been done for securities, it is not realistic to hope for a repeal of the Basel 8 percent requirement[12]. This rule has unfortunately been enshrined into law by the European Union[13] and imposed on all member countries. It has also been adopted in the regulatory framework of the United States via the FDICIA[14].
5. The problems connected with the implementation of the 8 percent rule will, however, fade away. It will be just still another useless rule imposed on the credit system in need of effective regulation. Market (securities) risk has been well taken care of by allowing each financial institution to adopt a reasonable own recipe (internal model). This procedure not only is able to impose risk-control discipline, it also allows a diversification of behavior across financial intermediaries that could streamline systemic danger. Up to now market risk accounts however only for a very small percentage of total bank risk.
6. In spite of the monopoly of the payment system held by banks, the public is voting with its feet by shifting funds away from banks into mutual funds. For instance, U.S. banks' share of total assets has been declining from 40 percent to about 20 percent between 1973 and today. Since banks are financially supported by public funds via deposit insurance as well as other safety nets, by moving out of the banking system, the public is essentially giving up a state gift. This implies that banks are so inefficient that mutual funds investments are perceived to be more advantageous than publicly supported bank accounts. This flow of funds away from banks is obviously making the Ponzi's schemes described in Sec. 3 less and less sustainable.

Through the bank monopoly of the payment system, the taxpayer is forced to support an inefficient and obsolete bank-centered financial intermediation system. I shall next propose three alternative scenarios:

- Fully deregulate the payment by dismantling the bank monopoly, eliminate all public support of deposit guaranties, either extend the central banks support of the payment system to all participants or abolish it.
- Leave things as they are.
- Re-regulate the system in order to force the structure that would be reached through full deregulation and antitrust intervention.

In the first scenario, that of deregulation, we can anticipate that MMMF, credit card companies, and new electronic money providers will become the major players of the system. Some banks will decide to retain their position in the payment system, to become narrow banks[15] and to phase out their credit operations. Both banks as well as the MMMF can easily provide, at a cost, a floor on the level of the customers accounts. The current technological developments, e-cash, chip cards, and the electronic commerce of financial services via the Internet or some alternative or complementary proprietary nets, will be the likely Trojan horse of the current system. This will happen if they will not be regulated out of the market, according to the best tradition[16]. Right now in the United States, a major credit card company is offering an innovative securities trading system via the Internet[17]. The securities and cash accounts owned by the clients feed a credit card. This is the only example I know of a payment system completely disconnected from the banking system, but unfortunately limited to the payments that can be charged on the credit card.

The second scenario assumes infinitely tolerant taxpayers and very strong lobbying from the banks. Under this scenario not much will change. Technically insolvent banks, either too large or too rotten to fail, are resurrected by an infusion of public money and will soon go back to their old ways[18]. An insolvent bank is like a plant almost killed by parasites, just before its death the parasites abandon it, ready to come back when the plant is healed!

A very likely possibility is that internal models for credit control will indeed be imposed. Their implementation depends, however, on the possibility of setting up an efficient supervisory system. The use of credit risk control methods does not eliminate the moral hazards that we have pointed out[19]. The last option is to force by law the implementation of the financial intermediation system, which would be naturally adopted in a deregulated environment. If government decides to stop shoring up the uncontrollable, obsolete, and costly banking system, it should adopt a multitier system[20]. This would allow only Tier one intermediaries with no risk beside technical errors and criminal behavior (i.e., institutions not granting loans— (like MMMF, debit cards companies, e-cash or narrow banks) to become members of the payment system. They would offer only money markets and not demand deposit accounts. Complete or partial floors on the account level could be separately offered to the clients. Thus a zero-risk demand deposit account will be synthesized. No statutory reserve will have to be imposed[21]. In this system, credit will be granted by specialized Tier two institutions, which will be financed only via non preredeemable time deposits, bonds, or equities. To break through the conflict of interests that causes the perverse forbearance and concentration bias, loans will have to be accompanied by a separate rating of the credit worthiness of the potential borrowers. The rating will have to consider not only the risk associated with the single client but also with its business sector and geographic location. Supervision will be centered on very objective facts, in particular on the separation between the two tiers of financial institutions, in view of possible common ownership. The reregulation of financial intermediaries should lead to the same system, which would be autonomously enacted if all state interventions were abolished. Following the argument presented in some previous works[22], I would like to show next that vice-versa in this system there exist such effective internal balances that no government intervention would be needed; it is a self-controlling system[23]. We must first of all recall the pretext for public intervention in financial markets are essentially two: depositors' protection and control of systemic risk. The former is achieved via deposit insurance, the latter by controlling the payment system. The existence of such public safety net is then adopted as a justification for government controls. The monopoly of the payment system to Tier one institutions and, as an additional safety measure, the adoption of gross settlement procedures fully protected depositors and rules out the most scary systemic scenario: the breakdown of the payment system[24]. What about the Tier two credit institutions? Can we leave them to their tricks? Are we sure that, even if completely separated from the payment system, some too-big-to-fail Tier twos will not unload horrendous bills on the taxpayers? For those reasons we have proposed the introduction of cross-checks performed by parties characterized by conflicting interests. The procedures, adopted by the securities primary markets, could be extended to loans. In the former an underwriter or a syndicate of underwriters issues securities in the markets on behalf of a client. There is no conflict between client and underwriter. The securities are then placed in the market and no collusion is possible between an underwriter and the potential buyers; the investors independently reassess the value of the securities. The key element, which must be borrowed by Tier two credit institutions from the primary market, is the underwriter. This intermediary has essentially the function of rating the securities. In a similar way, loans will have to be rated either by specialized institutions or by Tier two intermediaries, which will be, however, financially penalized if they keep their loans in their portfolios. They will have to either resell them to other (unrelated) credit institutions or securitize them. In this case a complete separation between credit-granting and monitoring can be achieved. The forbearance bias is reduced but not eliminated since the ones responsible for the purchase of the loan may be inclined to defend their decisions. This bias will however decline with the increase in the frequency of loan trades: the potential losses are smaller the more frequently the loans are traded. Forbearance could be completely eliminated if an institution owning a credit at any given time could be prevented from extending new finance to the same borrower.

Technological innovation could considerably simplify the management of such credit system. All loans will be dematerialized, stored, or assessed by a centralized system, which can serve as continuous monitor of the ownership of the loans as well as the financial state of each borrower. If and how this data will be accessible to the rating companies will depend of the legislation in each country[25].

7. CONCLUSIONS

One of the probable reasons for the shift of funds from banks into mutual funds is that investors have come of age and want to be masters of their destiny. Indeed, mutual funds, if properly supervised, must do what they pledged to do in their prospectus both in terms of fund allocation as well as of benchmarking. It is against antitrust principles that households and companies be obliged to transfer a certain portion of their wealth into the hands of fully discretionary and inefficient intermediaries with very tainted records: the banks. Banks do not make any commitments about how to invest customers' money, but they need public support to survive. Exactly for this reason, mutual funds and credit cards issuing institutions have so far not been pressured to become members of the payment system[26], but have used (small and captive) banks to handle their clients money flows: Why should they give up to a free state gift?

Having discounted the persistence of the Basle rule, would it be possible to abolish its most distorting element: the cost of capital and make banks fiscally neutral between equity and debt financing[27]. The role of capital in financial institutions is quite different than for other firms. The authorities should become aware of this point and, following the logic of public dole, introduce a fiscal level playing field. It is inconceivable that in the third millennium, taxpayer money should be spent to keep afloat these relics from the past, the traditional banks, when other financial intermediaries, at no cost to the public could easily perform their tasks.

ACKNOWLEDGMENTS

This paper is the offspring of a research started in 1992, while at the Research Department of the International Monetary Fund in Washington and devoted to the cost and benefits of the Basle capital requirements in view of their possible adoption on former centrally planned economies. The results of this research were presented at a seminar at Harvard University in May 1993. The study leading to this paper considerably benefitted from my appointment in May 1995 to a unique observation point, the Board of Directors of the Bank of Naples. This experience reinforced the conclusions I reached at IMF: that the banking system does need pills but a scalpel. I wish to thank for their comments, without making them in any way responsible for my conclusions, Dr. Allen Berger of the Board of Governors of the

Federal Reserve System, Prof. Richard Herring of the Wharton School, Prof. Merton Miller of the University of Chicago, Prof. Robert Merton of Harvard University. I also wish to thank Prof. George Kaufman of Loyola University for his helpful dissenting views: it is never too late to change opinions!

NOTES

1. See, for instance, Berg.
2. Since 1994, consolidation has lost the characteristic of the salvation of troubled banks, but it has been more along the lines of typical M&A.
3. See a recent report by J.P. Morgan, 1997.
4. This result has been obtained for U.S. data by Saunders and Yourougou and confirmed for all major markets. This trend has reversed itself in UK since 1994 and in the USA since 1996. See, NcCauley and White, 1997, Table 3. Note that the data given are not risk-adjusted.
5. See the papers by Nichols and by Ledingham, 1995.
6. A short description of the Suffolk system can be found in Lamoureax, 1994.
7. The existence of different positions is a guaranty also in case of panics and speculative bubbles.
8. See, for instance, Szego, 1996.
9. The group of ten plus Switzerland and Luxembourg.
10. See Shah, 1996.
11. This is one of the basic contributions of George Stigler. *The Citizen and the State. Essays on Regulation*," Chicago Un. Press, Chicago, 1975.

Additional dissenting views on the Basle rule, notably by Merton Miller and A. Berger, R. Herring and G. Szego can be found in N. 3–4, Vol. 19 (June 1995) of the *Journal of Banking and Finance*, which is devoted to "The Role of Capital in Financial Institutions".

12. While in its first accord on market risk the Basle Committee suggested precise risk control mechanisms, which have been incorporated into the EU CAD directive 93/6, very wisely the same committee has amended the accord allowing the use of internal models, albeit approved by the local supervision authorities. Is there any hope for a similar correction for the 8 percent rule? I have been privately informed that there has been a serious attempt to include a repeal of risk-adjusted capital requirements in the 1992 electoral platform of the Democratic Party. This attempt was unfortunately not successful.
13. Through the Directive 89/646 and 89/647.
14. The Federal Deposit Insurance Corporation Improvement Act, Public Law 102–104, Dec. 19, 1991, introduced a grid of risk-adjusted capital ratios. The bill contemplated the mandatory closure of severely undercapitalized banks. At the end of 1993 when the senate banking committee was supposed to act on this matter, almost all such banks had some way or another recovered. See Garcia, 1995.
15. The concept of narrow bank was introduced by R. Litan.
16. The important impact of technological innovation on financial intermediation has been the subject of the 33rd (May 1997) Annual Conference on Bank Structure and Competition of the Federal Reserve Bank of Chicago. Regarding the problem of competitive regulation, we refer again to G. Stigler's views. See note 10.
17. We refer to the Financial Direct service, introduced by American Express.
18. See Kumar and Morgan, 1993.
19. The first formalized model is the so-called Credit Metrics proposed by J.P. Morgan in cooperation with other important banks.
20. The multitier is fully described in Szego, 1994.
21. While it would be a wise business practice for Tier one intermediaries to maintain a certain liquid percentage of their assets, of course within limits stated in their prospectus, no statutory reserve requirements will be needed. This will avoid the next dubious practice of sweeping demand deposits in order to reduce reserve levels. See Fed. Res. Bank of New York, April 1997.
22. See, for instance, Szego, 1996.

23. The regulatory systems introduced in 1933–34 in the USA, while very intrusive, were internally coherent (deposit insurance counterweighted by interest rate limits). We cannot say the same thing about the current capital based regulations.
24. See, for instance, Angelini, Maresca, and Russo, 1993, for an assessment of the systemic risk in a payment system.
25. In Italy all the major loans are accounted for at the Centrale dei Rischi of the Bank of Italy, the budgets of all Plcs are stored by the Centrale dei Bilanci, which has also produced a very advanced bankruptcy prediction models. All the data and the models to minimize credit risk are therefore available to the banks, which deliberately refuse to use them.
The bank managers do not want to reduce even minimally their dictatorial power on credit allocation.
26. Indeed the famous NOW have practically been abandoned and mutual funds use captive banks to allow their clients to withdraw and transfer funds. The same applies to one of the main credit cards issuers in the USA: AT&T!
27. If financing via equity would be just as costly as via debt, the signalling effect associated with equity would disappear.

REFERENCES

Angelini, Paolo, G. Maresca, and D. Russo (1993). "An Assessment of the Systemic Risk in the Italian Clearing System," *Temi dei Discussione* N. 207, Banca d'Italia, Rome, July.

Berg, S.A. (1993). "The Banking Crisis in the Scandinavian Countries," Proc. XXIX Annual Conference on Bank Structure and Competition, Fed Res. Bank of Chicago, Chicago, 441–5.

Berger, Allen, Richard Herring, and Giorgio Szego (1995). "The Role of Capital in Financial Institutions," *Journal of Banking and Finance*, N. 3–4, Vol. 19 (June), 393–430.

Federal Reserve Bank of Chicago (1997). "Technology, Policy Implications for the Future of Financial Services," 33rd Annual Conference on Bank Structure and Competition, Chicago, May.

Federal Reserve Bank of New York (1997). "Falling Reserve Balances and the Federal Funds Rate," *Current Issues in Economics and Finance*, N. 5, Vol. 3, New York, April.

Garcia, Lillian (1995). "Implementing FDICIA's Mandatory Closure Rule," *Journal of Banking and Finance*, N. 3–4, Vol. 19 (June), 723–726.

Ledingham, Peter (1995). "The Review of Bank Supervision Arrangements in New Zealand: The Main Elements of the Debate," Paper presented at the OECD Committee on Financial Markets, Paris June 20–21.

Journal of Banking and Finance, Special Issue (1995). Edited by A. Berger, R. Herring, and G.P. Szego, "The Role of Capital in Financial Institutions," N. 3–4, Vol. 19 (June).

Kumar, R., and G.E. Morgan (1993). "A Moral Hazard Rationale for Early Closure in FDICIA," Proc. XXIX Annual Conference on Bank Structure and Competition, Fed Res. Bank of Chicago, Chicago, 421–31.

Lamoureax, N.R. (1997). *Insider Lending*. Cambridge Univ. Press, Cambridge.

Morgan, J.P., (1997). "The End Game Has Started for Japan's banks," *Asian Financial Markets*, Tokyo, April.

Morgan J.P. (1997). *Credit Metrics*. New York, April 2.

McCauley, Robert, and William White (1997). "The EURO and European Financial Markets," Presented at the Conference on EMU and the International Monetary System, IMF, Washington, March.

Saunders, Anthony, and Pierre Yourougou (1990). "Are Banks Special?" *J. Eco. Bus.*, Vol. 42 171–182.

Shah, Atul (1996). "Why Capital Adequacy Regulation for Banks," Mimeo, Dept. Acc. and Fin. Mgt., Univ. Essex, April.

Szego, G. (1992). "Pseudo Risk-adjusted Capital Requirements: Many Thorns and Little Flowers," Mimeo, Harvard Bus. School, May.

Szego, G. (1994). "Financial regulation and multi-tier financial intermediation system," Proc. Euro Working Group in Financial Modeling, *Physica Verlag*, Heidelberg.

Szego, G. (1996). "Il Frankenstein di Basilea," *Rivista di Politica Economica*, Apr. 122–140.

8. THE IMPLEMENTATION IN THE UK OF THE BASEL ACCORD REGARDING MARKET RISK

CLIFFORD SMOUT

I am delighted to be here today to give you a personal perspective on some of the issues that are likely to arise in implementing the Basel market risk package over the coming months and years. In some ways this project is like a forward contract: although the time for implementation has not yet arrived, we can nevertheless use current information from the market to estimate with some confidence the most likely outcome in the future. Before I start on the details however, I'll make some preliminary remarks.

First, I shall assume that capital requirements have a role to play in banking supervision, not least to limit the extent to which banks might otherwise take advantage of what is sometimes called the "safety net": the implicit subsidy offered by deposit protection or bail-out arrangements, arrangements that have grown up in response to the externalities involved in banking. These externalities are necessary, although not sufficient, to any case for official intervention, although they certainly do not provide a rationale for any particular set of requirements, which may impose costs on the economic system greater than the benefits they bring.

Second, I do *not* propose to dwell at any length on the position that those of us in the European Union face, where we already have a Directive in place that sets capital requirements on market risk, but that does not allow for some of the techniques contained in the Basel market risk package. This means that there is a real risk that amendments to allow the full-scale use of value-at-risk models may not be finalized in Europe until after the implementation date of the Basel market risk package: a matter of deep interest and some concern to banking supervisors within

Europe but not, I think, an issue that any of you in this audience need find particularly captivating.

So, what are the main features of the Basel market risk package?

First, as others have explained already, while the world may have been created in six days, the market risk package has taken rather longer! Some of these delays have reflected the technical nature of these issues, as well as an attempt by banking and securities regulators to agree on common standards, discussions that paved the way for agreement within Europe on the Capital Adequacy Directive, or CAD, but that did not lead to wider agreement outside the EU. But it also reflected a lengthy consultation process with the industry, at the end of which Basel produced not only a standardized measurement framework for market risk, revised slightly so as to incorporate options and commodities risks, but also an approach under which capital changes were based on internal value-at-risk models, subject to a number of qualitative and quantitative tests. Even in the medium-term many of the smaller banks in the UK are likely to use the standardized approach, but we expect the larger firms with diversified portfolios to opt for the value-at-risk approach (not least because tests suggest that on average this may result in a 30 percent reduction in these capital requirements). The rest of my talk will therefore focus on the models approach, which in many ways marks a real innovation in supervisory techniques, and the implementation issues that it raises.

As you will have heard already, value at risk is an estimate of the likely maximum loss on a given portfolio over a specified period with a certain level of statistical confidence. In other words, rather than speaking about a bank being $100 mn long Deutschemarks, value at risk looks at the possible loss on that position over (say) the next 24 hours, which would not be exceeded (say) 95 times in 100. By so doing, risks can be expressed in a common numeraire—so that the risk on the DM position can be compared meaningfully with the risk on $30 mn of five-year Treasury bonds. Moreover, if coupled with appropriate correlation assumptions, to pick up the effects of diversification and of hedging, the figures can be aggregated meaningfully.

The key features of this approach are that

- the firm has an effective internal risk model, which it uses to calibrate and manage risk
- key inputs to this model (such as position and price data) are accurate
- estimates of volatility (needed to translate nominal positions to amounts "at risk") are well based
- correlation estimates are robust

Underlying this are two key assumptions: the past is the best available guide to the future, and the model contains an essentially *subjective* judgment (perhaps dressed up in the guise of a confidence interval or multiplicative factor) on the appropriate protection against loss.

Within this generic description a wide variety of models exists. Some rely on a variance/covariance approach under which a normal distribution is assumed, and confidence levels are derived as a multiple of the standard deviation of the variable. Others use historic simulation, in which the given confidence interval is observed directly from the observations in the particular period chosen. Similarly the degree of sophistication in the treatment of correlation differs markedly between models, some using a variety of simplifying assumptions, while others use a more precise but computationally complex calculation. And I could—but won't—talk for several days about the wide variety of approaches used to model the risk on options books, approaches that require dexterity not just in English or Hebrew but also most of the Greek alphabet.

In some ways this variety can make the value-at-risk approach more powerful as a supervisory tool, since it goes more with the grain of what the firms themselves have decided is the most efficient way of analysing the risks in their particular business. Nevertheless, the Basel Committee felt it right to set a number of quantitative and qualitative parameters; the key ones are highlighted in the Annex. Note in particular that the choice of a scalar of 3 is no more subjective than the choice of a confidence interval of 99 percent (although the latter somehow sounds more respectable); what it says is that supervisors want to be confident that a firm does not lose more than one-third of the capital it allocates to market risk more often than one fortnight in 100 (i.e., once every four years). Note also that a feedback loop has been incorporated into the arrangements; a model that does not track reality well will be subject to a higher scalar than one that does. This provides a powerful mechanism to encourage firms to improve the accuracy of their models, while still having in place the safeguard implied by the minimum standards: such a safeguard is judged necessary since reliance *only* on backtesting would mean a bank that put far too little capital aside might be discovered as having insufficient capital via backtesting only after losses had exceeded the capital concerned.

Nevertheless, it is in many ways the qualitative parameters set out in the Annex that are the key to the success of the market risk package. Many of these are inevitably subjective, but that does not make them any the less important.

First let us remind ourselves of four key pitfalls in risk management:

- It is cheaper to talk about a model than to make one work.
- Some risks cannot be quantified; there is more to risk management than capital calculations.
- No solution is 100 percent reliable; a well-run bank will use a variety of techniques to manage any set of risks.
- While risk management principles are generally agreed, there is no model that suits every bank.

Let me briefly expand on each.

Risk management is all about actions rather than words. While in many banks there has been significant progress in recent years in getting the basics in place, there is a general acceptance that it has not been easy to get even this far. For instance, it is vital for banks to use consistent and accurate data, but to collect these can be an immensely time-consuming task, whether or not they are then used to calculate capital requirements in a model-based system. More generally, creating high-quality risk management is not something that can be done on the cheap; it requires significant resources in both IT and human terms.

Second, risk management is about far more than market risk, credit risk, or indeed any other risk that is potentially susceptible to mathematical analysis. Operational and reputational issues can wipe out a firm and must never be ignored, even by those at the forefront of risk management technology. Risk management is the key to control in any organization, especially one in which values or volumes fluctuate sharply. And it is about something much more fundamental than internal capital allocation or regulatory capital requirements. Exactly why market incentives do not always deliver effective risk management is an interesting conundrum for the academics, and one of the central issues we face as regulators is to consider whether we can sharpen these already powerful incentives to ensure that management invest in the people and resources needed to run a global firm effectively.

Since no formula or approach to risk management is fail safe, banks must use a variety of techniques to control risk. Moreover, risk management must be a continuous process—testing assumptions both against the past (e.g., via backtesting, investigation of control problems) and also against possibilities in the future (dynamic stress testing and proactive internal audit), and adjusting procedures accordingly. And since no one model fits all businesses in one firm, neither will it be appropriate to every individual bank. This has significant implications: appropriate supervision will not in the future mean applying identical rules to all, but rather creating a framework in which decisions stem from a common set of broad principles.

In considering the implementation of value at risk, the easiest place for me to start is by analyzing the experience of our Traded Markets Team over the last two years, in reviewing those models already allowed under the CAD, some of which are similar to value at risk (for instance, foreign exchange) and others which are—in the jargon—more of a preprocessing nature (e.g., interest rate sensitivities on derivative books, or options). This work forms a test bed that is not available to many other countries that have yet to grapple with implementing a market risk package, and reinforces us in our view that it is the *use* of the model that is as important as the mathematics. Put more bluntly, qualitative factors matter in any model, be it called VAR or something else.

The starting point for any model has to be the data. For a VAR model this means *consistent* data; as we have seen, the value-at-risk approach converts everything into a single numeraire. This is easier said than done. First, the data has to arrive all in one place. Second, it has to be timely (a real challenge in a major global house); at present we expect risk and profit-and-loss information to be available to those who need it by noon on the following day, but all of us would like to do better than this. Third, the myriad of systems that use different measures of risk have to be made consistent with one another. For instance, the interest rate risk on a derivatives book may be measured by using the present value of a basis point, on the bond desk by futures equivalent and on the forward FX desk by gap analysis. Different traders are used to different measures and so either need to be reeducated or understand what risk management is doing if they convert these concepts into a uniform format and set limits accordingly.

The next issue is independence, particularly independence of the risk management function that should have a reporting line outside the Treasury operation, but should not be so independent it becomes detached from reality on the trading floor. Similar issues can relate to the compliance function and to internal audit, although here at least the issues are better known.

The fourth issue is one that the techies like to refer to as granularity. How do you group together the data you receive for interest rate risk: day by day, month by month, year by year? The so-called standardized approach in the CAD makes similar assumptions: *why* should a maturity band be from 1–3 months? These assumptions will become even more important in a VAR framework, where there will be a choice between estimating correlations on an empirical basis, and imposing these by lumping together the observations into a single time bucket. Indeed, there is a whole section on this subject, (called—rather unenticingly—"Specification of Market Risk Factors") in the Basel market risk document.

Fifth, is stress testing properly proactive? Or does it merely replicate past disasters rather than thinking of those in the future? How far is credit risk incorporated into such scenarios; and are the effects of shocks limited to the size of exposures, or do they include the impact on the *creditworthiness* of counterparties themselves? Are there any tests for a *combination* of unfavourable events?

Finally, and crucially, there are all the well-known issues relating to data integrity and more generally to internal controls. Are the valuations independent? Are they accurate? How much cross-checking is there? Do reported profits meeting the plausibility test (e.g., does a trader whose job is to take positions on volatility rather than market direction make unexpected profits in quiet markets?) Is backtesting carried out by rote as a mechanical exercise, or does risk management use it as a tool to ask unpredictable questions? What is the role of audit? Is it forward looking and risk-based, or unimaginative and reactive?

None of this will get any easier in the future. In particular, value-at-risk models are constantly being refined and improved, and the regulatory process must accommodate, indeed encourage this to happen. Even so, major changes will still need to be reviewed if regulators are being asked to base capital charges on them, not least because many of the particular risks associated with new products can also apply to new models designed to capture their risks (or, indeed, the risks on older lines of business). This will require a certain amount of give and take on both sides. However, there will be certain minimum standards: for instance, there will need to be sufficient runs of data to capture the relevant risks, which can be a particular issue for certain emerging markets or for some types of implied volatility. More generally, a VAR model can only get you so far; it has to be supplemented by proactive and questioning stress tests formulated by a truly independent risk management function.

But I would not wish to strike too negative a note so far as VAR models are concerned. Of course there will always be difficult questions of detail: which products are covered and which not, how exactly backtesting will operate, what does the word *independent* in fact mean, how far one should allow a model to adjust to levels of abnormally low (or high) volatility and so on. But let us not lose sight of the very real advantages of the VAR approach.

1. It is a step backwards from the obsessive detail towards which requests for "a level playing field" and "certainty" were driving us, and which was increasing compliance costs for all involved, the regulators as much as the regulated.
2. It represents a more flexible and easily adjustable approach, which is much less likely to be rendered irrelevant by technological advance (or evaded by regulatory arbitrage); in short it is both more durable and more comprehensive an approach than any standardised set of rules.
3. It is much more accurate in its treatment of hedged and partially hedged positions.
4. It is, at least in theory, fair between different types of risk and should reward diversification appropriately.

Of course, not all banks have the systems in place to allow them to calculate capital on this basis, and it is not necessarily an approach that will work well in every country in the world: simplicity on paper is not always matched by simplicity in practice. Moreover, it is undeniably a challenge for regulators to attract and retain the talent needed to make this system work, in a way whereby banks are challenged to justify their procedures in an expert, constructive and totally independent fashion. Nevertheless, so long as the regulators set out the basic ground rules and parameters in advance (be they qualitative or quantitative) and then are able to apply these to the particular circumstances of an individual bank in an appropriate and consistent fashion, it is well worth the effort to follow this approach.

Question: *I wanted to ask Mr. Smout how far along banks in the UK are in implementing the* VAR *(value at risk) system?*

Mr. Clifford Smout: The story in the UK is that there are, I would say, 60 banks in the UK with trading books. Of those 30 to 35 have models that require a review under the capital adequacy directive. At this stage in 1997, I would say that no more than a third of those are plausible candidates for value-at-risk methodologies. Now, some are quite well advanced. A few of those are what you and I would think of as British banks. A few of them are what would seem to us very much like American banks, sometimes because all the people who work for them are American, but they are not, in fact. owned by American firms. More typically, however, they are, for instance, firms such as Bankers Trust International, which is incorporated in the UK but is a subsidiary of the Bankers Trust group. So I would say that at this moment, if you force me to give a number, there are twelve or so firms which are candidates for their approach. Now, no bank in the UK can yet use the value-at-risk approach for its regulatory risk calcutions across all risk classes as allowed for by Basel because that is not consistent with the capital adequacy directive. So that means that in some of those cases we have claims of models rather than anything much more than that. And looking at some of our experience before the implementation of the capital adequacy directive, I would say with some confidence that it will be less than twelve firms who had anything of any substance in place at the moment. But we do see this as a dynamic situation and we do think that the lower capital requirements resulting from models would, of course, be an incentive for firms to get up to speed. So I would anticipate that within two or three years that number would have risen. I don't think however that of the various banks that we have in the UK—we have perhaps just over 200 which are incorporated in the UK—I don't expect most of those to be using value at risk models even in ten years time because I don't expect most of them to have significant trading operations on that time scale.

V. PROBLEMS IN FINANCIAL REGULATION

9. RECENT US EXPERIENCE IN REGULATING FINANCIAL RISK

JOHN G. HEIMANN

Mr. John Heimann: Thank you very much for that generous introduction. I am really delighted to be here and it is a particular pleasure for me to see Ze'ev Abeles again. We have known each other for many years and I hold him in the highest regard.

Perhaps one of the toughest jobs in the world is that of a bank regulator. When you do things right, nobody knows about it. When something goes wrong, everybody knows about it. You only get criticism, you never get applause. I think Ze'ev deserves a great deal of applause, for he has performed admirably in sometimes-difficult conditions.

The title of today's session is "Risk Management in Regulation and Banking." I'd like to change that slightly to "Risk Management and the Regulation of Financial Intermediaries," which includes banks, investment banking and securities firms, insurance companies, and others who are intermediaries in the global financial market. Using my own firm as an example, Merrill Lynch's balance sheet is in excess of $300 billion, larger than most banks in the world. In addition, within Merrill Lynch we hold about 2 percent of the total household savings of the United States, over a trillion dollars! We have 60,000 people, and we operate in 45 countries. The question of risk management is as critically important to us as it is to any commercial bank.

This is a view of risk management from the battlefield, from the front line. Risk management and control is one of the hottest topics in the United States for the financial supervisors—the Federal Reserve, the Office of the Comptroller of the

Currency, the FDIC, the Securities and Exchange Commission, the Commodity Futures Trading Corporation, and others. This concern rues from the globalization of finance, particularly in the wholesale or the capital markets area. Risk, therefore, and risk management are not peculiarly U.S. concerns. It is a worldwide phenomenon. Capital markets are inexplicably intertwined and linked by technology, and goaded by competition. I would like to give some examples in recent years which were highly disruptive to the financial system and which could have led to a systemic breakdown if it had not been stemmed by prompt supervisory action.

In the United States, we had Continental Illinois, the Savings and Loan crisis, Drexel Burnam, Orange County, Procter and Gamble, the computer problems of the Bank of New York. In Japan, the Jusen problem, and the status of the Japanese banks in general; Daiwa, had a breakdown in management information systems; Sumitomo Copper suffered from a rogue trader. In the UK, there was BCCI and Barings. And at Deutsche Morgan Grenfeld, a rogue money manager caused Deutsche Bank to bail out its affiliate.

Also of German origin, Herstatt, the grandfather of global crises; and Metal Gesellschaft. In France. Credit Lyonnais and IndoSuez. And in Spain, Banesto, which had to be sold. Please note that I have mentioned six of the G7 countries. This is not a problem unique to one nation.

In the non-G7 countries, I note the problems in Scandinavia, Russia, the Czech Republic, Venezuela, Mexico, Brazil, Thailand, Korea, China, and, of course, Israel in the mid-1980s. Everyone had problems. What this leads you to conclude is there is a shift in the underlying tectonic plates of the world's financial system. Hence, the role of the risk management.

In the U.S., there was a growing awareness of the problems of risk management. It is today the primary concern for the management of financial institutions as well as their supervisors. What risks? Well, we have had a lot of them listed for us today, but let me just run down them again. Credit risk, market risk, operational risk, technological risk, reputational risk, people risk, legal risk, suitability risk, liquidity risk, and settlement risk. Time does not permit me to deal with all of them today. So, I would like to concentrate on credit and market risks.

I would like to focus on the model approach to risk management that in many ways represents an innovation in supervisory techniques. It also gives rise to a whole new series of implementation questions. I was a member of the Steering Committee of the Group of Thirty's pioneering study on derivatives. Subsequently, the SEC and the CFTC asked the six major Wall Street firms to create a voluntary system for the oversight of derivatives activities, the Derivatives Policy Group. Within that report, there is a section called Management and Control. Even though the thrust of that report was aimed at derivatives, it is an absolutely perfect template of how to manage risk within a financial institution. How do you organize for risk management? It starts with the Board of Directors. They have to have a role in deciding the risk profile of the organization, which is then implemented and enforced by management. There is also a role for the external auditors to make sure that these things are being done. Of course, finally, the supervisors who have the ultimate responsibility to make sure that these institutions are being run in a safe and sound manner. Therefore, the ideal risk management system for a financial institution is one that is centralized and integrated but not based solely on legal entities.

In many countries, foreign financial institutions are required to have separate legal entities. The supervisor may well require credit and risk management systems independent of the parent, but the reality is that for a global institution, risk management, must be centralized. In every financial institution, there should be a risk-policy committee of the Board of Directors. Their task is to set the limits of risk. This committee is supplemented by a risk management group that tends to be of the business unit as it is only the business unit that actually knows best how to manage their risks. Finally, there is the risk control function. That is the group that approves the marks of the traders. But since you cannot mark everything to market because in many cases there is no market, and because, in the derivative area particularly, you have the creation of uniquely singular instruments, this group not only checks the market but also values these specialized individual instruments. Furthermore, they approve new products for their risk parameters and approve the additions to old products, which could very well increase risk. This group, the risk control group, must be independent of the business units. By independent, I mean independent! Risk control cannot report to a business unit. It cannot report to the Chief Financial Officer, if the Chief Financial Officer is also running a profit-making treasury department. The head of risk control must 1) report only to the Chief Executive Officer or to the Chief Operating Officer, and 2) risk control must have unimpaired access to the Board of Directors. If you do not have that, you will not have independent risk control.

Risk control is a process. It is not a periodic snapshot. It is not an accounting technique. It is a 24-hour-a-day job for people who are overseeing the risk profile of an organization. Yes, you need the mathematicians, but you also need common sense and experience. Senior management must clearly communicate risk tolerance levels and risk philosophy to the entire organization. Risk tolerance must be clearly defined so that it is understandable to all. Unfortunately, most members of senior management in this rapidly evolving world do not quite understand all of the new instruments or techniques for risk management. My theory on that is very simple: if you don't understand it, don't do it.

The second point is communications. Risk management starts at the lowest level of an organization and communication is the key. But it is not just sending out memoranda. You have to look further. For example, compensation practices: how are traders compensated? Are they compensated for taking risks? Do they get rewarded for successful risk assumption but not penalized for loss? Is compensation a one-way street? If so, why?

Controls are the third point. The limits should be in risk terms, not in nominal terms or in notional terms. Most organizations use gross limits of 100. Today, the more sophisticated organizations talk in terms of tolerable loss. They do not set notional limits. Therefore, the traders and their managers are responsible for keeping whatever loss might occur within that acceptable tolerable level.

The next trend in the United States, which was mentioned this morning, is the portfolio approach, or the evaluation of probabilities. Now credit analysis has always relied on unit levels. How much do you have exposed to this company? How much do you have exposed to this country? It is a name by name approach. Very important. But in the new systems it is a building block to, what you might call, advance portfolio analysis. Concentration does not only include the traditional measures; you know, credit rating, maturity, etc.; but concentration as to currencies, industries, or commodities, the possibility of contagion and effects, and so forth. For example, what if the southeastern Asian countries devalued their currencies by 10 percent? What does that do to the risk profile? Or, what if the Deutsche Mark appreciates 15 percent against the dollar? What industries within Germany suffer? Which counter party will be deeply affected by this move? Portfolio analysis also requires discipline. If your coverage to a counter party in a diversification sector goes above the tolerable loss limits that you have set, that requires you to reduce your exposure to counter parties in the same sector. It is not a total add on, it means if you add and breach the tolerable loss limit, you have to subtract from somewhere else, otherwise risk profile will be skewed.

Finally, and I think very importantly, there has to be independent evaluation of the models from outside of your own organization. All professionals fall in love with their work. They can't help it. They just think they have done a bang up job and they may well have done that, and yet, they become wedded to the concepts or the assumptions that they have fed into the models. This happens not only in the risk areas. It is prudent and wise to test these assumptions outside of your organization with experts to make sure that your models have not become outdated.

When setting risk limits or the tolerable loss limits, management must ask itself a series of questions. What is the value added to my business by this transaction? If the answer is just the spread, then it is probably not a good piece of business. It has to be more than that. Or, what is the economic value optimization of values and client relations? I think that management has to understand far better the importance of value at risk and what it means and should cast a very jaundiced eye on residual valuations, which cannot be identified with precision. Management should also have a thoughtful evaluation of all of the factors behind the assumptions that are being made in their own organization and then ask the question, How do these assumptions stand up in the market place? What are my competitors doing? Does this make sense or not? And, finally, as somebody else pointed out this morning, how much is too much? There has to be a level at which senior management says, "Enough." Everyone knows that there has been a substantial narrowing of spreads, particularly in the emerging growth markets. I don't see how money can be made at some of these spreads. I have a sense that, once again, bankers are exercising their notoriously short memories, compounded by the "youth quake" within most organizations. And, in many organizations, senior management do not quite understand what is happening down on the trading floors as the young quandts innovate and originate.

As an ex-regulator, I am always concerned to hear from the financial sector of a country the phrase: "We are different. Our culture, our tradition makes our financial system different from everybody else's." That is always wrong. If you wish to a part of the global financial system, then the same rules apply to all. They must understand that the basic ground rules of banking apply to them. The excuse of culture and tradition usually hides practices that do not stand up to scrutiny. I commend to you some of the lessons we have learned in the United States or are in the process of learning and I would be delighted in the time that is remaining, to answer any questions that you might have. Thank you very much.

Question: *I would like to put to you two questions. One general and one more specific. My impression is that after the catastrophe of Bankers Trust and Procter and Gamble, all the succeeding incidents, many of which you listed, have not involved American institutions and have been focused in Germany, Britain, and Japan. Is it therefore valid to say that American institutions are much more advanced in risk management and/or have absorbed the lessons of their own disasters much more rapidly than the rest of the world? And specifically with regard to the Sumitomo business, you categorize that as a rogue dealer, but the impression one got from the media was that there was senior management, if not involved, then at least turning a blind eye and that they were very happy with what Hacker was doing, and that that raises questions from Sumitomo and that the Japanese really do not understand very much about risk management.*

Mr. John Heimann: Let me try to break down this series of very good questions. I'll answer the first question last, and deal with rogue traders. When there is a rogue trader, and they often exist, the key is catching them quickly through sophisticated MIS. In the case of Sumitomo, I do not know if there was suitability on the part of senior management. I read the same newspapers you read, but clearly, Sumitomo MIS was distressingly lacking. Furthermore, another lesson can be learned from this mess. The primary supervisory is the Ministry of Finance. The violations were in capital markets activities, actions which were not caught by the Inspectors from the Banking Bureau. If MOF had sent people from the Securities Bureau, this problem may have been uncovered earlier. However, the historical division of Banking and Securities Activity replicated in many other countries is no longer functionable in a world of melded financial activities. This has cost the Japanese heavily. We should all learn from this as the British have by their creation of the Financial Services Authority which will oversee all financial intermediation.

Question: *Should regulators have a hand in setting compensation?*

Mr. John Heimann: The answer is No, you have to let the private sector do that. But what the regulators can do, is to see whether compensation practices are such as to increase the risk profile without offsetting corrective policies. No, regulators should not be telling the private sector what to pay. I do not believe that at all. On the other hand, if I were a regulator today, I would look to see if the disparity of pay between producers and risk managers was such to indicate senior management's attitudes downplaying the risk management activities. The supervisors are in a unique position. They can look into all organizations within their jurisdiction and get a sense of best practices, domestically and internationally. Regulators are no smarter than bankers are. I do not mean that. They just see everything and almost by default, they learn what is good practice and what is bad practice.

At Merrill Lynch, when profitability in a product zooms out of the normal range, we send in our controllers to figure out what is going on. It could happen that the trader just got it right. That does happen from time to time. But not to investigate is usually a costly error on the part of senior management.

I suppose most importantly now we come back to management knowing what is going on. There is a question of language here that is very important. I heard today at least five definitions of portfolio approach. So what does that mean? In your organization you have to make sure that the words you use are understood by the organization for what they are, not for what they think they are. If you choose a portfolio approach, spell it out so that everybody has the same knowledge of what management means by portfolio approach. It is the same way on the concept of independence of the risk control unit. What do you mean by independence? People have lots of different definitions for that word, to suit their own particular quirks.

In closing, make sure that your organization understands fully the tolerable limits of risk. Don't assume that they understand. Make sure they do.

10. A RECENT CASE HISTORY OF INTERNATIONAL BANK FRAUD

BRIAN SMOUHA

I come here with some trepidation, following some erudite and fluent speakers. The perspective from which I speak is one of the foot soldiers in the trenches, or maybe I am just the light relief at the end of two very hard days of serious consideration. For the last two days, speakers have been concentrating on the risks arising in the ordinary course of business and how to control them, to identify them, measure them, and limit them. There have been a few references to rogue banks, but mostly they have not been considered. It is now my turn to talk about the biggest and most frightening of all risks, which is fraud. Fraud is not always so damaging. You can have it in small measures, someone cheating on expenses or one step up, the diversion of small or not worryingly larger sums of money from institutions. So to restrict this huge subject, I will not talk about frauds that take place in a bank by one or a small number of employees, which could be called fraud in a bank. I will be talking about fraud by a bank. A bank where a large number of people including top management make the bank a fraudulent bank as a whole and the bank loses sight of normal commercial considerations.

In BCCI, even though it is nearly six years since it has occurred, a reasonable number of senior management have been found guilty of a variety of crimes and have spent or are spending time in jail; some criminal and civil litigation is still in process.

So, as you would expect, it is not possible for me to deal with certain aspects of the cases because they are sub judice. But I still think there's plenty left to talk about. I propose, therefore, to refer to a number of factors, just very quickly to touch on controls and regulation. In BCCI I will pick up some of the signals which were going around in the marketplace and the media which proved not to be untrue. A concern that is expressed by many bankers is that supervisors treat all banks as if they were of the same standing. By implication that means that they rank the banks by sector rather than by risk. It is not the same way as bankers would necessarily treat all their credit situations.

So when I speak, I would like you to consider, or the regulators to consider, whether it is not appropriate to identify banks which are risky, not from the point of view of the way they trade, but risky as to the integrity of the institution as a whole. Your reaction when I talk about Ambrosiano and BCCI may be to ask two questions: 1 where were the controls? And 2 if an institution is riddled with fraud, what can anyone do about it?

This talk is not about controls. It is about banks which spin out of control. And let me just record, though, the importance of all controls. John Hyman yesterday spoke about high level controls. None of these controls were working in the two banks which I am talking about.

The second question that I raised, if an institution is riddled with fraud, can anyone do anything about it, let me just pick up with that at the end of this talk and you will, I hope, have, from what I say, some of the answers.

A few words, if I may, about the completeness and reliability of financial information. It would be an understatement to say that the Ambrosiano and BCCI's information was incomplete. There is one point, though, that seems to escape many people from countries with well-developed cultures of accounting, reporting, supervision, and honesty between individuals. Organizations which are in high-risk countries will suffer from a compounding effect of the high risk of the country as a whole, of the culture, which creates that risk, of the expected level or different levels of integrity and reliability and the lower level of financial sophistication. So the conduct of an institution, if it performs to the norm in the country in which it is located, would have controls which will be weaker, internal and external audits, which will have a lower standard, regulators who may not have the same sort of resources or knowledge, and would not put up such a challenge against an institution. And you put all these together and they compound so that you have to be that much more careful. And even if, and I will mention a case, even if a small part of the organization that you might consider to be immaterial is located outside strong supervision areas, you are at very serious risk because that small, or what you thought was small, subsidiary or branch, may conceal a large black hole.

Let me tell you about a real case. In 1974, I was asked by one of my bank clients to go and see some regulators because they were having problems in getting some information across to the regulators. The bank had a complicated structure. It had been a private group; it had been very successful and been built up and it was operating in a number of different countries. The bank's structure was not designed to be attractive to analysts or investors because, as I said, it was a private group.

And what my client wanted me to do was to go and see two different regulators, including the main regulators to explain the group. When I got down to the details, I found both regulators were looking at the institution in their country alone. Neither was looking at the consolidated accounts, which were being sent to them. Now I know we have moved on quite a bit, but it still illustrates the point.

For the meetings it was not difficult for me to create a model of the actual information of this bank and with that model I demonstrated to both those regulators how they could be made fools of if they restricted themselves to the single companies only. I do not know if they were very pleased with my approach, but they listened to me very quietly and they accepted what I said. Subsequently my client was regulated much better because my client was regulated on the consolidated statements, and the regulators were also happier because they understood what was going on inside the group.

So let me remind you, that was 1974. We have since then had much more concentration on consolidated supervision, but the rules still stay the same. Unless you get your arms around the whole situation, you really do not know what you are missing. Situations such as related-party transactions, and trades with friendly groups, can conceal some of the most frightening situations.

On the other hand, because of complications that arise from where groups are located, you should not automatically assume that they are fraudulent or that there is something wrong. There may be good reasons.

I will now move on to Ambrosiano. Some of you will remember Banco Ambrosiano. I would describe it as the Italian bank that collapsed in 1982, most famous for its chairman, Roberto Calvi, being found hanging under a bridge in London. Also for its close connection with the Vatican and the Vatican's bank, the IOR, the Institute for Religious Work, and the payment that the Vatican made of $250 million to the liquidation as part of the payment to the creditors.

At the time I started to look at Ambrosiano, I had already investigated a number of frauds. In some cases, frauds where the frauds were not endemic. Ambrosiano was my first experience of an institution that was so riddled with fraud that almost everything that you touched had something wrong with it.

Ambrosiano itself was an Italian bank, a retail bank in Italy with a Luxembourg subsidiary, that was created to hold all of the worldwide organizations situated outside Italy. At the collapse, the retail bank was separated out by the Bank of Italy and was rescued by a consortium.

At the behest of the 109 banks that remained, creditors of the Luxembourg holding company, we took control as liquidators, that is, of the subsidiaries in the rest of the world. None of the frauds in Ambrosiano was very complex. That was the strange thing. Finally and to a greater extent, in the final stages of the bank, large sums of money were transferred out of the bank, from one account to another, sometimes through six, seven, or eight accounts across three continents and back again, and into the personal pockets of individuals or organizations. In one case, the funds ended up, when we found them, in the name of one of the wrongdoers' mistresses. We were successful in most, but not all, cases of tracing and recovering the funds.

The next stage of complexity, if you were trying to grade them, it was the creation of a large number of Liechtenstein trusts or Panamanian companies. The companies had no share capital, so nothing appeared on the balance sheet or in their accounts. So-called loans were made, obviously, for no good reason, for no assets, with no backing, no security and no documentation, and the funds were plundered. In one case, $20 million was moved through the group and then suddenly converted itself into income and started coming back through the group as profits and, therefore, dividends to show what kind of prosperous group it was. In fact, it was only their own money being recycled.

Investments were made in a number of Italian media companies. These included the famous Corriera de la Sera, which was one of Italy's top-selling newspapers and was and is a famous publishing group. Our analysis was that this formed part of the Italian right-wing battle in Italy against the liberals and left, which was being waged in that period of the late-1970s. Much of the control and corruption were intricately entwined with the illegal P2 Masonic lodge to which a majority of Italy's top military, political and businessmen belonged.

The investments were not only overvalued, the companies that they were put into made dramatic losses, and further loans were made to keep them afloat. This happened in Rizzoli, which was undergoing a battle with the unions at the time. So nothing was really simple or on its own. Although Ambrosiano was putting more and more liquidity into the group, no provisions were made for losses, and the interest was rolled up with the addition of some large fees. This income that enhanced Ambrosiano's financial balances was quite uncollectible. In other cases, some investments were sold at inflated prices with separated buyback agreements. The buybacks were not of course shown in the books of Ambrosiano. Back-to-back loans were made with a variety of banks around the world, and I was amused to find later that one of them was with part of BCCI. So together all these false transactions created a beautiful appearance of liquidity in the group.

The main companies in the group all had different auditors, and different year ends. Funds seemed to move around the group at very convenient times, just to fit with the financial statements. There was no proper consolidation, and there were no pro forma accounts. Ambrosiano had a controlling stake in Banco del Gottardo, which was at that time about the tenth biggest Swiss bank. Banco del Gottardo was not detached from some of the goings on and dealings of the group, and acted as a very convenient vehicle for these purposes.

So all in all, this was a very straightforward series of frauds that left the creditor banks short by $1.6 billion. When we moved in, there was less than $60 million in cash and many of the assets appeared to have little value.

Let us move on now to BCCI. As I have said, the saga is not yet over, so it is difficult to comment on some of the things. What I want to do, though, is focus on what was known about BCCI while it was trading and what was behind the rumors, or some of the media comments.

There was always something mysterious about BCCI, and it's very existence. Who owned it? How did it grow so fast? What was its business? Why was it so opulent? It almost appeared as if it levitated. I remember seeing these luxurious offices and asking, and no one seemed to know.

There was a U.S. bank that had a significant holding in BCCI, but they sold that strategic holding in 1978, and it was not until quite a bit later that anyone found out about the sale. As you know, bankers and regulators correctly distrust information that comes out much later. Late information was a regular event with BCCI. The press reports at the time were that the U.S. bank had received critical reports on BCCI's lending and provisioning, and that was why they were selling. And who were the purchasers? Nobody knew. As it happened, the rumors were right. BCCI, even in those days, had bad debt problems and were not provisioning properly. And who were the purchasers of this holding that was being sold? The shares actually were warehoused in the Cayman group of foundations and companies, which formed part of BCCI and were under the control of BCCI's management. So there was nothing too tangible, but there were rumors, and they were just about true.

In 1978 BCCI had been refused permission to bank in the United States, but a series of acquisitions of banks in the U.S., starting with Financial and General Bank, were rumored to have BCCI behind them. John Heimann said he remembered from his position at the OCC, refusing to allow them BCCI into the U.S. BCCI of course denied any connection with these banks being purchased, although it was the same group of people who went on to acquire six other banks in the United States under the leadership of First American Bankshares, Washington's biggest bank. In spite of the Federal Reserve's best efforts, it was not until 1991 that the regulators could prove that the rumors had been true. The whole operation had been organized by BCCI in disguise. BCCI had been refused permission throughout to bank in the U.S., but they found a way around—not very satisfactorily.

Also in 1978, which you might say was a busy year for them, the press reported rumors that the loans amounted to twice BCCI's capital. You may have seen reports in the last month of the trial of Abbas Gokal, the head of a family and group that conspired with the management of BCCI. Abbas Gokal was found guilty and is now well into his fourteen-year sentence. The lending by BCCI to the Gokal group ended up at $1.2 billion, the majority of which appears now to be almost irrecoverable. However you had measured BCCI's capital when that rumor was going around, they were so deeply into the Gokal group, that if the Gokal group had gone down, so would have BCCI.

In 1984–85 there were reports of excessive trading losses, treasury losses, and other losses in financial and commodity markets. These reports were true. There were very heavy losses during that time with the information only coming out late. Of course, nobody was very happy that the regulators seemed to be the last to know. There were also a series of reports around the world of breaches of local regulations: Nigeria, fraudulent transactions, 1985; India, foreign exchange breaches, 1986/87/8; Kenya, foreign exchange and fraud, 1987; Jamaica, breaches of currency rules, 1988.

All were true. Interestingly, banks did not feature very largely as creditors of BCCI. In fact, none lost materially from the collapse; none of them were in there as none of them like dealing with BCCI.

Then finally in 1988 there was the Tampa, Florida, incident. The corporation itself and some of its officers were found guilty of money laundering. This was three full years before closure. Let me briefly tell you how they were caught. A U.S. agent was trying to infiltrate drug cartels to find how they were moving the drugs, offering the cartels his services to help them with laundering their funds. And by chance, as he went along the street in Tampa, he found the Bank of Credit and Commerce International. It sounded like a nice international sounding name, so he opened an account there. After a few visits, to his surprise and concern, he was told that the manager wanted to see him. So he was steered in to see the manager. Before he could say anything, the manager said, "We know what you are doing. You are not doing it very well. We will do all the work and you just do what we say and it will all be done. We can do the laundering much better than you can." And they did. That is the way that BCCI was caught.

Throughout its life, control of BCCI was an enigma. I have referred to shares transactions in 1978. The analysis of ownership of the group itself is really a major study. To this day there are arguments whether it was owned by the foundations or whether it owned the foundations, and you can go on ad infinitum. So people were absolutely right to be suspicious.

I will talk a little bit about the culture of the two banks. BCCI, first. I have been asked whether in my opinion, the founder of BCCI (Abedi) set out to be fraudulent when he incorporated the bank in 1972. Strangely enough, I do not actually think he did. It may not have mattered to him if he lied, cheated, or stole, or how he conducted his affairs. He was a very clever, scheming, dishonest man. The frauds were necessary to keep the bank alive. I am no psychoanalyst, and I have no firsthand knowledge of cults. But there were many facets in BCCI which would match a cultlike behavior. Abedi was a mystic leader, who would hold his audience of managers and staff, sometimes for house—four or five hours—with the most extraordinary speeches. I have heard one or two tapes of those speeches. And most of the content hardly makes sense, let alone has anything to do with banking. Much of the senior management, showed huge loyalty to the cause. How else could they have covered up these frauds for so long? One or two of them broke away, and true to form, blackmailed the management for a large payoff. Their threat was that they would disclose all. But other than those few people, there was great discipline and loyalty, and that is why I match it with a cult.

There was one other thing, which was very interesting, and bankers will find this worrying and interesting. There was extremely good cross-selling in the group, maybe because there were no profit centers and no control of costs. So clients of one part of the group would be beautifully cared for wherever they went in the world by any other part of the group, even if it was not the same legal entity. The bank looked after them very well, including what I believe is called extra services.

In many cases there was a different culture of honesty where much of the management came from. Many employees were from the same families or villages with different ethical standards from those which we are used to. Many of them spoke perfect English. They were beautifully tailored, they looked and sounded like model bankers. I met many in the early days, before they went to prison.

As for BCCI, also for Ambrosiano, I do not think Ambrosiano was conducted with fraud and enrichment as its prime aim. Since that time Italian establishment has been shown by a series of trials to have been riddled at that time by fraud, deceit, and power struggles, and there were no restrictions on the methods used. In the late-1970s and early-1980s, these attitudes seemed to be the norm there. P2, to which I have referred, probably had similar objectives to the Roman Catholic Church, but for quite different reasons. Ambrosiano ended up as a pawn in this big national game. Strangely, Calvi and Ambrosiano followed Sindona and Franklin National Bank, another fraudulent bank. There were connections and similarities, but there was no real affiliation between the two. Sindona ended up poisoned in an Italian jail, so he also met an untimely death.

Calvi was well known in international banking circles. He had access to many senior politicians and gave the impression of being a very serious and successful banker. A number of people that I have met have told me how they were taken in by him. In Italy, he was pushing forward with an ambitious acquisition strategy, probably to cover up some of the deficit. And he was probably also being blackmailed at the same time. So Ambrosiano is another example of a bank under the sole control of a single dictatorial person.

The internal controls outside Italy were nonexistent, and as I told you, huge sums of money were moved around at will. The main board, or some of them, may have known little of what was going on in Luxembourg, and the Luxembourg board was there for the formality and I suppose fees, but it did not seem to do anything else. Earlier I said I would come back to the question of how to identify banks that have high risks or are not what they look like. I will not dwell on these but I would just like to touch on the main things that need to be looked at, and the questions that need to be answered. They are some of the hardest things to answer.

You can get superficial answers, but these are the things you have to get to the bottom of, if you want to know what is happening.

If you do not understand an institution, you go on until you do understand it. If you do not understand the reason for the structure of the institution, you go on till you find the reason. If you do not understand the location of the activities or regulations, which may, just by chance, happen to be in a location with an under resource supervisor, you go on until you find out why it is there. Where do its profits come from? You need to know. You need to go on and on till you have got absolute satisfaction. You may need to use a whole number of specialists in different areas outside your own field, whichever role you are playing, till you actually can be satisfied how profits are generated One sign may be when results go against the industry trend. For any nonconformity, go on to find out why the institution is different from others. Being the same, by the way, does not mean it is all right, but being different may mean there is something unusual going on. So you need to pursue on, and go on till you find the answers.

I should tell you, I was actually talking to one bank recently that fitted a whole number of these situations. In fact, it is a very ethical, very careful, very well-controlled bank. So you must not always assume it is bad, but you have got to be that bit more careful, and of course as I have illustrated with the market intelligence on BCCI. You must listen to the market and the press. They may not always be right, but if you want to sleep well at night, do not move till you know you have got your satisfactory answers to those questions. Just to finalize very quickly then, I will ask myself a question. Are we all fully equipped to combat and catch these major frauds? And the answer is as you would expect, yes and no. Each time there is a fraud, new tools are added and I would say, usefully so. The Basel Committee actually put out new directives after the failures of each of these two banks. But from my experience, it is not enough just to add extra controls. There is the need to use all the tools which are available. I am also glad to refer to the silent majority of problem banks, the ones which were stopped before they could do any serious damage, the ones you do not hear about. Better communication between regulators and stronger powers do help. In all these cases, there has been resistance to regulators inquiries, but never absolute refusal. You should take resistance as a very strong warning.

The *no* is because theoretically it is possible to construct a fraudulent bank. It is possible, if everyone conspires, and the records are very carefully put together, to create such a situation. So, would that be undiscoverable? In theory, yes. I have never seen anything even in part of a fraudulent bank that would approach something like this. So will there be further instances in the developed world of a major bank being built on fraud in the way these have with the consequential collapse? I do not know, but I hope it is very unlikely. In places where regulation is weak, nonexistent, or conducted only by the rule book rather than by intelligence, understanding, and diligence, I would expect there to be fraudulent institutions. And I would expect there to be failures as a result. There is much that I have not covered that I would be happy to try and answer any questions. Thank you.

Mr. Aryeh Shapiro: Let me now suggest that questions can now be addressed to both our speakers. By all means ask anything.

Question: *I want to ask Mr. Smouha, where were the auditors in these two banks?*

Mr. Brian Smouha: In Italy, there were a small number of individuals, I think two or three, who were the auditors. They have been condemned in the report on the criminal case that came out. They, as I say, are individuals who are not affiliated to major firms. There were not consolidated accounts. At the Luxembourg holdings level, there were no consolidated accounts. The auditors of individual companies were various, at various times as I have described to you. There were also a large number of companies, which were not audited at all. In BCCI, there is litigation in process against the auditors.

Question: *You raised the point of the fact that the regulators were always the last to know. And indeed, in this country as well, although it's regrettably from the point of view of* *the press, we haven't had a collapse for twelve years. The last bank to go down the tubes was from downtown Jerusalem, which everybody knew about and the very last people to act on it were the regulators. I'd like to have your view as it were, and your own impressions, Mr. Smouha, why do you think that is?*

Mr. Aryeh Shapiro: I can only add to what you've asked now, that in an article, the *Financial Times* I believe it was in November of 1991, the watchdogs that didn't bark. And by that they meant not just, I think, the central bankers, but they also meant the auditors, the independent board of directors, and others who also share some of the responsibility.

Mr. Brian Smouha: It's a good question, it's a difficult question. First, there are cases where people said at the time that there is a problem with an organization. There are not as many cases as where after the event people say that it was obvious there was a problem. Now, I'm not talking about your downtown Jerusalem bank necessarily, but I am aware of a number of cases where things were so obvious and they were drawn to the attention of the regulators. I think there are some cases where that is not true. We of course only see a small sample. There are some cases where the supervisor does see that there is a problem and does take action and where the information never gets out into the press or into the public domain at all. I can think of a number of cases which were resolved satisfactorily without a thing appearing in print at the time or even after the event. And so there are those cases as well, so you are seeing only a partial picture. The question you raise is a good one. I think, however, that a bank cannot be closed down just on the basis of rumors. It is the job of the supervisor in that case to try and establish the facts and that is something which we can argue about the most effective way of doing and the speed with which it is done. But simply because someone is making an allegation against a bank, one cannot close it down. Now, I don't think I want to say very much more than that, but all I would like to say is that I think the banking acts in most countries do put in certain safeguards. That said, of course, it is the regulator's responsibility to try and limit the risk to depositors and it is their responsibility, when necessary, to act in a robust fashion. But what I'm suggesting is that it is not always possible to act as rapidly as one might like.

VI. MANAGING MARKET RISKS: THE CASE OF ISRAEL

11. MARKET RISKS—THE AMENDMENT TO THE BASEL CAPITAL ACCORD AND INTERNAL MODEL APPROACH: THE ISRAELI CASE

YORAM LANDSKRONER, DAVID RUTHENBERG, and DAVID ZAKEN

1. INTRODUCTION

Starting in 1998, banks in the G-10 countries will be required to measure and apply capital charges to the market risks they incur.[1] This supplements the 1988 Basel Accord, which focused on capital charges in respect to credit risk.[2] Market risks are defined as risk of losses in on- and off-balance-sheet positions resulting from movements in market prices. The market risks subject to these requirements are interest rate risk of debt instruments and price risk of equities in the trading book; foreign exchange risk and commodities price risk throughout the bank.[3]

In measuring market risks, banks will have a choice between two methods (models). One alternative is to measure risks using the Standardized Measurement Method using the measurement framework described in the Amendment. The alternative method allows banks to use risk measures derived from their own internal risk management models. The method has to be approved explicitly by the supervisory authority. Banks wishing to use the internal models method will have to meet certain qualitative and quantitative standards before they are permitted to use internal models. The ***qualitative criteria*** include

1. The bank should have an independent risk control unit that is responsible for the bank's risk management system.
2. The unit should regularly test the model by comparing the risk measure generated by the model against actual changes in the portfolio value.

3. The board of directors and senior management should be actively involved in the control of risk.
4. The internal risk model should be an integral part of the risk management process of the bank.
5. Routine stress tests should be conducted to supplement the risk measurement model.
6. The overall risk management process should be reviewed at regular intervals.

For the calculation of capital charges, bank's internal models will have to meet also some minimum ***quantitative standards***. First, the requirements concerning the measurement of risk include the following:

1. Value at risk (VaR) must be computed daily.
2. In calculating VaR, a 99 percent, one-tailed confidence interval is to be used.
3. In calculating VaR, a minimum 10-day holding period should be used.
4. The (historical) sample period for calculating VaR should be at least one year, and the data updated at least every three months.
5. Banks can use risk models based on variance-covariance matrices, historical simulations, or Monte Carlo simulations.
6. Banks will be allowed to recognize empirical correlations within broad risk categories (Internet rates, exchange rates, etc.) and across risk categories.
7. Bank's models must capture the unique risks of options.

The second part of the requirements concern the capital requirements. These include the following:

1. Banks must meet daily a capital requirement expressed as the higher of the previous day's VaR or an average of the daily VaR on each of the preceding 60 business days multiplied by a supervisory *multiplication factor* set at a minimum of 3.
2. Banks will be required to add to this multiplication factor a "plus" related to the ex-post performance (backtesting) of their model. The plus will range from 0 to 1.
3. Banks will be subject to separate capital charges to cover *specific risk* owing to factors related to the individual issues of debt and equity securities (credit risk).

The capital requirement can thus be expressed as

$$K \geq 3(2.33\sigma - \mu),$$

where, K = capital requirement
3 = multiplication factor
2.33 = Z of a 99% one-tailed confidence interval
σ = standard deviation of return (change in value)
μ = expected return

The expression in parenthesis is the VaR of the bank for a 99 percent interval estimated over a 10-day period. That is, the bank is required to hold three times the maximum possible loss with a probability of 1 percent.

In calculating market risk using an internal model, two approaches are possible. First, a simplified approach where each risk category (interest rate, exchange rate, inflation rate, etc.) is measured separately and then summed up to obtain total risk. (See Landskroner and Ruthenberg, 1991, for an example of such an approach.) The second is portfolio approach, in which the covariances among the different risk categories is taken into account in the calculation of total risk.

In what follows, we present an internal model based on the portfolio approach. Importantly, we define risk as the unexpected (surprise) component of the random variable, as opposed to total change in the random variable. The risks are estimated using historical data. The estimates are applied to the balance sheets of a sample of banks in Israel. Based on these estimates, capital requirements are calculated based on principles of the 1996 Amendment to the Basel Accord for the trading and banking books of the banks.

In Section 2, we present the model and derive the risk measure. In Section 3, we define the components of the risk measure and estimate them empirically. In Section 4, the capital requirement for market risk is defined and calculated for a sample of the five largest Israeli banks. Concluding Remarks are presented in Section 5.

2. THE MODEL

2.1. The objective function

The bank's overall measure of risk is defined in terms of its net worth. Thus, risks are measured in terms of their effect on the change in net worth, and the objective function of the bank, defined as a change in net worth (in real terms) is used as the framework for risk measurement. The change in net worth consists of two parts: 1) net financial income, which is determined by the interest margin and the net position in the different segments and is affected by changes in inflation and exchange rates; and 2) change in net worth due to a change in interest rates.[4] The banking firm is assumed to operate in three segments of intermediation: local currency, foreign currency, and local currency linked to a general price index (CPI).[5] The equation for the change in economic net worth in real terms (ΔNW) for a single period can be written as

$$\begin{aligned}\Delta NW = {} & [A(1+r_A) - L(1+r_L) + F] - \delta_p \frac{d\tilde{r}}{1+r}(A - L + F) \\ & + [a(1+i_a) - l(1+i_l) + f]\,\tilde{q} - \delta \frac{d\tilde{i}}{1+i}(a - l + f) \\ & + [a^*(1+i_a^*) - l^*(1+i_l^*) + f^*]\frac{\tilde{X}_1}{X_0}\tilde{q} - \delta^* \frac{d\tilde{i}^*}{1+i^*}(a^* - l^* + f^*) - NW_0, \qquad (1)\end{aligned}$$

where,

A, a, a* denote indexed (real), nonindexed (nominal), and foreign-currency assets (loans) respectively.

Similarly L, l, l* denote the liabilities (deposits) in the three segments of intermediation.

F, f, f* denote the net off-balance sheet positions (e.g., forward contracts, swaps and options) in the three segments.

r is the domestic market real (indexed) interest rate and i and i* are nominal interest rates in local and foreign currency respectively. Subscripts on the rate variables denote the interest rates on assets and liabilities (r_A is the real interest rate on the bank's indexed assets, for example).

δ_p, δ, δ^* denote the duration measures of the net position (net worth) of the real, nominal and foreign currency segments respectively.

$d\tilde{r}$, $d\tilde{i}$, $d\tilde{i}^*$ denote the random (unexpected) changes of the market interest rates; in each segment they are assumed to be the same for assets and liabilities.

$\tilde{X}_1$ and X_0 are the exchange rates at the end and beginning of the period, respectively.

$\tilde{q} = 1/(1 + \tilde{\pi})$ is a purchasing-power index where π is the inflation rate; tildes denote random variables.

The components of equation 1 are as follows. The first term on the RHS ($A(1 + r_A) - L(1 + r_L) + F$) is the net financial income of the indexed segment and the second term δ_p ($d\tilde{r}/1 + r$) ($A - L + F$) is the change in net worth of this segment due to unexpected changes in interest rates. The other terms in equation 1 are similar expressions for the local-currency (nonindexed) and foreign-currency segments respectively. However, the financial income in those segments are also affected by unexpected changes in inflation and foreign exchange rates. Interest-rate risk is defined here as the effect of an unexpected change in interest rates on the net worth of each segment (or net position in each segment). This effect has two components: the first is the unexpected change in interest rates; the second is the sensitivity of net worth to changes in interest rates measured as the duration of net worth[6]. Thus, for the nominal (nonindexed) sector:

$$dV = -\delta \frac{d\tilde{i}}{1+i} \cdot V,$$

where $V = (a - l + f)$ is the net position in the segment and dV is the change in the net position. The duration of the net position is

$$\delta = W_a\delta_a - W_l\delta_l + W_f\delta_f$$

where $W_a = a/V$, $W_l = l/V$ and $W_f = f/V$ are the weights of the assets, liabilities, and off-balance-sheet positions respectively; δ_a, δ_l and δ_f are the duration measures of the assets, liabilities and net off-balance sheet positions respectively. Similar measures are obtained for the other two segments of intermediation.[7]

Equation 1 presents the effects of the different sources of uncertainty on the change in net worth for each of the three segments. It is subject to the balance sheet constraint, namely, that total assets equal total liabilities. However, for each segment this equality does not necessarily hold, that is, the bank may have a net open position (short or long) in the different segments. These open positions expose it to inflation, exchange-rate, and interest-rate risks. For example, a bank that obtains local currency deposits linked to a general price index (L) and uses them to extend credit (a), which is not linked (nonindexed), is exposed to inflation risk and interest-rate risk simultaneously.

2.2. The measure of risk

The measure of overall risk is taken to be the variance of the portfolio of risks. This measure follows the concept of overall risk used in this paper, namely, it considers the three types of risk in our model and takes the covariances among the different sources of risk into account.[8] The variance of the change in net worth is defined as

$$\text{Variance}\ (\Delta NW) = \sum_{j=1}^{5} \beta_j^2 \text{Var}(R_j) + 2\sum_{\substack{j \\ k}}^{5} \sum_{\substack{k \\ >j}}^{5} \beta_j \beta_k \text{COV}(R_j R_k), \tag{2}$$

where the constant coefficients or the weights (β) and random variables (R) are defined as follows:

$$\begin{aligned}
\beta_0 &= [A(1+r_A) - L(1+r_1) + F] & R_0 &= 1 \\
\beta_1 &= -\delta_p (A - L + F)/(1+r); & R_1 &= d\tilde{r} \\
\beta_2 &= [a(1+i_a) - l(1+i_1) + f]; & R_2 &= \tilde{q} \\
\beta_3 &= -\delta(a - 1 + f)/(1+i); & R_3 &= d\tilde{i} \\
\beta_4 &= [a^*(1+i_a^* - l^*(1+i_1^* + f^*)]; & R_4 &= \frac{\tilde{X}_1}{X_0}\tilde{q} \\
\beta_5 &= -\delta^*(a^* - l^* + f^*)/(1+i^*) & R_5 &= d\tilde{i}^*
\end{aligned}$$

Similarly, we can define the expected value of the change in net worth as

$$\text{avg}(\Delta NW) = \sum_{i=0}^{5} \beta_i \overline{R}_i - NW_0, \tag{2a}$$

where $\overline{R}_i$ is the expected value of the different random variables, and β_i is the weight of these variables as defined earlier. Note that avgΔNW includes an additional term, β_0, the weight of the indexed segment, which does not appear in the variance since it does not involve uncertainty in real terms, ($R_0 = 1$).[9]

3. ESTIMATIONS OF THE RISK VARIABLES

The overall measure of risk defined in equation 2 is estimated in three steps. First, we define and estimate the different sources of uncertainty, decomposing the risks into an expected and an unexpected part. Second, the weights of the various risks in the portfolio are estimated. Last, the different risks and their weights are combined in the portfolio of the bank's risks.

3.1 Random variables

There are five sources of uncertainty in our model, and the random variables are $\tilde{q}$, $\tilde{X}_{1p}$, $d\tilde{r}$, $d\tilde{i}$, $d\tilde{i}^*$. To estimate the risks, we consider only the surprise, or unexpected, part of the actual change in the random variable (interest rate, inflation rate, and exchange rate). It is assumed that the bank takes into account only the expected part in its planning and pricing, while the surprise, which is unexpected by definition, is therefore the more appropriate measure of risk. Thus, we decompose the actual change to an expected part and an unexpected part.

In general, for each of the random variables we have

$$\tilde{R} = \overline{R} + \tilde{e},$$

where $\tilde{R}$ is the actual (realized) random variable, $\overline{R}$ is its expected value, and $\tilde{e}$ is a random residual ("surprise") with a zero mean. Following the decomposition of the random variables we use the surprise part of each of these variables to estimate the variance and covariance terms of equation 2. To estimate the expected value of the change in net worth, equation 2a, we use the means of the realized values of random variables. Note that by construction, the expected value of the surprise is zero.

Inflation risk

We decompose the actual (realized) change in the purchasing-power rate ($\tilde{q}$) into two parts: an expected rate ($\overline{q}$) and a surprise (error) term (e):

$$\tilde{q} = \overline{q} + e,$$

where $\tilde{q} = 1/(1 + \tilde{\pi})$. The decomposition of the purchasing power variable is based on the Fisher equation, i.e., $(1 + i) = (1 + r)\ (1 + \tilde{\pi})$, obtaining for the expected purchasing-power rate:

$$\overline{q} = \frac{1+r}{1+i}.$$

It follows that the surprise part is given by

$$e = \frac{1}{1+\pi} - \frac{1+r}{1+i}. \tag{3}$$

In estimating the surprise purchasing power rate we used the consumer price as an estimate of inflation, for the real interest rate we used the interest rate on an index-linked government bond and for the nominal interest rate we used short-term government (treasury) bill rates. The data used for r, i, π are defined in the Data Appendix.

Exchange-rate risk

Since the change in net worth in equation 1 is defined in real terms, we must also define the random variables in real terms. We define a random real end-of-period exchange rate as

$$\tilde{X}_{p1} = \tilde{X}_1\tilde{q},$$

where $\tilde{X}_1$ is the end-or-period exchange rate. We now decompose the real exchange rate into an expected real exchange rate ($\bar{X}_{p1}$) and a surprise (error) component (ε_p)

$$\tilde{X}_{p1} = \bar{X}_{p1} + \varepsilon_p,$$

where by definition $\bar{X}_{p1} = \bar{X}_1\bar{q}$[10]. We assume a naive model where the forward rate is an unbiased estimate of the expected rate. The forward rate is derived from the interest rate parity theorem in real terms, where the expected change in the real exchange rate can be written as

$$\frac{\bar{X}_{p1}}{X_0} = \left[\frac{1+i}{1+i^*}\right]\bar{q} + \left[\frac{1+i}{1+i^*}\right].$$

The surprise change in the real exchange rate can be written as

$$\frac{\varepsilon_p}{X_0} = \frac{\tilde{X}_{p1}}{X_0} - \frac{1+r}{1+i^*}. \qquad (3a)$$

Since most foreign exchange transactions of Israeli banks are denominated in US$, we have used the US$/NIS (New Israeli Sheqel) exchange rate to estimate exchange-rate risk, and the dollar LIBOR interest rate for the foreign interest rate. See Data Appendix for details.

Interest-rate uncertainty

The change in the nominal interest rate ($d\tilde{i}$) is decomposed into an expected change ($d\bar{i}$) and an error term (unexpected change) (u), as follows:

$$d\tilde{i} = d\bar{i} + u.$$

We assume that the term structure of interest rates is consistent with the unbiased expectations theory of interest rates, that is, the expected future (one period) spot rate (${}_1\bar{i}_1$) is equal to the implied forward rate:

$${}_1\bar{i}_1 = \frac{(1+i_2)^2}{(1+i_1)} - 1,$$

where i_2 and i_1 are two period and one period current spot interest rates respectively. The surprise change in the interest rate is thus:

$$u = (1 + \tilde{i}) - \frac{(1 + i_2)^2}{(1 + i_1)}, \tag{3b}$$

where ${}_1\tilde{i}_1$ is the actual future spot rate.[11]

Similarly, the change in the real rate is decomposed into an expected and an error term,

$$d\tilde{r} = d\bar{r} + u_p, \tag{3c}$$

while the expected future spot rate is assumed to equal the implied forward real rate. The change in the foreign currency interest rate is decomposed as:[12]

$$d\tilde{i}^* = d\bar{i}^* + u^*, \tag{3d}$$

Table 1 presents summary statistics of the random variables. For each variable we present the statistics for the actual, and surprise (error) values. As expected, the means

Table 1. Summary Statistics. Estimates for period Nov. 1989–Dec. 1995 (74 monthly observations, in annual terms).

	A. Actual	
Variable	Mean	Std. Dev.
$q = 1/(1 + \pi)$	0.8799*	0.0306
$(X_1/X_0)q$	0.9517*	0.0600
$d\tilde{r}$	0.0074	0.0187
$d\tilde{i}$	0.0021	0.0300
$d\tilde{i}^*$	−0.0025	0.0097
	B. "Surprise" = actual-expected.	
Variable	Mean	Std. Dev.
e	−0.0061	0.0292
ε_p/X_0	−0.0014	0.0582
u_p	−0.0005	0.0182
u	−0.0053	0.0289
u^*	−0.0077	0.0095

* significant at 5% level,
where $q_t = CPI_t/CPI_{t+12}$ is the purchasing-power index (CPI is the consumer price index).
X_1 and X_0 is the dollar/sheqel exchange rate at the end and beginning of a year, respectively.
$\tilde{r}$ is the real rate of interest on a one-year government indexed bond.
$\tilde{i}$ is the nominal rate on a one-year Treasury bill.
$\tilde{i}^*$ is the one-year dollar LIBOR rate.
e is the surprise (residual) of q.
ε_p is the surprise of the real exchange rate X_1q.
u_p, u, u^* are the surprises of the real interest rate, the nominal rate, and the dollar interest rate, respectively.

of the surprise values are not significantly different from zero. The standard deviations are of a similar magnitude (0.95% – 5.82%) where the dollar interest rate (LIBOR) surprise has the smallest standard deviation and the real exchange rate the largest.

3.2. Portfolio weights

To estimate the variance of the change in net worth, we need also to estimate the constant coefficients, or weights, β, in equation 2. These are bank-specific, since they are determined by the position the bank is taking in the different segments of intermediation.

Our sample consists of data for the five largest banks in Israel for the years 1992–1995.[13] The data comes from two sources: consolidated financial statements and reports to the Supervisor of Banks.

Assets, liabilities, and off-balance-sheet positions

In the calculation of net financial income, assets, and liabilities were taken at their book value. However, following the definition of interest-rate risk, when estimating the effect of a change in interest rates on net worth (calculations involving duration), we used market values of assets and liabilities, i.e., we calculated the values of the assets and liabilities as the present value of their future cash flows. The discount rates used here were market interest rates taking into account the term structure of interest rates. For example, one-year interest rates on government indexed bonds were used to calculate the present value of one-year index-linked loans and deposits of banks.

Interest rates

Interest rates on the banks assets (loans) and liabilities (deposits) were calculated as weighted average interest rates of different maturities and types in each of the segments.

Duration

The duration of assets and liabilities in each of the segments was calculated as the weighted average of assets and liabilities according to their maturity buckets.

3.3. Variance-covariance matrix

Having estimated the surprise components of the random variables, we then estimated the variance-covariance matrix, following equation 2. The findings are presented in Table 2. The variance and covariance terms are of a similar magnitude; the covariances are mostly positive, but for the terms involving foreign interest rate; the covariance terms involving the LIBOR rate are mostly negative, but near zero. Because of the relative contribution of the covariance terms, they have a significant effect on the new measure of risk we propose. As pointed out earlier, our portfolio approach to risk considers not only the individual sources of risk, but

Table 2. Variance—Covariance Matrix of the Surprise Terms.

	e	ε_p/X_0	u_p	u	u*
e	0.000839				
ε_p/X_0	0.000630	0.003336			
u_p	6.25E-5	−2.88E-5	0.000328		
u	−0.000268	−0.00037	4.24E-5	0.000826	
u*	−0.000128	−0.000151	−4.88E-5	0.000120	8.90E-S

For definition of variables, see Table 1.

also the interaction between them; and it turns out empirically that they are important.

3.4. Banks' risk

The next step is to incorporate the variance and covariance estimates of risk into the specific positions of the five banks in our sample, thus obtaining portfolio risk estimates for the banks. The results of the estimation of the variance of ΔNW for the five banks in our sample are presented in Table 3. First, we present the weights in the calculation of ΔNW, the expected value of ΔNW, which was calculated following eq. 2a, and finally, the standard deviation of the ΔNW was calculated following eq. 2. It is interesting to note that the banks differ in their positions (weights), and the result being that they have different exposures to overall risk. The differences in the coefficient of variation are significant between the banks, ranging from 0.05 to 0.74 for the bank with the greatest overall risk exposure.

4. CAPITAL REQUIREMENTS

The estimation of the banks' overall risk is the first step in the supervision of these risks. The next step the banking authority may take in order to regulate these risk exposures is to impose capital requirements. The capital standard proposed here is derived from a criterion imposed by the banking authority. This authority determines, for a given probability, (confidence interval), the maximum level of losses a bank may have relative to its capital. These determine the adequacy of the bank's capital. Specifically, the two parameters, which are determined by the supervisor, are a confidence interval parameter, Z (score) and a scaling parameter, α^0 ($0 < \alpha^0 < 1$), reflecting the risk aversion of the banking supervisor. The criterion can be stated as

$$NW_0 + [\text{avg}(\Delta NW) - Z\text{std}\,(\Delta NW)] \geq (1 - \alpha^0)NW_0, \tag{4}$$

or,

$$\alpha^0 NW_0 \geq [Z\text{std}(\Delta BW) - \text{avg}(\Delta NW)] = \alpha NW_0, \tag{4a}$$

where, avg (ΔNW) is the expected change in net worth as defined by (2a), Std(ΔNW) is the standard deviation of the change in net worth obtained in (2),

Table 3. Expected Value and Standard Deviation of Change in Net Worth for the Five Banks for 1995 (Millions NIS).

Weights	Leumi	Hapoalim	Discount	Mizrachi	First International
β_0	3691.7	3846.8	528.0	1753.9	1761.3
β_1	−39616.5	−5726.8	−12164.7	−160.2	−4048.8
β_2	1784.0	1318.8	848.8	−441.0	−142.3
β_3	1403.8	−3322.5	113.1	0.5	274.9
β_4	1409.1	1350.7	818.4	148.7	377.2
β_5	4059.4	−3072.2	−58.1	−348.3	−1087.6
Avg (ΔNW)	145.4	113.6	16.6	151.5	36.0
Std (ΔNW)	725.4	164.1	220.3	19.1	72.2
NW_0	2069.6	3133.7	1020.1	120.2	988.2

where,
$\beta_0 = (AR_A - Lr_L + F)$ net position in the linked segment.
$\beta_1 = -\delta_p\ (A - L + F)/(1 + r)$ the change in the net worth for a given change in the relevant interest rate in that segment.
A, L, and F are the assets, liabilities, and futures positions respectively in the indexed segment, r_A and r_L are the interest rates, and δ_p is the duration of NW of the segment.
$\beta_2 = [a(1 + i_a) - l(1 + i_l) + f]$.
$\beta_3 = -\delta(a - f)/(1 + i)$.
$\beta_4 = [a^*(1 + i_a^*) - l^*(1 + r_l^*) + f^*]$.
$\beta_5 = \delta^*(a^* - l^* + f^*)/(1 + i^*)$.
β_2 and β_3 are the weights of teh nonindexed segment, and β_4 and β_5 are the weights of the foreign-currency segment.

α^0 is the maximum allowable erosion rate of capital (net worth), and α is the actual erosion as estimated by VaR.

The sum of the first two terms on the LHS of (4) is the expected end-of-period net worth: $avg(NW_1) = NW_0 + avg(\Delta NW)$; Z standard deviations are deducted from it to obtain a possible actual end-of-period NW or a confidence interval for net-worth. Since we are concerned only with a deterioration of the NW we consider only the possibility of a negative deviation of Z standard deviations from the expected value of NW. The terms in the brackets (4a) is the Value at Risk (VaR) $VaR \equiv [Z\ std(\Delta NW) - avg(\Delta NW)$, this is the estimated change in NW for a given confidence interval (Z score). The banking supervisor, based on his/her attitude towards risk, determines a maximum allowable rate of erosion in net-worth α^0 that is a minimum (critical) level of capital is established.

If the inequality in (4) does not hold, the bank has a capital deficiency (or is undercapitalized) and will be asked to add capital to enhance safety and soundness. The additional required capital $\Delta\ NW_0^0$, is defined by the following equation:

$$\alpha^0[NW_0 + \Delta NW_0^0] = VaR \tag{4b}$$

We can now compute the additional capital in two alternative ways, first it can be derived from equations 4 and 4b:

$$\Delta NW_0^0 = \left(\frac{\alpha}{\alpha^0} - 1\right) NW_0 \tag{5}$$

where α^0 is the maximum erosion rate of capital, and α is the actual erosion rate obtained in equation 4a.

Following (4a) and (4b) we can rewrite the capital requirement as:

$$NW_0^0 \geq \frac{1}{\alpha^0}[Z\text{std}(\Delta NW) - \text{avg}(\Delta NW)] = \frac{\alpha}{\alpha^0} NW_0, \tag{5a}$$

where $NW_0^0 = NW_0 + \Delta NW_0^0$ is the required level of capital and $1/\alpha^0$ is the multiplication factor of the VaR. From (5a) it follows, that the more lenient the supervisory authority is (a larger α^0) the smaller will be the multiplication factor and hence the lower the required capital. Equation 5a is consistent with the Basel 1996 Amendment, under this amendment, the multiplication factor of the VaR is equal to 3, and $Z = 2.33$, that is an implied allowable rate of depletion of capital of 1/3.

The next step is to examine the adequacy of capital of the banks with respect to the types of risks analyzed here (i.e., excluding credit risk). Setting the decision rule of (4) in its equality form we have calculated Z levels (confidence level parameter) for different values of α, the scaling parameter. The lower α (for given Z) the higher is the implied risk aversion and the less is the allowed level of capital erosion. Table 5 presents combinations of α and Z values for the five banks in our sample.

Assume that the supervisor has decided on a value of 0.99 for the α parameter, that is a permissible maximum loss of 1% in terms of NW, and a 99% confidence interval (i.e., $Z = 2.33$, under normality assumption). Table 4 presents α values for different Z values for the five largest banks in Israel for the years 1992–1995.

Let us consider the Discount Bank in 1995 where for a Z value of 2.33 the bank incurred a corresponding α value of 0.487, indicating a potential loss of 51.3%. This loss is greater than the critical level of 1% that the supervising authority has imposed.

Following equations 5 and 5a, we can now calculate the additional capital required ΔNW_0^0 for a given initial level of capital (NW_0). For the Discount Bank where $NW_0 = 1{,}020$ in 1995, thus

$$\begin{aligned}\Delta NW_0^0 &= 3(0.487 - 0.333)1{,}020 \\ &= 3(496.7) - 1{,}020 = 470.1\end{aligned}$$

To calculate the comprehensive capital requirements, we combine the new capital charge for market risks with the existing capital requirement for credit risk. Continuing the case of the Discount Bank, the existing capital ratio is[14]

$$\frac{\text{Capital}}{\text{Risk weighted assets}} = \frac{3{,}371}{38{,}746} = 8.7\%$$

According to the new approach, the capital required for market risks is NIS 470.1 million. This is deducted from the bank's capital to obtain the comprehensive capital ratio,

Table 4. Z Values for Different α Values from Equation 4: $NW_0 + [Avg(\Delta NW) - Z\ std(\Delta NW)] = (1 - \alpha^0)NW_0$.

α	Leumi	Hapoalim	Discount	Mizrahi	First International
			1992		
0.20	0.62	1.23	3.08	5.48	9.39
0.30	1.03	1.84	4.30	5.94	13.3
0.40	1.43	2.46	5.52	6.39	17.2
0.50	1.84	3.07	6.75	6.85	21.1
0.60	2.24	3.69	7.97	7.31	24.9
			1993		
0.20	2.21	1.59	1.95	3.92	3.86
0.30	3.33	2.46	2.56	4.32	5.36
0.40	4.45	3.34	3.17	4.73	6.86
0.50	5.58	4.22	3.78	5.14	8.35
0.60	6.70	5.10	4.39	5.55	9.85
			1994		
0.20	0.71	1.48	1.78	8.86	2.05
0.30	1.09	2.28	2.56	10.1	2.94
0.40	1.47	3.08	3.34	11.3	3.84
0.50	1.85	3.88	4.12	12.6	4.74
0.60	2.23	4.68	4.90	13.8	5.63
			1995		
0.20	0.37	4.51	1.00	9.17	3.23
0.30	0.66	6.42	1.46	9.80	4.61
0.40	0.94	8.33	1.93	10.4	5.97
0.50	1.23	10.2	2.39	11.1	7.34
0.60	1.51	12.2	2.85	11.7	8.71

$$\frac{3,371 - 470.1}{38,746} = 7.49\%,$$

which means that the bank is not adequately capitalized, when market risks are taken into account. Its capital ratio was reduced by 1.2% due to the new capital charge.

It should be noted that the risk-based capital ratio, calculated according to the 1988 Basel Accord, is 8.7 percent. This means that the bank is adequately capitalized only when credit risk only is considered. The bank is, however, undercapitalized, when also market risks are considered.

Thus, we demonstrate that modifying existing measures of risk may affect the bank's capital requirements. The incorporation of market risks into a new capital standard may have an effect on the capital adequacy of banks.

5. CONCLUDING REMARKS

The main motivation of this paper was the increase in the magnitude of market risks as reflected by the high volatility of exchange rates and interest rates. This paper adopts a portfolio approach to the measurement of market risks, thereby taking the covariances among the different risks into account. The estimation of the overall market risk considers the bank's total balance sheet (including on, as well as off-balance sheet items), and not only on the bank's trading portfolio. The Basel Committee on Banking Supervision and U.S. banking agencies have recently proposed ways of measuring those risks but treating interest rate risk separately from other market risks. Our approach is consistent with the alternative given in the Basel Amendment (1996), which allows banks to use internal risk models.

We incorporate the market risks into a capital requirement. Our proposed risk-adjusted capital standard is comprised of an objective factor, which is derived empirically from money and capital market data, and a subjective factor, which reflects the degree of risk aversion of the banking supervisor (or of the banks' managements if the model is used for internal control of risks). The degree of risk aversion is reflected by the maximum allowable deterioration of the initial net worth (α) for a given confidence interval (z value) that the decision making body (banking authority or bank management) is willing to bear.

The Israeli example suggests that broadening the definition of risk and establishing new capital standards is not just a technical exercise but might also have implications for the capital adequacy of banks throughout the world.

Note that although the model was applied to Israeli banks, which are exposed to a large variety of market risks, including inflation risk, it can easily be implemented by other banking systems, which are exposed mainly to exchange-rate and interest-rate risks.

NOTES

1. See Amendment to the Capital Accord to Incorporate Market Risks, Basel Committee on Banking Supervision, January 1996.
2. Allen, Jagtiani, and Landskroner (1996) have analyzed and estimated the impact of the implicit interest rate subsidy on bank risk taking, due to the Basel Accord, which considered only credit risk.
3. In the U.S., concern about interest rate was reflected in the Federal Deposit Insurance Corporation Improvement Act (FDICIA) of 1991. The Federal Reserve issued a proposal for capital requirements for market risk. U.S. regulators are expected to implement the Basel Amendment in general and use the internal models for some of the largest U.S. banks (see also, Levonian (1994)).
4. Grammatikos, Saunders, and Swary (1986) in an analysis of the foreign exchange activities of banks derive the impact of interest rate and foreign exchange risk on net worth.
5. As noted before the indexed segment of intermediation is unique to Israel, while the other two are common to banking firms in other western economies who operate in domestic as well as foreign currencies. The relative share of the three segments of intermediation in Israeli banking (December 1995) is: 26%—nonindexed, 42% indexed and 32%—foreign currency.
6. For an analysis of the concept of duration and its applications see, Bierwag (1987). For an application of the concept to banking and some problems, see Landskroner and Ruthenberg (1989).
7. The bank is assumed to maximize expected utility of the change in net worth. In our analysis we assume that the first order conditions w.r.t. to the decision variables: quantities or interest rates (prices) on assets and deposits are met.

8. The main difference between this paper and Landskroner and Ruthenberg (1991), who incorporate exchange-rate and interest-rate risks into capital adequacy requirements is that the current paper takes the covariation between the different risks into account.

9. Obviously, these definitions can be expanded to the case of multiple assets and liabilities in each segment of intermediation.

10. The error term of the *real* exchange rate is defined as

$$\varepsilon_p = \bar{X}e + \bar{q}\varepsilon + e\varepsilon \quad \text{where} \quad \varepsilon = \tilde{X}_1 - \bar{X}_1$$

is the error term of the exchange rate.

11. where $d\tilde{i} = {}_1\tilde{i}_1 - i_1$ and $d\bar{i} = {}_1\bar{i}_1 - i_1$

12. The variance terms of the variables are thus defined as: var(dr) = Var(up); Var(q) = Var(e); Var(di) = Var(u); $\text{Var}\left(\frac{X_1}{X_0}q\right) = \text{Var}\left(\frac{\varepsilon p}{X_0}\right)$; Var (d_1^*) = Var(u^*).

13. Total assets of these banks as of 12.31. 1995 in US$ billion were: Leumi 36.0; Hapoalim 44.5; Discount 22.3; Mizrachi 12.6; First International 7.9. Total assets of the five banks represent about 96% of total assets of the banking system in Israel. The exchange rate at that date was $1 = 3.135 New Israeli Sheqels.

14. The risk-adjusted capital ratios as of 12.31. 1995 for the other banks in the sample were: Leumi 9.8%; Hapoalim 9.4%; Discount 8.7%; Mizrachi 9.8%; First International 12.1%. That is all the banks are adequately capitalized according to the Basel Accord.

REFERENCES

Allen, L., J. Jagthani, and Y. Landskroner (1996). "Interest Rate Risk Subsidization in International Capital Standards," *Journal of Economics and Business* 48(3), August, 251–267.

Basel Committee on Banking Supervision (1996). Amendment to the Capital Accord to Incorporate Market Risk.

Berger, A.N., R.J. Herring, and G.P. Szego (1995). "The Role of Capital in Financial Institutions," *Journal of Banking and Finance*, 19, 3–4, June, 393–430.

Board of Governors of the Federal Reserve System (1995). "Proposed Capital Requirements for Market Risk."

Grammatikos, T., A. Saunders, and I. Swary. (1986). "Returns and Risks of U.S. Bank Foreign Currency Activities," *Journal of Finance*, 41, 3, July, 671–681.

Landskroner, Yoram, and Ruthenberg, David (1989). "How Variable Interest Rates Affect Bank Duration and Immunization," *Financial Analysts Journal*, July–August.

Landskroner, Yoram, and Ruthenberg, David (1991). Incorporating Foreign Exchange and Interest Rate Risks in Capital Adequacy Requirements," *Issues in Banking* (Hebrew), Bank of Israel, 10, 17–34.

Levonian, Mark E. (1994). "Bank Capital Standards for Foreign Exchange and Other Market Risks," *Federal Reserve Bank San Francisco Economic Review*, No. 1.

APPENDIX

The sample used in the study consists of monthly observations (in annual terms) of interest rates, exchange rates, and rates of inflation for the period May 1989 through December 1995. All interest rates here are market rates.

1) The actual and expected purchasing-power annual rate of changes at time (month) *t* were estimated as follows:

$$\tilde{q}_t = \left[\frac{CPI_{t+12}}{CPI_t}\right]^{-1} \quad \text{and } \bar{q} = \frac{1 + r_{t,12}}{1 + i_{t,12}},$$

where CPI_t is the consumer price index for month t, and $r_{t,12}$ is the real interest rate on a government bond linked to the CPI with one year remaining to maturity; $i_{t,12}$ is the nominal interest rate on a Treasury bill with a one-year remaining to maturity.

2) The change in the actual and expected real exchange rate, in annual terms, was estimated as:

$$\frac{X_{t+12}}{X_t} \cdot q_t = \frac{X_{t+12}}{X_t} \cdot \frac{CPI_t}{CPI_{t+12}} \quad \text{and} \quad \frac{\overline{X}_{p,t+12}}{X_t} = \frac{1+r_{t,12}}{1+i^*_{t,12}}.$$

The expected change in the real US$/Sheqel exchange rate was estimated using the US$ LIBOR interest rate on a 12-month instrument ($i^*_{t,12}$), and the real interest rate on a government bond linked to the CPI with one year to maturity ($r_{t,12}$).

3) To estimate (3b) the nominal rate we used the annualized Treasury bill rate (MAKAM). The expected future spot rate on a 6-month Treasury bill 6 months hence was calculated as

$$\bar{i}_{t+6,6} = \frac{(1+i_{t,12})^2}{1+i_{t,6}} - 1,$$

where $i_{t,12}$ is the one-year spot rate at t, and $i_{t,6}$ ("two-period rate") is the six-month rate (in annual terms) at *t* ("one-period rate"). Similarly, for the expected foreign interest rate we used one-year and six-month spot US$ LIBOR rates. For the longer term real bonds we used the rates on two- and one-year government index linked-bonds, respectively. The actual interest rate used to calculate the surprise is $i_{t+6,6}$, i.e., the future spot rate.

12. RISK MANAGEMENT WITH DERIVATIVES TRADED AT THE TEL AVIV STOCK EXCHANGE[1]

YAIR E. ORGLER

The objective of this presentation is to describe the financial derivatives available at the Tel Aviv Stock Exchange (TASE) and those planned for introduction in the near future. I will discuss the main features of all these derivatives and provide some data on those presently traded. In addition, I will try to explain why certain contracts did not take off.

OPTIONS ON TA-25 INDEX[2]

The TA-25 share list includes the 25 shares having the highest market value and is updated twice a year. At the end of 1997 total market value of these shares was $26 billion and represented about 56 percent of total market capitalization. Since December 1997 they are traded continuously using the new TACT (Tel Aviv Continuous Trading) system. The index is computed by the TASE according to its rules and published by the TASE and the Central Bureau of Statistics.[3]

The underlying asset multiplier is 100 new Israeli Shekels (NIS) so that the size of a contract at the end of 1997 was 30,400 Shekels or about $8,600. A series of options include Call and Put options with at least seven different exercise prices, one equal to the closing TA-25 index on the day preceding the date of issue and at least three above and below that level. Options are issued bimonthly for terms of four months with expiration dates on the last Fridays of all uneven months. The closing price is based on the TA-25 index determined at the opening session of the last trading day prior to the expiration date. Exercise style is European where an

Table 1. The TA-25 Index Options, 1994–1997.

Year	Trading Volume: No. of Contracts Traded (Thousands)	In Underlying Asset Value Terms: US $ Millions	% of TA-25 Shares	% of TA-25 Shares Delta Weighted*	Maximum No. of Open Interest Contracts (Thousands)	Maximum No. of Investors' Accounts
1994	4,326	26,835	399%	177%	276	11,723
1995	5,654	34,357	945%	421%	322	10,383
1996	5,814	37,626	1,110%	476%	322	8,076
1997	5,743	44,008	791%	340%	329	8,482

* This ratio takes into account the probability of exercising the options.

option contract can be exercised only on the last trading day prior to expiration, and settlement is in cash.

The TA-25 index options were the first derivatives traded at the TASE, beginning in August 1993. They have caught on rather quickly so that six months after introduction, by February 1994, a daily average of over 7,000 contracts was already traded. As shown in Table 1, the total number of contracts traded reached 4.3 million in 1994 and increased to over 5.6 million in 1995, 1996 and 1997.

The rapid integration of stock index option trading at the TASE can be attributed to several reasons. First, the detailed planning and training that has been undertaken by the TASE prior to the introduction of the new financial instrument. Second, the existence of similar instruments, that were introduced and traded over the counter at a much lower scale by one of the commercial banks in Israel (the United Mizrahi Bank) so professional investors were already familiar with stock options. Third, the high level of professionals working at Israel's banks and brokerage houses, some of which had experience in this area in the U.S. and the U.K. Fourth, since short sales of shares are not common in Israel for a variety of reasons, the index options provide a substitute for selling the market short. Fifth, the volatility of the TA-25 index provided excellent opportunities for options trading as can be seen in Figure 1. Finally, there is a strong demand by sophisticated Israeli investors for high-risk, high-return financial instruments.

Trading volume in terms of underlying asset value increased from over $26 billion in 1994 to over $44 billion in 1997. Moreover, in comparison with the trading volume of the underlying assets, the notional volume of the options was four times larger in 1994 and over 9, 11, and 8 times larger, respectively, in 1995, 1996, and 1997. Even if these ratios are delta weighted, that is, taking into account the probability of exercising the options, the ratio was still close to five in 1996, which is extremely high by any international standard. This development is due not only to the popularity of the index options but also to the decline in trading volume in the underlying assets in 1995 and 1996. Indeed, in 1997, as trading of the underlying assets picked up, the delta weighted ratio has declined to 3.4. For more details

Figure 1. The TA-25 Index 1-Aug-93 to 30-June-98.

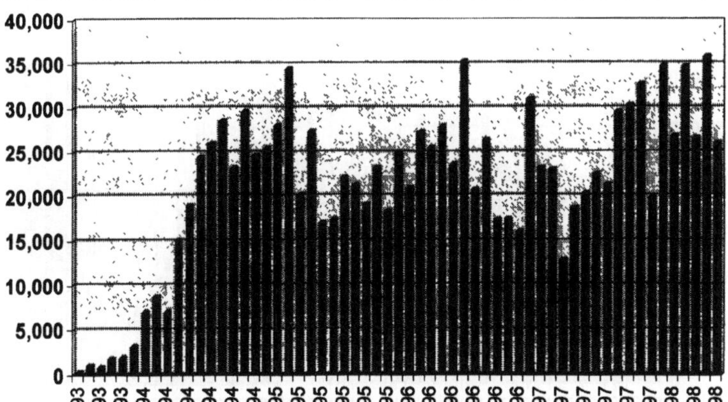

Figure 2. Options on the TA-25 Index (Average daily volume).

on average daily trading volume in terms of number of contracts see Figure 2 and in terms of turnover ratio see Figure 3 and Table 1.

The maximum number of open contracts has also increased rapidly and exceeded 100,000 already in March 1994. It reached a peak of over 340,000 open contracts in May 1998. Since May 1994, the maximum number of open contracts has fluctuated between 150,000 and 340,000. For more details see Figure 4.

Another interesting figure is the maximum number of customers' accounts. It also rose quickly to a peak of close to 12,000 in July 1994. Since then, it has gradually

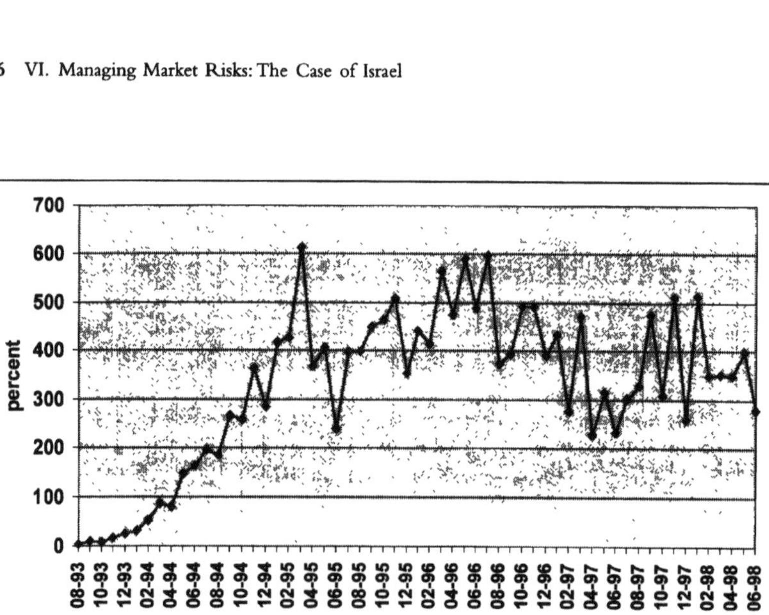

Figure 3. Options on the TA-25 Index. Ratio of turnover in underlying asset terms (Delta weighted) to TA-25 shares turnover.

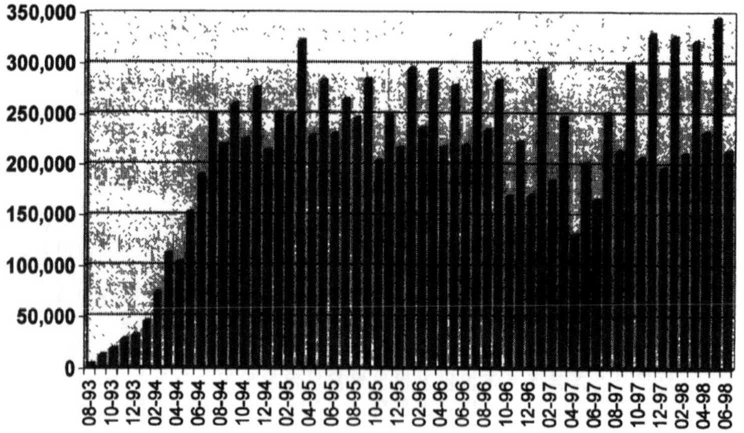

Figure 4. Options on the TA-25 Index (Max. open interest).

declined and was over 6,000 in December 1997. This decline, in contrast with the increase in trading volume, may be explained by the increased professionalism of investors and traders in options and the elimination of mediocre players (for more details, see Figure 5). Still, institutional investors could play a much larger role in the market. For instance, provident funds which hold a substantial amount of shares are not yet allowed to write options.

As of December 1997, the shares comprising the TA-25 index are traded via TACT. This has improved the quality of trading in options, since the underlying assets are now traded simultaneously and continuously.

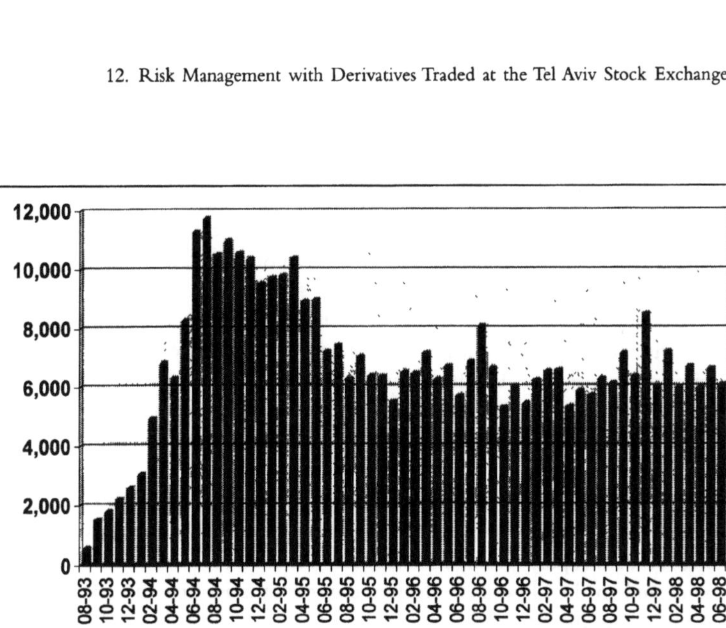

Figure 5. Options on the TA-25 Index (Max. No. of customer accounts).

The following advantages of trading in the underlying assets via TACT, has led traders in index options to adapt their activity to the new system:

- The TA-25 index is updated in real time. Since the shares comprising the TA-25 index are traded continuously and simultaneously, the index expresses, at any given moment, the most recent price of each security.
- Immediate activity in the underlying asset. TACT enables option traders to enter simultaneous orders for buying and selling the underlying assets. This facilitates trading, both in options and their underlying assets, while significantly reducing the risk that traders were exposed to when these assets were traded in the semi-continuous system prior to the introduction of TACT.

Due to fluctuations in the trading volume of the underlying assets during the short period since the TACT system has been launched, it is difficult to determine its precise impact on the volume of option trading. Nevertheless, it is quite obvious that the trading volume has increased. In the first six months of 1998, the average daily trading volume in index options was 31,000, a 20% increase compared with the last six months of 1997 and a 40% increase compared with first half of 1997.

FUTURES ON TA-25 INDEX

Futures on the TA-25 index were introduced in October 1995 (for a brief description see Appendix B).[4] Unlike the options, futures never picked up at the TASE. In the last three months of 1995 a total of about one thousand contracts were traded. In 1996, the number of contracts traded gradually declined and trading stopped completely as of August 1996. This development is surprising, especially in comparison with other derivative markets where the volume of futures trading is at least equal to that of options. Moreover, since options trading at present at the TASE is not simultaneous, it is very difficult to create synthetic contracts using options while this could be easily done with futures. One possible explanation for this phenomenon is the order of introduction of these two instruments, which at the TASE was the opposite of the common approach of starting with futures and adding options at a later stage. Once Israeli investors and traders got used to options they fell in love with this type of contract, and did not feel the need to add futures to their derivative portfolios. Another possible explanation is that private Israeli investors, who dominate this market, are unused or unwilling to hold an instrument that is marked to market, which means that their accounts are debited (or credited) daily.

In concluding this section it should be emphasized that throughout the entire period when options and futures were traded on the TASE, there have not been any failures or bankruptcy problems. This can be attributed to the strict margin requirements and to the close and effective controls imposed by the TASE and the TA Clearing House members.

OPTIONS AND FUTURES ON THE NIS/US $ EXCHANGE RATE

The size of the option contract is $10,000 US and it is quoted in Shekels (NIS) per US Dollar; that is, the options are linked to the U.S. Dollar but traded in Shekels. Expiration date is the last Wednesday of every even month. New series of options for periods of six months are issued every second (even) month. Exercise style is European and settlement is in cash.[5]

Dollar options were introduced in April 1994 and were very slow to pick up as can be seen in Table 2. Average daily volume during the first 24 months never exceeded 1000 contracts. Trading volume increased rapidly only in the second half of 1996 reaching a daily average of over 5600 contracts in December 1996 (for more details, see Figure 6). In April 1998, the volatility of the exchange rate increased in expectation for the liberalization of foreign currency trading in Israel. Consequently, trading in dollar options reached a record of 29,000 contracts in a single trading day.

Maximum daily open interest reached over 174 thousand contracts in April 1998, representing underlying assets of over $1.74 billion (for more details, see Figure 7).

Table 2. The Foreign Exchange (NIS/US $) Options, 1994–1997.

	Trading Volume			
Year	No. of Contracts Traded (Thousands)	In Underlying Asset Value Terms (US $ Millions)	Maximum No. of open Interest Contracts (Thousands)	Maximum No. of Investors' Accounts
1994	66	657	21	1,765
1995	69	695	19	1,367
1996	568	5,681	168	4,528
1997	508	5,078	159	5,834

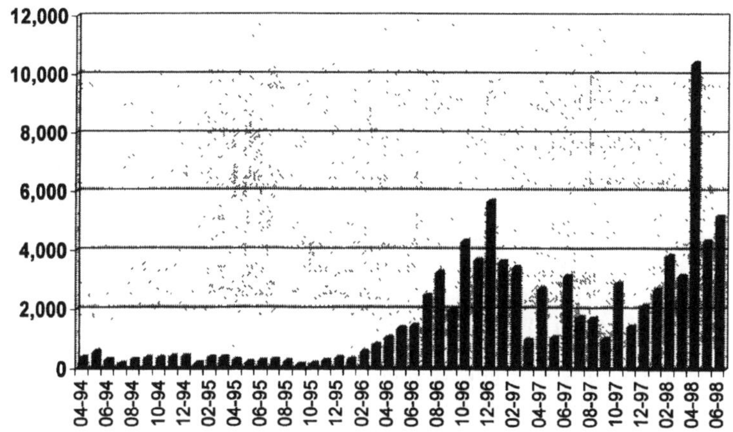

Figure 6. Options on the NIS/US$ Ex. rate (Average daily volume).

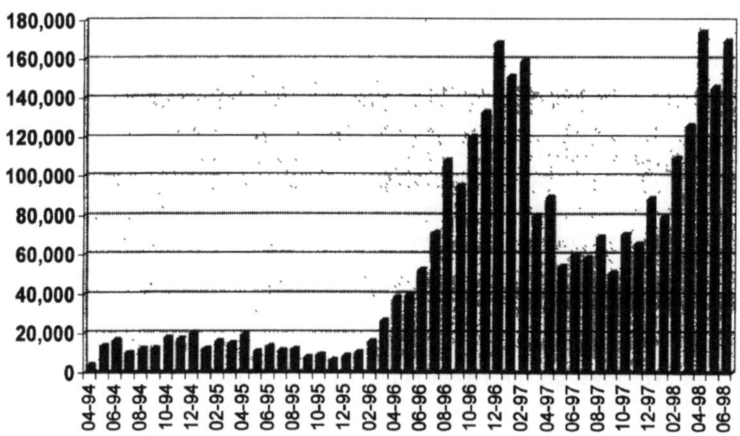

Figure 7. Options on the NIS/US$ Ex. rate (Max. open interest).

We note that the ratio of open interest to trading volume is much higher than for the TA-25 index options, indicating that dollar option investors are mostly interested in protection from currency fluctuations.

The maximum number of customer accounts also increased slowly reaching a peak of close to 6000 in February 1997. Since then, the number declined, reaching 1,500 in September 1997. It has, however, picked up again and in April 1998 reached over 4,500 accounts (for more details, see Figure 8). Considering the value of open interest, this is an indication that investors in currency options are larger, on average, than those investing in TA-25 index options.

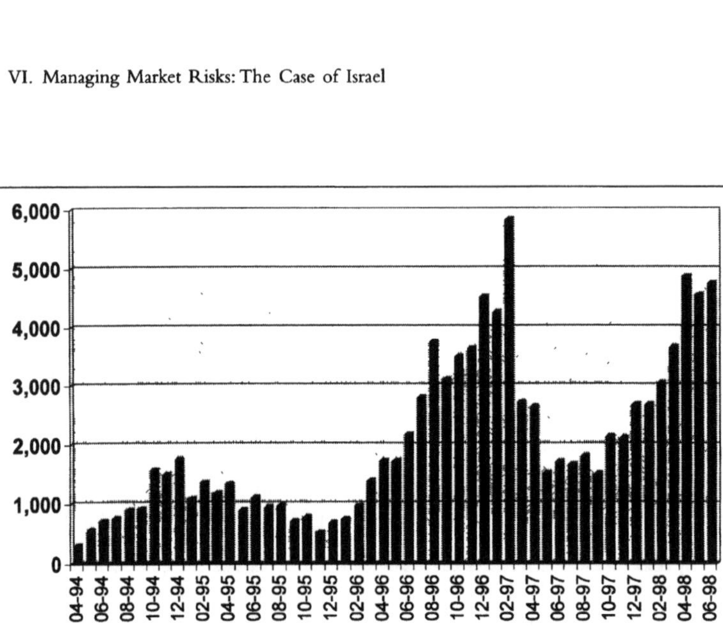

Figure 8. Options on the NIS/US$ Ex. rate (Max. No. of customer accounts).

In November 1996, US Dollar futures were introduced (for a short description see Appendix D). It was hoped that these contracts will attract large institutional investors and sophisticated corporations who would not mind that their accounts will be marked to market on a daily basis. So far, none of this has happened. At the beginning, there were some quotations but no trades whatsoever. The reason is probably competition from commercial banks, which offer tailormade forwards and other foreign currency products at very competitive rates.

PLANS FOR THE FUTURE

Simultaneous and computerized trading

Trading in derivatives on the TA-25 index and on the NIS/US $ Exchange rate is conducted in open outcry. Trading in the latter is simultaneous, whereas the trading system in the former allows for only one option to be traded at each point in time. At the beginning of 1999, the TASE has begun preparations for computerizing trading in derivatives, following the success of TACT. This process is expected to take about one or two more years, so that at the beginning of the third millennium, all securities and derivatives listed on the TASE will be traded continuously and simultaneously, using a most advanced computerized system.

Introducing additional contracts

The first contract to be introduced is a 90-day interest rate future with treasury bills (MAKAM) serving as the underlying asset. This type of contract, which is very popular worldwide, is expected to be successful also in Israel. There is a demand for such a product, especially from large institutional investors. For example, commercial banks could use it for asset-liability management. As yet, no competitive instruments of this type and scope are available in Israel. Most of the preparations for launching this contract have been completed and it is expected to start trading in the year 2000.

Another new instrument that has been approved is a future contract on the consumer price index (CPI). Since in Israel many financial and other business transactions are linked to the CPI, it is expected that this instrument will be attractive, especially for hedging purposes by institutional investors and large corporations. Since the CPI is updated once a month, the volume of trading is likely to be limited. At a later stage, options on CPI futures may be added.

Other contracts that are in initial stages of planning include futures on long-term interest rates. The underlying assets for these contracts are long-term government bonds that are linked to the CPI. Additional instruments include options and futures on the ISX (Index of the US listed Israeli securities which is traded on the CBOE); options and futures on sector indices and options on a number of highly liquid stocks, such as Teva and Koor, on which options are already traded in U.S. markets.

Overall, these additions will substantially expand the volume and scope of derivatives trading at the TASE. We also hope that once the new futures are successfully traded, investors will become familiar with this type of instrument so that existing futures on the TA-25 index and foreign currency will also be traded.

NOTES

1. I would like to thank Dror Shalit, Vice President and Head of Trading & Clearing for his assistance in preparing this article.
2. For a detailed description see *Profile of Call and Put Options on MAOF-25 Index*, MAOF Clearing House Ltd., November 1995. A brief description appears in Appendix A. Note that the TA-25 index is commonly referred to as MAOF-25 index where MAOF are the Hebrew initials for futures and financial instruments.
3. For a detailed description see S. Mizrahi and K. Meshkati, *Securities Indices*, Central Bureau of Statistics and the Tel-Aviv Stock Exchange, February 1996.
4. A detailed description appears in the *Profile of MAOF-25 Index Futures*, MAOF Clearing House, Ltd., November 1995.
5. For more details see Appendix C.

APPENDIX A

TA-25 Index options

Year Contract Began Trading	August, 1993
Trading Hours	10:00 A.M. to 4:30 P.M. Tel Aviv time (Sunday through Thursday).
Underlying Asset	The TA-25 Index is a capitalization-weighted index of 25 stocks with the highest market value.
Contract Unit	NIS 100 multiplied by the index level.

Expiration Months	Uneven months: January, March, May, July, September, November.
Options Lifetime	Once every two months (in uneven months) new series of options for periods of four months are issued.
Price Quotation	Stated in points. One point equals NIS 1.
Minimum Price Fluctuation	NIS 1 (for prices up to 20 NIS) NIS 5 (for prices 20–200 NIS) NIS 10 (for prices 200–1,500 NIS) NIS 20 (for prices over 1,500 NIS)
Strike Price Increment	At least seven different prices.
Last Trading Day	Wednesday before the last Friday of the expiration month.
Expiration Date	Last Friday of the expiration month.
Exercise Style	European. Option contract can be exercised only on the last business day prior to expiration.
Settlement	Cash settlement.
Position Limits	12,000.
Strike Price Increments	10 Points. During the expiration month—5 points.
Automatic Exercise	All in-the-money options.

APPENDIX B

TA-25 Index futures

Year Contract Began Trading	October, 1995.
Trading Hours	10:00 A.M. to 4:30 P.M. Tel Aviv time (Sunday through Thursday).
Underlying Asset	The TA-25 Index is a capitalzation-weighted index of 25 stocks with the highest market value.
Contract Unit	NIS 100 multiplied by the index level.
Expiration Months	Uneven months: January, March, May, July September, November.
Futures Lifetime	Once every two months (in uneven months) new series of futures for periods of four months are issued.
Price Quotation	Stated in points. One point equals NIS 1.
Minimum Price Fluctuation	NIS 10.
Last Trading Day	Wednesday before the last Friday of the expiration month.
Expiration Date	Last Friday of the expiration month.
Settlement	Cash settlement.
Position Limits	12,000.

APPENDIX C

U.S. dollar options

Year Contract Began Trading	October, 1994.
Trading Hours	10:30 A.M. to 4:00 P.M. Tel Aviv time (Sunday through Thursday).
Contract Unit	10,000 U.S. dollar.
Expiration Months	Even months: February, April, June, August, October, December.
Options Lifetime	Once every two months (in even months) new series of options for periods of six months are issued.
Price Quotation	In terms of shekels (NIS) per U.S. dollars.
Minimum Price Fluctuation	NIS 1 (for prices up to 20 NIS) NIS 5 (for prices 20–200 NIS) NIS 10 (for prices 200–1,500 NIS) NIS 20 (for prices over 1,500 NIS)
Strike Price Increment	Stated in points. One point equals NIS 1.
Last Trading Day	Tuesday before the last Wednesday of the expiration month.
Expiration Date	Last Wednesday of the expiration month.
Exercise Style	European. Option contract can be exercised only on the last business day prior to expiration.
Settlement	Cash settlement.
Position Limits	48,000.
Strike Price Increments	10 points plus 5 points around the money
Automatic Exercise	All in-the-money options.

APPENDIX D

U.S. dollar futures

Year Contract Began Trading	November, 1996.
Trading Hours	10:30 A.M. to 4:00 P.M. Tel Aviv time (Sunday through Thursday).
Contract Unit	10,000 U.S. dollars.
Expiration Months	Even months: February, April, June, August, October, December.
Futures Lifetime	Once every two months (in even months) new series of futures for periods of six months are issued.
Price Quotation	In terms of shekels (NIS) per U.S. dollars.
Minimum Price Fluctuation	NIS 10.

Last Trading Day	Tuesday before the last Wednesday of the expiration month.
Expiration Date	Last Wednesday of the expiration month.
Settlement	Cash settlement.
Position Limits	48,000.

MIX
Papier aus verantwortungsvollen Quellen
Paper from responsible sources
FSC® C105338

If you have any concerns about our products,
you can contact us on
ProductSafety@springernature.com

In case Publisher is established outside the EU,
the EU authorized representative is:
Springer Nature Customer Service Center GmbH
Europaplatz 3, 69115 Heidelberg, Germany

Printed by Libri Plureos GmbH
in Hamburg, Germany